Finding Your Voice:
How to Put Personality
in Your Writing

finding your
voice

how to put **personality** in your writing

LES EDGERTON

WRITER'S DIGEST BOOKS
CINCINNATI, OHIO

www.writersdigestbooks.com

Visit our Web site at www.writersdigest.com for information on more resources for writers.

To receive a free weekly e-mail newsletter delivering tips and updates about writing and about Writer's Digest products, register directly at our Web site at http://newsletters.fwpub lications.com.

07   06   05   04   03   5   4   3   2   1

Library of Congress Cataloging-in-Publication Data

Edgerton, Leslie.
   Finding your voice: how to put personality in your writing / Les Edgerton.
      p.   cm.
   Includes index.
   ISBN 1-58297-174-9 (alk. paper)—ISBN 1-58297-173-0 (pbk.: alk. paper)
   1. Authorship. 2. Creative writing. I. Title
PN147.E28   2003
808′.02—dc21   2002191020

Edited by Meg Leder, Rachel Vater
Cover design by Brian Roeth
Interior design by Sandy Conopeotis Kent
Production coordinated by Michelle Ruberg

Dedication

This book is dedicated to all those who were in my psychic "gang" back in public school. You know, the kids teachers called the "Underachievers." All us poor souls who didn't live up to our "promise" (whatever that was) or our "potential." Which, translated, meant all of those poor slobs who didn't fit *their* mold. The daydreamers. The ones who didn't know from kindergarten that selling insurance or being President was their shining goal. That's the gang I was forced into . . . and I'm glad I was.

It left my imagination in working order and I trust it did yours, too. After all, it's our reward for being the daydreamers.

Acknowledgments

With grateful thanks to Jack Heffron who saw this as a book writers might find useful and to Meg Leder who guided me through rewrites with a particularly gentle and knowing hand and made it a much better book for her editing brilliance. Thanks also to Rachel Vater, Kelly Nickell, Donya Dickerson, Liz Carpenter and all the other wonderful folks at Writer's Digest Books who've contributed much to "our" book.

And . . . a very special note of gratitude to a hulking mouthbreather I only remember as "Waldo" in the fourth grade in Freeport, Texas, who used to viciously bully my skinny scared butt in front of the other kids. I began writing little humorous vignettes about Waldo (*he* may not have found them humorous . . .) and passing them around to my schoolmates, and that had two major effects on my life. Waldo quit bullying me because of the resultant public derision and I found out the truly awesome power of the written word and became a writer. Wherever Waldo is today (prison, I hope) I say, "Thanks, creep." I think he learned that old nursery rhyme about sticks and stones just isn't true. Words *can* hurt you.

They can also help.

A lot.

Just ask Waldo.

About the Author

Les Edgerton lives with his wife Mary and son Mike in Fort Wayne, Indiana, where he writes full-time and teaches creative writing online for Vermont College (where he received his MFA in Writing) and for Painted Rock. He formerly taught online for the UCLA Writer's Program.

He has two daughters; Britney, who works in the computer industry in Louisville, and Sienna, an artist who lives in Indianapolis and who just gave Les his first grandson. Besides writing and teaching, Les coaches youth baseball and his son Mike, who is something of a baseball prodigy, his fastball being timed at 78 mph when he was eleven and 86 mph when he had just turned twelve and who plans to attend Stanford to become a doctor (after his playing days with the Dodgers).

Les writes short stories, articles, essays, novels, and screenplays. His fiction has been nominated for the Pushcart Prize, O. Henry Award, Edgar Allan Poe Award (short story category), Jesse Jones Award, PEN/Faulkner Award, and the Violet Crown Book Award, among others. One of his screenplays was a semifinalist in the Academy Awards Foundation's Nicholl Fellowships and a finalist in the Writer's Guild's "Best American Screenplays" competition.

Table of Contents

Introduction

I've written all my life (in my case, that began just about the same time as dinosaurs were put on the "endangered list") and have also been privileged to teach several hundred writers of all levels and abilities as an online teacher of creative fiction writing in the famed UCLA Extension Writer's Program and these days for Vermont College and Painted Rock, as well as for The Neighborhood Connection, local adult education classes here in Fort Wayne, Indiana. Even though I'd enjoyed success myself as a writer and teacher, I was much like most of my students—searching for a "secret" that would guarantee for my work the light of publication. I hunted along all the canyons and woodlands wherein such a secret might lie . . . workshops, writing magazines, "how-to" books, queries to published authors I met . . . and so on. Even though I'd been published, I was still convinced that others met success without as much blood and sweat as I had. There just had to be some kind of "secret" Tim O'Brien and Kurt Vonnegut and Barbara Kingsolver weren't sharing—were holding close to the vest, so to speak.

Well, there was.

I discovered that secret in the most unlikely of places. In the Indiana state prison at Pendleton.

In my wild and tempestuous youth, I had gone afoul of the law and ended up serving time in that institution. I'd come home from four years in the Navy, the last two spent in Bermuda, and just kind of went crazy "back home in Indiana." I fell in with some other guys who were very pleased to let me go insane right along with them and ended up committing a bunch of burglaries and robberies and getting my very own personalized number on my blue denim state-issued shirt. They say you remember your social security number all your life, as well as your military number. Along with those numbers, I find it hard to forget an additional series of digits . . . #49028. That was my "personality" for the next couple of years.

Decades later, having straightened up my own mess of an existence,

I felt I owed something of a debt to the guys I'd left behind and so, a few years ago, I began to pay visits to the inmates downstate. I'd offer up my own life as proof that anyone can overcome the label of ex-con and go on to contribute to society rather than simply take from it.

What began to happen was that after many of those visits, an inmate would write me a lengthy letter, telling me that he, too, had ambitions to become a writer and could I advise him on how to go about learning the craft. These letters would also go into great detail about how the unlucky incarcerate had personally been "bum-rapped on the litigous" (a term I coined in one of my short stories titled "Dream Flyer", available in my collection titled *Monday's Meal,* a copy of which would make a marvelous Christmas or birthday present for someone should you be filling out such a list . . .). The letters would tell marvelously-inventive stories of how society had dumped on the inmate and how it wasn't his fault that he found himself in a six-by-eight-foot cell, painted an unfashionable gray. A con job, but what good writing isn't?

The thing was, these stories had all the elements of great fiction. They were rollicking, exhilarating tales of car chases, lawyerly ineptitude, shootouts, and judges they were convinced had been "fixed" or just politically motivated to be perceived by the voting public as "crime-fighters." I might also add that many of the letters were rife with misspellings, along with grammatical and punctuation errors, but through all the slag and dross that might cause an English teacher to cringe, shone the unmistakable luster of literary gold. These guys were writers! I wrote each of them back, asking them to create for me a short story and we'd go from there.

I felt like a budding Maxwell Perkins. I was "discovering" writers and would have a major hand in shaping their craft. At least one of these guys was going to emerge a major American author, when I was done. Eat your heart out, Normie Mailer—my cons were more better than yours ever were, dude . . .

Not so. The stories I invariably got back could never possibly be matched to the authors of those original letters. In every single case, the author had opted to become "writerly." I could imagine the earnest tyro sitting on his bunk, hunched over a yellow legal pad, scribbling with a blue-capped Bic . . . with a Webster's Collegiate Dictionary and Random House Thesaurus open beside him. Plus a copy of a coverless Zane Grey glommed from the prison library's priceless collection. Instead of the stories so passionately expressed in their letters, I was given tales of rustlers in the Wild West and Sam Spade retreads in Los Angeles and "Noo" York City . . . written in a hand unmistakable as an imitation of the original . . .

The same thing happened when I began teaching for UCLA in the nineties. I'd get these great letters at the beginning of the class in response to the bios I asked for from my students . . . and then the stories that began to emerge utilized an entirely different voice.

It dawned on me what had happened. Faced with writing something an "authority" (that would be moi . . .) would actually be reading (and judging), they had fled from their own natural, wondrous voices and succumbed to what I started to recognize as the "writer's inferiority complex." An inferiority complex I began to see everywhere in beginning writers and even in some fairly-seasoned pros.

As time went on and I began to teach more, I saw the malaise among beginning writers everywhere. Universally, it manifests itself in definite patterns.

The writers afflicted with this most wretched of all writer's maladies almost always "hold themselves back" from their best writing (read: natural voice) because they approach their craft with overmuch respect for the published word and/or to satisfy the critical voices they hear in their heads from all the writing teachers or mentors they've had, and end up trying to create prose they feel is in what they see to be a "writerly" style.

Instead of the very likable voice that is unique to each of them, they try to be a William Faulkner or a Sandra Cisneros clone, or, in the case of many of my inmate friends, a Zane Grey-ite, as well as for all those writing "authorities" sprinkled in their pasts, and in the process do much good for their mail carriers' end-of-year bonuses, keep the papermill industry profitable and amass a significant collection of editor's rejection slips, but do little for their own careers.

Some of these folks do get published, but many times only because they've learned how to be technically perfect. The piece of writing accepted didn't hit any of the editor's "hot" buttons, those buttons that allow them to get through that humongous pile of manuscripts staring at them from across the desk. The buttons I'm referring to are the "don't's" of writing, i.e., improper format, misspellings, grammatical mistakes, etc.

Editors are busy folks and to get through the mass of manuscripts most use an internal checklist of "mistakes" to automatically reject a manuscript. If a story or an article makes it through that minefield, it sometimes gets published simply because it didn't hit any of those buttons or "mines." As an editor of *The Crescent Review,* I see stories like that being accepted every now and then. Sometimes, I wish we'd published the writers' cover letters instead since those were in their natural voices and much more interesting reading.

About that "natural voice . . ." The theory I've arrived at through these observations is that readers select certain authors to read in much the same way as they select their personal friends: on the basis of the "voice" (personality) of that person. All human beings in the world have a circle of people who like them and want to be around them . . . and they also have folks who don't like them all that much. The same is true of an author's readership. They are the "friends" he or she will accumulate. Contrary to what many think, I don't believe readers are attracted nearly so much to plots and characters as much as they are to the personality of the person regaling them on the page. The same holds true for nonfiction—a reader may initially be attracted because of the subject or to the basic "facts" revealed, but unless the author provides a personality to the material, many won't stick around till the end.

Think about it. Remember when you were a kid and your mom wanted you to eat all your peas and you balked? Maybe even threw a wee fit, one of those minor seismic domestic disturbances that registered, say, a 4.5 on the Richter Scale? What'd she tell you? That you ought to eat 'em because "there were eight million starving people in China," right? Well, that's an example of a "basic fact" (even if it wasn't true . . .) that writers sometimes rely on. What was the result? Went in one ear and out the other, unless I miss my guess.

Now . . . what if she'd said, "Eat your goshdarned peas, Harvey/ Maybellina! You know, the Millers next door would kill for those peas! Especially since both the mister and missus have been laid off for six months and they've been buying day-old bread to go with their gruel and last night I heard the Miller boy rooting around in our garbage can." Now, that's something I bet would have had an influence on your pea-eating career! Why? Because, "eight million starving people in China" is basically meaningless and just too impersonal. If you hadn't heard that fact before, it *might* have been an interesting fact . . . for about a nanosecond. After that . . . zzzzzzzz. But, if Mom would have personalized the example as I did, it most likely would have struck home and you would have experienced a real emotion and it may have even prompted you to finish your peas.

Same way in writing. Which doesn't mean that every single person who picks up your article or story will be fascinated and mesmerized to the very last word, but lots more will than if you don't make the story or piece unmistakably yours and yours alone.

Although some won't . . .

That's not bad, folks. Just as in "real life" you don't honestly expect everyone to like you or want to join your "gang," neither should you expect everyone who picks up your story or article or novel to feel a rapport with you. That's just not reasonable to expect. Don't worry about it whatsoever. You'll pick up lots more friends (readers) by being yourself than you will be by writing in a beige voice. Lots and lots more!

What *is* reasonable for you to expect is that no matter how idiosyncratic or "different" your own, particular voice may be, there will be a number of readers who *will* like it. Who will be drawn to the personality on the page.

It's usually a mistake in any business to try to be "something to everyone," and that's kind of what writing in a neutral or colorless voice is kind of doing. Trying not to offend by being so bland that the readers' emotions are left untouched.

I think that's a mistake. By being yourself on the page, you'll more than likely attract more readers because of your individuality than you would by hiding your personality behind a neutral style. Consider the departed Howard Cosell. He got it right when he said he didn't care if viewers hated him or loved him . . . just so long as they watched him. In fact, for those of you too young to remember Howard or those of you who couldn't care a fig less about sports, there were vast legions of people who actively hated the man and his nasal voice and belligerent projection of superior attitude. Cosell-haters probably made up half his audience! He actively cultivated those folks and they helped pay his salary by tuning in and increasing his Nielsen numbers to be much, much higher than those numbers would have been if he'd been a more neutral and unbiased observer and commentator. Providing commentary in a "beige" voice, so-to-speak . . .

Do you suppose everyone in America loves John Grisham's voice? Or Stephen King's voice? These are authors who are megasellers as we all know . . . and yet, there are lots and lots of readers who wouldn't dream of picking up their books. Think that bothers Grisham or King? Not on your life! They're very much aware that you can't be all things to all people. By developing their own personalities in their writing, they don't attract every single reader there is . . . but, boy, do they attract a lot of others!

And you will, too.

Much of this writing thing is in the delivery. Professional comics realize this. They know all too well that two comedians can tell the same joke and one will get belly laughs and the other mute stares. Think about your own experience. Remember in the third grade when Joey Dultoid told a joke and everyone just stared at him and an hour later, in the lunchroom, Anna-Banana Smith told the very same joke . . .

and had the gang hooting until they cried? Different personalities at work . . .

Even though Joey bombed with one audience, however, chances are he was a hit with his own circle of friends, a different audience with different sensibilities. Kind of like authors and their readerships. Anna-Banana may be the Stephen King of the lunchroom and may enjoy a large and appreciative audience because she just happens to have the kind of personality that appeals to more people, but Joey also probably has an audience, albeit smaller. If Joey tried to imitate Anna-Banana's style of delivery, chances are not only would he fail to gain any fans in that group, he'd also lose his own audience, albeit smaller. Even if the number of people who enjoy his jokes is smaller, it's still an audience, one that would probably disappear if he tried to be something he wasn't.

Kind of the same deal in writing.

Employ your own personality and, to steal a popular saying that came from the movie, *Field of Dreams*, "they will come." Be someone else on the page . . . and they won't.

This is where I think many books on writing leave a hole in the advice given. Granted, it's vitally important to know the nuts and bolts of writing, but more importantly and universally neglected, is the tremendous role your personality plays when you arrange words and sentences. *How* you tell a story is at least as important as the content of that story and I contend it's quite possibly even more vital. The most important concept we can grasp as writers is sublime in its simplicity—*to be yourself on the page*!

And this is what the book you hold in your hands will concern itself with. Not only the critical importance of being yourself on the page instead of trying to emulate someone else or writing in a neutral voice, but also to offer up some concrete methods by which you can accomplish this goal.

To discover that your own voice is desirable is incredibly liberating and empowering. It will bring out some of the best work you've ever done. Writing that has a much higher possibility of being published.

In my own experience, ever since I've discovered this and incorporated my theories in my teaching, my students' efforts, without exception, have improved exponentially and perhaps even more important, the percentage of those getting their work published has risen dramatically. In my files, I have dozens of letters attesting to that from students who tell me my classes are head and shoulders above every other class they've ever taken and chiefly because I forever challenge them to find their own, unique voice. Now it's time to find yours.

◆ ◆ ◆

You know what's really, *really* cool? The exhilarating sense of confidence you'll gain when you learn your own voice is perhaps just as good as anyone who just got a rave review in the *Times*. Maybe it's even better. You can't hold back a writer who grasps this about him or herself. That writer is off to the races, writing-wise.

That's why I wanted to write this book. There are hordes of genuinely talented and gifted writers who simply don't realize they've placed a roadblock in the path of their success. It's a simple thing to just reach out and fling that wretched plastic barricade into the weeds and be on the way to magnificent successes.

And what about those of you out there who're the lucky ones and have already discovered the power of your own voice? Stick around . . . I believe you'll find the advice in this book to be worth your time. Time well spent in that you'll learn some ways to make yourself even more powerful on the page. And you'll be reinforced in your confidence in that terrific voice only you possess.

This is a book I wish had been available to me those many years ago when I first began to create fiction and nonfiction.

You know . . . when dinosaurs first went on the endangered list . . .

◆ ◆ ◆

A final word before we begin seeing exactly how to get to our own voices, lurking within.

Relax.

Yep. That's the word. Relax. Even though there are lots of exercises and examples and other nifty ways to get to your voice in the following pages, what we'll be involved in isn't thermonuclear physics or household plumbing or anything like those two incredibly complicated sciences. This is all about the voice you already own and have the owner's manual for. What we'll be trying to do here is have you simply *remember* stuff you already know to a T but have just misplaced in the basement of your mind.

So . . . sit back and enjoy the trip down the stairs!

You won't even need a flashlight. I've already switched on the light for you.

Just use the handrail . . .

CHAPTER ONE

Why Writers Lose Their Original Voices

I did not begin to write novels until I had forgotten all I had learned at school and college.—JOHN GALSWORTHY

Da rules.

That's how we lose our voices. One of the ways, anyway. One of the biggest ways.

Huh? (I can hear you now.) Whaddya mean, *da rules?*

Way back in P.S. 101, the rules are what Missus Grundy drummed into our pointy little heads. You know—those carved-in-granite commands of the English language—as administered by that well-meaning, sweetheart dragon in the third grade.

In this chapter, we'll take a look at just how those rules keep us from getting to our individual voice in our writing. We'll also look at some ways to overcome what may appear at first glance to be a formidable obstacle in our journey toward publication, but is actually easily overcome, as you'll see.

Now . . . I don't mean to impugn each and every English teacher that ever drew squeaky chalk across the blackboard as she explained sentence diagramming . . . but, boy! There sure are more than one of those characters who did his or her very best to drum all the creativity and original expression out of their charges by over-relying on the rules of grammar and formal writing. To be fair, there are also more than a few who inspired their students to become wondrous scribes. To be even fairer, I think a great teacher is behind most of us who have decided to become writers.

Alas, I think those wonderful mentors sometimes find themselves sharing caffeine in the teacher's lounge with a few more unimaginative colleagues . . .

Example: "Johnny, this is an incomplete sentence. A sentence requires a subject and a predicate. A noun and a verb. What is this I see? *Simple, Jack?* Here's the way this should be written: *It is simple, Jack.* See the difference? Now, go back to your seat, and write *It is simple, Jack.*

Remember that day? Do you realize also, that after that day, that a little evil genie (Critic Nag Dude) popped up on your shoulder and every blessed time after that incident when your fingers typed out an incomplete sentence, Critic Nag Dude smacked you up alongside your stupid head? Think about it. Bet it's true, isn't it? Oops. Sorry, Missus Grundy. I meant to say, *I will* bet it is true, isn't it?

Well, if you want to write prose containing 100 percent genuine, certified complete sentences, don't expect to be paid for your work. Why? *Simple, Jack.* The reader is guaranteed to fall asleep. Editors realize that. And editors are the ladies and gentlemen who decide if your work gets published. And they don't usually buy prose that makes people nod off after the third or fourth paragraph unless they're related to you or you have something incriminating on them.

On the tails' side of that coin, how many times did you get a paper back with "run-on sentence" or "this sentence is too long—break it up" marked in glaring red? More than once, I betcha. Maybe Jamaica Kincaid missed that admonishment—she must have, or she could have never written her brilliant short story titled "Girl"—which is a *single sentence of six hundred and eighty-six words.* (How'd you like to diagram that puppy?)

Those are but a couple of the dozens of examples of how Missus Grundy hammered your own, original, peculiar, particular, *unique* writing style into submission, driving it closer and closer to the accepted standard. Throughout the course of this book I'll get into more such examples of how the brakes are applied to the engine of creativity.

Taking you further and further from your own voice . . .

A caveat: Don't take this to mean that you should disregard every single "rule" you've been told to follow in writing. Lots of those rules and conventions make sense, and, if followed, help you to get published. Run-on sentences aren't the kind of thing you want to break the rules with. The example of Kincaid's story isn't really a run-on sentence, but actually a very complex sentence. She's used the correct punctuation to make it work.

There are lots of other instances in which the rules and conventions of writing are sound and should be followed. We're not quarreling with most of those. Just the ones that are designed to force you to deliver that bland voice. And the way that sometimes trying too hard to follow those rules in drafts can lead to stiff writing or no writing at all.

How can you tell which "rules" to follow and which ones to ignore or break? That's a great question and a difficult one to answer. First of all, you need to recognize when a particular rule or custom may apply and you should follow it and there are other instances when it's best to forget you ever heard of the rule or the customary usage. Remember that tradition keeps changing as well as customs. It's the nature of the beast (language and prose structure—both fiction and nonfiction) we're dealing with. Keep in mind that for many of the so-called rules of writing, the particular situation at hand is the key factor in determining whether you should employ it or not. There are several ways to ascertain what the particular situation calls for.

Trust Your Instincts!

First and foremost; trust your instincts. I keep relearning this. More than anything else, your own gut feeling may be the best guide to what you should do. Most of us as writers are readers and just about all of us have read a great deal of material in our lives. Just plain reading lots of stuff is the single best way to learn how to write. All that reading

Rules and Techniques That Will Help Take You Away From Your Voice

Some of those rules and writing techniques being taught are:

1. Always use complete sentences.

2. Combine actions with "as" and "-ing" sentence constructions. Example: "As I stepped into the tent, I began pulling my trousers off, yanking out my choppers and blowing my nose." First of all, many times the actions described cannot possibly be performed simultaneously as the writer intends to show. The reason I know students are being taught this is that my then-sixth-grade-son Mike had a homework assignment last year in which they were to do just that—create sentences combining actions with "as" and "-ing" constructions! Made me fume a bit, as I spend time with my writing class students urging them to quit doing that very thing! (Note: That was a *fictional* example. I don't have false teeth. I don't go near tents either, as they're usually located in mosquito-infested areas . . .)

3. Don't use run-on sentences. (Don't tell that to Jamaica Kincaid!)

4. Use the pyramid style for articles and essays. In some (many?) journalism classes, this is still being taught. Basically, it's a system of article-writing in which the most important info is included at the beginning of the article or story and the less important stuff at the end. The purpose of the pyramid is to allow the editor to lop off the latter paragraphs if space so dictates. As Pulitzer Prize-winning author and editor James B. Stewart clearly shows in his brilliant book, *Follow the Story: How to Write Successful Nonfiction* this method of article construction is guaranteed to lose the reader after a few paragraphs. He promulgates the technique used by writers of the publication he formerly edited, *The Wall Street Journal*, whereby articles are developed and written much like short stories, in which the important stuff is built up to and arrived in the end. This technique is the main reason the *Journal* enjoys the highest "read-through" percentages in the business (besides extraordinary writing talent by their reporters). (By the way, this is a superb book for fiction writers as well as nonfiction scribes and I cannot recommend it highly enough.)

5. Archaic dialogue tag constructions. "He/she/name said" is the accepted contemporary usage. "Said he/she/name is considered archaic. Also, using words other than "said" in speaker attributions. Said should be used 99.9 percent of the time, instead of all those other synonyms such as replied, stated, shouted, screamed, breathed, yelled, and so on. The word said is almost not a word anymore. The reader sees it more as a punctuation, and as such it becomes invisible and doesn't slow the read by making the reader aware that someone is writing the story or article.

6. Clichés. Last year, my son Mike brought home a sixth-grade creative-writing assignment that gave an example (of how they were to write their stories) consisting of a short-story excerpt. The example contained twenty-four sentences. And—I'm not making this up!—twenty-three of those sentences contained at least one cliché and some had several! (I had to be rushed to the hospital as I went into a deep coma from striking my head on the floor when I passed out.)

7. Wordiness. Students are often urged to "fluff up" essays by including lots of meaningless filler material.

8. Overemphasis on chunks of static descriptions. 'Nuff said.

9. Overemphasis on transitions between scenes. This especially applies to transitive sentences containing connective words such as "however," "therefore," "on the other hand," "furthermore," "thus," "in fact, "and," "similarly, "and "moreover." Again, a rather archaic concept, as nowadays, influenced as we are by jump cuts in movies and television, transitions are increasingly short and sweet or aren't used at all. Instead, we simply "go" to the next scene, signaled mostly by a simple line break.

10. Being "politically correct" in content and opinion expressed. This is (or should be!) the anathema of writers, at least those who aren't officially employed by *Pravda*. This kind of mindset is what drives us most away from our own voices—when we have to couch our language and thoughts to fit some group's sensibilities.

These are but a few of the rules and techniques of writing you may have been taught and encouraged to use that will keep you from effectively finding and using your own unique voice. There are many more and we'll get to most of them as we go along.

has honed our writing instincts to the point when our senses know when something we've written "feels right" or doesn't. Trust those senses! When you realize after you've written something that you've broken a rule, reread it and see if the passage is effective and does what you wanted it to do. If it does, then leave it alone. If it doesn't achieve your purpose, try rewriting it according to whatever rule you may have broken and see if that doesn't "fix" it.

Research the Rules

A second way to figure out which of those many rules are bogus is just by doing what you're doing now. Read all the writing "how-to" books and articles you can. By and by, you'll begin to see which advice is good for you and which isn't.

(Hint) If you don't yet have a standard by which to judge whether a writing book is good or not, this one is a particularly good one.

Get Another Opinion

A third way is to run your material by another reader. Running it by several readers is even better. Have them tell you any "mistakes" they may spot. If more than one of your friendly readers notes the same things—especially in places in the writing where you may have consciously or subconsciously broken a rule—then you should probably be adhering to the rule there.

Be aware that some readers may not "get" what you're doing." By that, and as an example, I mean that you may have included in your style incomplete sentences (hope so!) and your friendly readers, being trained just as you were to eliminate these critters, may easily misunderstand their usage. In cases like this, be polite and thank them, but follow your own credo.

In the case of a particular rule, ask yourself how long it's been "on the books." Usually, common sense and your own knowledge of your craft will tell you if it's been there forever or not. For instance, reading books like this and observing contemporary writing will help make you aware that "said he/she/name" is nowadays considered incorrect usage.

If the particular "rule" or usage has been there a long time, look at it suspiciously. English is a living, mutating language and it's important to realize that the rules go through many metamorphoses. Many times the textbooks and articles you find them stated in are simply lagging behind the times and the current usages.

For example, how about all that time Missus Grundy had you spend dreaming up the soufflés of writing—the similes and metaphors? Most English teachers of my acquaintance are absolutely batty about such things. Similes and metaphors by themselves ain't that bad, but what is bad is that the teach inevitably persuades the neophyte writer to include them in deadly-dull, static description breathlessly referred to as "poetry"—usually, the two-hundred-year-old brand of poetry. You know—that stale crap about "inundating waves, slithering up like molten fiery lava onto the golden shifting sands . . ." She may have even trotted out and held up for admiration and example that hoary and hopelessly syrupy-sweet paean that begins, "I think that I shall never see a poem as lovely as a tree . . ." Yuck! Who else feels acne begin popping out on their nose when they hear stuff like that? Feel the sugar rush? If you were the kind of kid who wanted to make note of Alphonse Dingus next door who beat his retarded son every Sunday before church to be sure he remained properly quiet during the homilies, you were doomed before you began with the tools you acquired in school. To be successful, such a subject requires words like "bastard" and "shithead" more than the language of Booth Tarkington.

In truth, that kind of writing language was okay at the time it was written. There was a period in literary history when it was okay to write like that and the reader of the time enjoyed it. But . . . things change. People change. Writing changes, which means *writers* need to change as well. And, many teachers just need to realize and incorporate into their reading recommendations and assignments the caveat to judge these authors and what they've produced in the context of their times.

It's certainly okay for you to enjoy prose that's now considered dated or archaic. But, it's counterproductive to produce material that's no longer in vogue if you expect to get your work published. Look at the old guys and gals, and be attentive to the stages writing techniques have progressed through, and you'll truly learn something about the craft, and what rules are still in action.

An Example of How Writing Stuff Has Changed . . .

Samuel Richardson's *Pamela; or Virtue Rewarded* (two volumes, over nine hundred pages) is considered by many to be the first fully-developed "psychological novel" ever written.

Written in an epistolary style, the novel is a series of letters from the title character back home to her mum from her post as a servant to Mr. B. who's trying to sleep with her, the fiction enjoyed huge success when it came out in Merrie Olde England in 1740. The good Mr. B. is doing his level best to bed the fair Pamela and she's frantically scribbling accounts of these attempts and how she's holding out for marriage. You can almost see her, trapped inside a closet, one hand on the door to keep out her amorous boss and the other writing furiously home to mom about what a pickle she's in. The fiction came out in serial form and when the last installment was released and Mr. B. finally broke down in defeat and asked for Pamela's hand in marriage, villagers rang the church bells and hooted and hollered all over England like their team had just won the NCAA national basketball championship. Pamela's "victory" represented a huge step forward for democracy. One of the lower classes managed to actually wed a member of the nobility, unheard of in that day. Stirring stuff, in those days. Readers couldn't wait for the next installment to see how Pam was making out.

Today, we'd kind of wonder why Pam even wanted to marry the boob. Why she didn't just hike on down to Starbucks and meet a nice young stockbroker . . . Or one of those cool creative types . . . like a writer. Today, it would bomb at the box office. That was then, this is now.

Besides being overlong, the other reason it would fail is because of the influence of television and the Internet affecting society's attention span. We no longer are willing (or have the time!) to wade through voluminous books such as *Pamela*. Even literary fiction has to move fast these days.

That's the point I'm trying to make here. Not that you shouldn't appreciate older writing, but that you should move ahead with the times. Also, it's not just older writing you probably shouldn't be imitating in your own efforts. Aping current authors is sometimes just as bad. Just be yourself!

The Problem With Synonyms

At this precise moment, my own son is being drilled on something called *synonyms* in class sessions. Only teachers are aware of such a thing as a synonym. Writers—at least *good* writers—find out early on that no such thing exists. There is only the one perfect word. Or, to paraphrase Mark Twain, "The difference between *lightning* and *lightning bug* be humongous, homeboy."

That's a bit facetious. Of course, there are such animals as synonyms. It's also probably important to know of their existence. The problem lies when we're advised to just pick up a thesaurus and choose a substitute. The result is usually a text loaded with those kinds of obvious substitutions. Which only mutilates your own voice and personality on the page. Instead of (your name here)'s voice, we get Mr. Roget's.

The Reason for Synonyms

In the case of synonyms, it would help if we were also aware of why exactly we use 'em.

Three reasons. Ranked in order of importance, for most cases.

1. We change to new words for meaning.

The original word didn't quite convey the exact meaning we were after. This is probably the best of all reasons to seek out a synonym. There is, after all, only one perfect word. Many times, in our first draft, we're just trying to get the material down. That deal where we turn off the left brain . . . Then, when we go back, we see the word we've chosen has been the choice that would have been made by a writer with the brain power of Cheez Doodles and doesn't say what we really mean to say. Or, we've got both sides of the skull engaged (as I prefer to do) and we stop until we figure out the only right word. Either way is fine. The problem comes when we get lazy again and just pick the first substitute that sounds half-way right. That's when our use of synonyms fails to reach the goal.

For an interesting "real-life" example of when a writer might change words, one of my editors at Writer's Digest Books told me of an incident that happened to her. In Rachel Vater's own words: "Once I interviewed an agent and I wanted to say in the article that she chose the authors she represented very carefully, that she was _____. I couldn't find the word. I put choosey for the first draft, and when I let the agent review it, she asked me to switch the word to 'discerning.' That still wasn't the word I wanted. It was more of a character trait than an adjective to describe the process rather than the agent. I tried again with 'particular,' but that sounded too snobbish. Finally, I had my 'Eureka!' experience when I found the exact word I meant: 'selective.' It adequately conveyed the meaning that she couldn't take everything that came across her desk. Not because she was mean, condescending or snobby, but because she had limited amounts of time and resources to devote to her clients."

As Raymond Obstfeld tells us in his excellent book, *Fiction First Aid,* voice is the most important element of style. It's the one component that is unique to the individual author. And, how you achieve your own voice is governed largely by the words you select to place on the page. When you select the *only* word *you* feel fits in a particular sentence, then you've made *your* choice—a choice many others wouldn't have made—and the accumulation of those choices is largely what determines your own style.

◆ ◆ ◆

Okay!
Cool!

That's all you need to do. Now, put this book down and get cracking, writing.

Kidding . . .

There's more.

✦ ✦ ✦

Obstfeld compares the writer's voice to Aristotle's definition of "*essence*," which was: "The essence of something is that special quality without which that something would no longer be what it is." He (Obstfeld, not Aristotle) gives the example of a horse to illustrate this. He tells us, "Though there are many possible ways to describe a horse (e.g., an animal with four legs, an animal that can be ridden), these descriptions aren't exclusive to a horse. A cow or even some dogs will fit. But there is something about a horse, its essence, that makes it uniquely a horse and not any other animal. Without that essence, it would cease being a horse."

And that's the only synonym you should want. The word that best fits the "horse" you're trying to convey to the reader. Your choice will be different than mine. Or, maybe not. But, when you apply this standard to all of your word choices and the synonyms you seek out, the accumulation of those choices will reveal your style and will be different from the choices I make. Or that anyone else will make.

Unless . . . Unless, you just pick the first handy substitute from your Roget's. That method of choosing is what gives synonyms a bad name and is the basis for my statement that, "good writers—find out early on that no such thing (a synonym) exists."

2. The second reason we reach for a synonym is for *sound*.
This is a very good reason for you to seek out a different word than the one you plunked down originally. As you know, reading is largely an *aural* experience. We "hear" the narrator relating the story. If the voice jars or bores or represents a cliché, we switch it off by putting down the story or article. It therefore behooves us as authors to provide a pleasant and interesting "sound" of our voices for the reader. One

of the reasons it's important to always read your stuff aloud when rewriting it. To give the piece the rhythm and pleasurable combinations of words that fall delightfully on the ear. To make the writing simply *sound* better is a wonderful reason to look for a synonym.

Example: *He was a big man.*

Better: *He was a fat man.*

No, wait! That wasn't the one.

Better: *He was an "I've-quit-counting-calories" man.*

Or, here's a great example from Francois Camoin, one of my mentors at Vermont College, in his short story, "Baby, Baby, Baby."

First, how *I* would have probably written it:

Bad example (mine): *On the far side of the room, under the frolicking dogs, the twins are playing.*

Francois's excellent version: *On the far side of the room, under the* moiling *dogs, the twins are playing.*

Moiling! What a fantastic word!

Here's one mo'. From my own story, "Blue Skies" in my collection titled *Monday's Meal.*

First writing: *I was getting anxious to get back to Houma and get out a canvas.*

Rewritten (and much better, I think): *I was getting* itchy *to get back to Houma and get out a canvas.*

A lot of poets know this. More fiction and nonfiction writers should.

Just watch that you don't sacrifice the perfect meaning of the word you want for its sound. Look for the only word—and there will be only one perfect word—that does both. Conveys the perfect meaning (according to your lamps)—*and* carries the right sound that reflects *your* voice.

3. Lastly, the third reason we use synonyms is because we want to avoid repetition.

This, I suspect, is the reason most of us look for a different word. The weakest of reasons. Not that it's not important to avoid overusing words, but not if the only reason you grab the thesaurus is that you've noticed you've used the word "beguiling" four times in the last three pages. It's a given that you don't want to use a word like this that much, but the sin is when the person who wrote this reaches for the thesaurus (or worse, clicks on the godawful ("godawful" in this instance is a synonym for "stupid") thesaurus in most word processing programs!) and uses the first word he or she sees for a substitute.

If you don't believe word processing program thesauruses are terrible (sorry, Mr. Gates), I just clicked mine on for the word "beguiling." Here's the choices it gave: *pleasant, gratifying, delightful, agreeable, enjoyable* and *amusing*. Huh? *Gratifying* means much the same thing as *beguiling*? Or any of those? I'd had some prior experience with these kinds of thesauruses, so I can't say I was knocked to the floor overcome with hysterical giggles by the choices offered—well, maybe just a titch—but it does make you kind of wonder who compiles these things, doesn't it! Curious, I keyed in the word "beguile" to see what Computer Thesaurus Monkey would give me. This proved a bit more accurate. The choices offered for that were: *deceive, hoax, trick, cheat, victimize, delude, mislead, swindle* and *seduce*. Do you suppose the same person came up with the synonyms for each form of the word? Maybe somebody on the same committee, but probably not the same person. My guess is that the author of the original list needs to hie himself to a dictionary first and learn the meaning of the word before he begins listing synonyms for it! At least talk to his co-committee pal.

Synonyms have their place in the writer's toolbox, but maybe not quite in the ways some of us have been instructed to use them. Certainly not in just substituting to avoid repetition, which is the most common reason to do so given by many of those in charge of our young, eager writer's minds.

Use synonyms . . . but use them for the right reasons. And, for gosh sakes!—use the only *perfect* word. Not the first one that looks halfway right. Don't stop looking until you find the only word that's right for what you're trying to say. To say in *your* voice.

Do you begin to see how the Stovetop Originality Stuffing was knocked out of you? The advice and instruction generally given just on synonyms is only one example, but I think an illustrative one.

The Role of Rules

Don't get the wrong idea. This isn't meant to be a harangue against the rules of the English language. Rules are important. The thing is, they're not IMPORTANT. Meaning, they're not all-inclusive, meant never to be broken. Therein lies much of the problem, said problem being an inflexible approach by more than one writing authority figure in her teaching of writing skills, bound by the chains of standardized writing.

The "standardized" version of writing taught in say, the sixth grade? "You must have five paragraphs in your essay, and the first paragraph must have a thesis sentence in which you specify the three main points of your paper, and each paragraph must have four to seven sentences, and each sentence must have eight to ten words."

Well, okay . . .

(You, there in the back row. Tracy Kidder. You just got an F . . . I don't care how many books you've sold, mister. . . .)

How We Learn vs. How We're Taught

Reading lots and lots of books and stories that have attained actual print is how published writers learn their craft. The more you read, the more you'll learn that what you're reading breaks just about every "rule" and goes against just about every example you were exposed to back in P.S. 101. Or in college, even, although the odds get better in higher education that you'll be exposed to a teacher who recognizes some of those things. For one thing, more than a few college creative writing profs are hired on the basis of their own publications. And that means they've figured out that what Missus Grundy taught them years ago was perhaps not altogether the Gospel According to Joshua The Wordsmith. Literature profs are a different story, however . . .

When I begin teaching a new class on creative writing, I'm always amazed at the one or two people who always show up who have just decided they have a burning ambition to become a writer . . . and haven't opened a book in years except maybe to attain a larger striking area to hit that pesky fly with. I don't think theirs is going to be an easy road to success . . .

I've spent some time here bashing English teachers and I apologize to those who don't fit the examples I've provided. For there are many teachers who do a wonderful job. Usually, they're up against it, as what they're teaching doesn't adhere to the pedagogy and they know going in they'll be in the minority of their colleagues. These are some downright brave souls! As a disclaimer, I really don't mean to create or perpetuate a stereotype of English teachers as a whole. The fact remains, however, that a certain number of those teachers are just about the worst thing that can appear in a budding writer's life.

Like many such things, the rationale behind teaching a set of rules is well-intentioned and has a worthy purpose at the heart of it. When we begin writing as kids, we're undisciplined in general and just haven't read all that much. Most five-year-olds have barely dipped into the canon, as a matter of fact . . . As writing is communication, it's the teacher's job to guide us so that we're understandable to others on paper. Almost all of the rules being taught were created with that purpose in mind.

Nothing wrong with that! In fact, for most students, a good thing. Most people aren't going to become writers. They're going to become engineers, dentists, retail clerks, cab drivers, arsonists and a million other things. Following the rules of writing is important to most folks so they can communicate on a basic level.

As writers who hope to be published, we're different. We *have* to be different! We have to escape a neutral, "faceless" voice and recapture our own if we want to be successful. Exactly what we're about here . . .

It's also one thing to cast aspersions at the behavior of a person or a group—that's easy enough to do—but the job is only half-done (and will appear "whiny") if it's left at that. To offer up a solution is the really important work of such a discourse.

And . . . I just happen to have a solution!

It's a simple one and can be described in one word: Context.

How It Was vs. How It Is

There is nothing wrong with reading and paying attention to, for example, the work of the past "masters" of literature as models for good writing. As one of our best writers, Jim Harrison said when asked for advice to beginning writers, "Just start at page one and write like a son of a bitch." No, wait. That was for something else. For our purpose here, he said, "*Be totally familiar with the entirety of the western literary tradition. How can you write well unless you know what passes for the best; in the last three or four hundred years?*" It's vitally important to be acquainted intimately with the work of those geniuses who preceded us, as Mr. Harrison so eloquently pointed out. The mistake many of us make in doing so, is to study these authors without a necessary caveat. A qualification of context. It's important to study Faulkner and Thackeray and Pope . . . but *in the context of the period in which they were writing.* That's the vital ingredient that's missing in most such instruction and advice to the writer. *In the context . . .*

If you're unfamiliar with Harrison's work, check out his collection of three novellas, titled *The Woman Lit by Fireflies* or any of his other novels and nonfiction books. You may also have seen the movie made of one of his novels by the same name, *Legends of the Fall.* He's a brilliant writer and worthy of study. He's also an epicurean and used to write a cooking column for *Esquire* magazine. Each year, he hosts a wild game feast at his home in the Upper Peninsula of Michigan and I have two recurring daydreams that will represent literary success for me should either occur—the first of which is being invited to Harrison's annual gourmet feast (I hear he's great with whitefish!)—and the second is knocking back brewskies with Woody Allen and Norman Mailer at Elaine's . . .

(If any of you guys are reading this, my phone number's listed and I can be there in a nanosecond . . .)

Stream-of-Consciousness Prose

For instance, the aforementioned Faulkner and Proust were the first to provide *"stream-of-consciousness"* in their prose. Alas, compared to the stream-of-consciousness of today's writers, their efforts were somewhat clunky. Just as the designers of the Model T and the Stutz-Bearcat came up with revolutionary and exciting designs for the automobile, those designs are regarded in today's eyes as awkward when compared to the sleek car models of today, so are Mssrs. Faulkner and Proust's efforts. This doesn't mean we shouldn't revere the earlier auto designs, nor should we pay less homage to earlier authors. The thing is, if Billy Faulkner were alive and writing in today's era, his books would be written much differently. He would have had the benefit of all the advances in writing craft since his day. And, being the genius he was, he would be pushing the envelop in an entirely different way. *That* information is what is usually not taken into account when we look at the example of *As I Lay Dying* for instance. Along with Mssrs. Faulkner and Proust, it'd be a good idea to take a look at a story or two of Gordon Lish's who does the stream-of-consciousness thing a whole lot slicker.

Hey, he (Lish) *should* be doing it better! He's a smart guy and he's also had the advantage of seeing stream-of-consciousness evolve from its early days until the present. If Faulkner had had the same advantage, who knows to what new heights he would have taken the technique!

There seems to often be a connection between the teaching of the rules of writing and the teaching of the canon itself. Sci-fi writers call this phenomenon "trapped in a time warp." (So do non-sci-fi writers . . .) Punctuation rules are a good example of this. The thing is, punctuation and syntax and all those things have changed, but sometimes you're not being apprised of that.

Have a look at the punctuation that's used in some older work. Notice anything? How about colons? Bet you a dollar, you spot at least a few of those puppies in work over fifty years old. *As I Lay Dying* is chock-full of them. Colons were a much-used punctuation in those days. Today, they've fallen into disfavor (as have semicolons) and when we encounter them, they have a kind of "musty" look to them. Today, the double dash or "em" dash has pretty well taken their place. Makes the work—especially fiction—look a lot less formal than it used to.

Syntax

Check out the noticeable paucity of sentence fragments in older work. You'll find a few, but by and large, sentences were complex (and complete) back in the "day." Check out anything by the James' brothers, Mssrs. Henry Jr. and William, those preeminent scholars, philosophers and psychologists, who wrote those weighty (literally!) tomes, *Portrait of a Lady* (Henry), and *The Meaning of Truth* (William).

Just one more thing that used to be a "rule" (complete sentences), that these days is considered fine and dandy to not follow. Your work needs partial and incomplete sentences to be contemporary. Necessary, if you want to provide the kind of voice that readers want these days. *Your* voice. How many complete sentences do *you* utter in the course of your average conversation?

Another good example might be Herman Melville's *Moby Dick*. While I personally think Mr. Melville would find it hard to get published under *any* circumstance today unless he was able to track down a consortium of English professors who owned a printing press, if he did, the editor would cut the first third of his "classic." It's basically a treatise on "everything you never wanted to know about whales." In his day, this was fascinating stuff.

Folks back then didn't have the Discovery Channel, for instance, and unless you lived in a whaling town in Massachusetts, you probably didn't know squat about whales, and the kind of info Herm gave in his book was doubtlessly riveting to the reader in that age. Again, Melville would have written the same book in a vastly different style and with totally different content for much of it, should he be alive and putting quill to paper today. (Although, he'd most likely be sitting down before a keyboard!) Also, *Moby Dick* (like most books of that era) is full of large chunks of languorous, slow-moving static description, a technique that has pretty near vanished these days. Today's description is active and doesn't interrupt the flow of the narrative as it did in

Herman's slower day when information and entertainment wasn't being blasted at folks from every quarter imaginable. Today's books have to compete with TV sitcoms, feature movies, direct-to-video offerings at Blockbuster, and presidential contests (and misdeeds) on CNN. Nobody's going to sit and read sixty pages of a whale's migrating habits unless they just have entirely too much time on their hands! Would you?

To repeat: The key component that's missing in much of the advice we're given in looking at past writers is simply *context*. Insert that into the equation, and we'll all be better off, writers *and* readers. You really should read those grand old dames and gents of the literary arts . . . but juxtapose what they did against the backdrop of their times and you'll come away from the experience with lots of worthwhile tips to help your own writing. Use that basic Model-T body you've just learned about to design a vehicle that looks more like something you'd see on Pacific Coast Highway or the Dan Ryan Expressway today.

Here's a fun exercise that will give you a clear idea of how writing has changed.

Context Exercise

Choose a book, a short story or an article from your favorite writer, one whose work is at least fifty years old. Select a favorite passage and type it out. Try to analyze how the sentences work. Compare it with a piece of your own that uses similar material, paying particular attention to how you both handle the elements listed below.

1. Scenery descriptions (active or passive?)
2. Dialogue
3. Flashbacks or backstory
4. Dialogue tags or attributions
5. Use of adverbs and adjectives
6. Use of punctuation and grammar
7. Elaborate transitions
8. Any idiosyncrasy that seems archaic or "odd" to you

Take notes on the differences. Underline the sentences, words, punctuation, etc., that seems to be "different," or that you felt violated current usage.

That done, rewrite your selected author's passage, this time in your own style, consulting the notes you took on the differences.

Here's an example of how to do this exercise. Let's say the author you picked was Charlotte Brontë and the book, her classic, *Jane Eyre*. You decided to type out a portion of chapter one and have underlined various sentences that you felt were dated or using techniques, punctuation, grammar, etc., that's not used these days. (I've numbered each instance for ease of reference in the commentary that follows.)

There was no possibility of taking a walk that day. We had been wandering, indeed, in the leafless shrubbery an hour in the morning;[1] but since dinner (*Mrs. Reed, when there was no company, dined early*)[2] the cold winter wind had brought with it clouds so sombre, and a rain so penetrating, that further *out-door*[3] exercise was now out of the question.

I was glad of it:[4] I never liked long walks, especially on chilly afternoons:[5] dreadful to me was the coming home in the raw twilight, with nipped fingers and toes, and a heart saddened by the chidings of Bessie, the nurse, and humbled by the consciousness of my physical inferiority to Eliza, John, and Georgiana Reed.

The said[6] Eliza, John, and Georgiana were now clustered round their mama in the drawing-room;[7] she lay reclined on a sofa by the fireside, and with her darlings about her (*for the time neither quarreling nor crying*)[8] looked perfectly happy. Me, she had dispensed from joining the group;[9] saying, "*She regretted to be under the necessity of keeping me at a distance;*[10] *but that until she heard from Bessie, and could discover by her own observation that I was endeavouring*[11] *in good earnest to acquire a more sociable and childlike disposition, a more attractive and sprightly manner,—*[12] something

*lighter, franker, more natural as it were—she really must ex-
clude me from privileges intended only for contented, happy,
little children[13]."[14]*

"What does Bessie say I have done?" *I asked*[15.]

I've marked fifteen different instances in which Brontë did something that we wouldn't see in contemporary prose. Language, spelling,
punctuation, etc., that were fine to use in 1847 but don't fly in the
early part of the twenty-first century. I could have pointed out more,
but this is enough to give you a good idea of how much writing has
changed. Let's go over each of them in the order they appear.

1. Semicolon: Here, Brontë has used a semicolon. Semicolons and
colons are considered mostly archaic punctuations in fiction these days.
They're still used in more formal writing forms such as company reports, research papers, academic papers, and the like, but in fiction
semicolons have been replaced by commas and colons have been replaced with double- or em-dashes. Or, sometimes by simply ending
the sentence at that point with a period. In this instance, a contemporary writer would most likely have used a comma instead of a semicolon
as Brontë did here.

2. Mrs. Reed, when there was no company, dined early: Here,
the offending punctuation is the use of parentheses. This is a form of
addressing the reader—that "Dear Reader" style that was very much
in vogue in those days. Writers (and readers) in the 1800s viewed such
a technique as a way to provide a kind of intimacy with the reader.
These days, we see such variations of the "Dear Reader" technique as
not desirable, as it interrupts the fictive dream by making the reader
aware that someone is writing it. *Jane Eyre* is chock-full of such paren-
thetical asides, as is much of the literature of that period. The "fictive
dream" refers to that "dream-like state" we want to transport our
readers into, which is the entire purpose of fiction and a large part
of effective nonfiction, a state in which the readers "suspend their
disbelief."

3. Out-door: This is relatively minor. Nowadays, this word wouldn't be hyphenated, but spelled "outdoor." Hyphenated words come about from pairing two words which weren't used in combination much before, but after repeated usage over time, the hyphen is dropped and the word is spelled as a single word. No biggie—it simply shows us a word that has evolved from Brontë's day.

4. and 5. Colons: We've already talked about semicolons and colons. While you may sometimes still see a semicolon from time-to-time, colons are pretty much out. A double-dash or an em dash is used today instead. (Em-dashes are like this—while double-dashes are like this--. Both do the same thing.) Where you might see such punctuation in current usage is usually in the work of an older writer, for whom, when they began writing, such punctuation was considered proper. You also might see it in the work of writers from other countries, particularly in the writings of those from England, Canada, and other societies with close cultural ties to western European countries. A writer such as the brilliant Canadian author Margaret Atwood, for instance, will be able to get away with these punctuations and that's fine for them. A newer Canadian writer and novelist, such as my buddy and classmate from Vermont College, Julie Brickman, may not.

6. The said: "The said" or "the aforementioned" is simply a case of dated language no longer used when referring to a character. It's just too stiffly formal these days.

7. through 10. Semicolons and parentheses: You'll notice these examples are used throughout the passage, and so won't be singled out here.

11. endeavouring: Archaic, "English" spelling. Still used in Canada and England and a few other countries, but the U.S. spelling would be "endeavoring."

12. comma, immediately followed by a double dash or an em dash: Most definitely an archaic form of punctuation! *Never* is a comma followed by a double dash or an em dash used today. The comma needs to disappear.

13. contented, happy, little children: Again, not a biggie and this one may be open to argument or a different interpretation. The "error"

I see here is in the profusion of adjectives. A common fault of many writers is to provide more than one adjective in a description in an effort to make the description "stronger." The same thing is often done with verbs and adverbs. What actually happens, is that with each addition, the effect desired is weakened by half. As great a writer as Brontë was, I think this applies also to her sentence above. The word "little" is not needed at all for the word "children" implies that they're little. Also, "happy" is a very similar synonym for "contented" and is likewise not necessary. I think her sentence would be more powerful if she completely lost the word "little" and also just used one of the two remaining adjectives. The style in her time was a more effusive, "wordy" kind of writing, and this wouldn't have jarred the sensibilities of a reader in 1847, but chances are pretty good it would today.

14. This refers to the dialogue as a whole: Brontë has given the reader summarized dialogue, but presented it as direct dialogue as evidenced by the quotation marks around it. Today, such summarized dialogue wouldn't be presented with quotation marks, but either in italics or more probably, just without the quote marks to indicate it isn't a direct quote from the character. The overall language is also decidedly of another era. Such ornate language today would be considered stifling and overly-formal. She's also pairing bunches of adjectives which we don't do much of these days, having found that with the addition of each new adjective the effect is weakened.

15. I asked: Again, this isn't a major example if it were simply an occasional usage, but I've included it because in Brontë's novels, this is an often-recurring technique of hers—using other verbs for dialogue attribution other than the ubiquitous "said." Today, writers are aware that he/she/name "said" should be used 99.9 percent of the time, as "said" has become nearly invisible with usage—it's almost a punctuation rather than a word these days—and so doesn't intrude upon the read, providing a speed bump in the fictive dream. Back in her day, writers were still encouraged to find substitutes for "said." Sadly, many teachers today are still providing the same mistaken encouragement. ■

Transitions

I didn't get into transitions with the above example, so will expound a bit on those puppies. Teachers used to (still do?) spend a lot of time on teaching neophyte writers how to create transitions between scenes. Don't use 'em these days. At least not as much and they're short if they're even in there. Why not? Well, because it seems that in this country, we spend a lot of time watching movies. We spend a lot of money at the ol' Bijou. Something like eighteen trillion dollars is spent per month at the theater in the U.S.A. (My figures could be a little off, but I think I'm in the ballpark here.) Anyway, check out old movies and look at the transitions made then—pretty much like the ones that used to be taught in writing. Long, labored and absolutely screaming to the viewer that, *Hey!, we're going someplace else now! Pay attention!* Then, check out how they make transitions in current flicks. Nowadays, instead of clever and lengthy transitions for when the movie goes from the bedroom of the lovers in midtown Manhattan to the war raging in Switzerland, the director uses a technique called a *jump cut.* Meaning, it just "jumps" to the next scene. No transition. Which is what we're doing in fiction these days. No transitions other than a space break, or at the most, skimpy transitions. We just leap forward to the next scene and the reader "gets it" just as the movie viewer does. We've been trained by the movies to do so. Makes the eighteen trillion we spend on them a month a worthwhile investment, doesn't it . . .

Getting back to the rest of the analysis shown earlier, this is the sort of scrutiny you should use when you perform your own exercise. What will happen is you will become more and more aware of how much writing has changed over the years, and knowing its evolution will only help you gain your own, *contemporary* voice. The voice that will get you published.

Each time you do this exercise you'll see more examples of archaic writing and writing technique than you did the previous time.

And what do you do with that information?

By becoming more and more aware of what *used* to pass as good writing and what is required in *today's* world, you'll begin to develop a more acute sense of what you may have picked up and included in your own writing that needs to be changed or updated.

A sense that gets you even closer to your own voice.

◆ ◆ ◆

Listen to what famed writer and playwright George Bernard Shaw has to say about gaining your own voice. Shaw says, "In literature, the ambition of the novice is to acquire the literary language; the struggle of the adept is to get rid of it."

He's nailed it.

◆ ◆ ◆

Da rules.
Understand 'em.
So you can break the shackles they impose.
Past masters in literature.
Know their work.
Know the context of their work.
So you can go beyond what they did.
Come with me as we learn how to do just that.

Exercise

Ready to do some writing? Let's begin by uncomplicating our language. Take a recent event in the news and write a three paragraph story or article about it as if you were involved as a character or participant.

Only . . . except for proper nouns, you're only allowed to use words of one syllable!

You'll find what you come up with to be minus the flowery verbiage and close to the voice you had long ago and have since misplaced, perhaps.

This is how we start to regain our voices. ■

CHAPTER TWO

Why Unpublished Writers Have an Inferiority Complex

One should never write up or down to people, but out of yourself.—CHRISTOPHER ISHERWOOD

According respect to those authors whose books we find on the library and bookstore shelves is a decent and honorable thing to do. In many, if not most cases, homage *should* be paid to those whose work has achieved print. (Except, maybe, in the case of books by writers like Lord Bulwer-Lytton . . . You know, that "dark and stormy night" dude . . . whose books were hopelessly overwritten with purple and melodramatic prose.)

As the majority of us have discovered soon after we began submitting our material, it's darned hard to get published. More so nowadays than at any time in literary history.

Respect, especially *over*respect however, can be an unhealthy thing for you. It can keep you from getting to your own voice.

Popular author Gloria Steinem had something to say about writers who respect too much when she observed, "Writing . . . keeps me from believing everything I read."

Because of that (over)veneration, you may be infected with a debilitating disease and not even know you're infected. The disease? A dread condition, peculiar to writers and other artist-types, known as *overadulation of the published word*, or the *writer's inferiority complex.*

This affliction, if untreated, can lead, even in its early stages, to a terminal condition known as *BEING UNPUBLISHED.*

Scary? You bet, but there is a cure. Soon to be FDA-Approved, with a little official seal, a song to be sung rousingly at the meetings of recovering nonpublished folks, and a secret handshake . . . The disease leads to a nondistinctive voice, or worse, an imitative voice. The RX for a complete recovery is available between the covers of the book you hold in your hand. Even better, the treatment is painless and doesn't require sharp needles or lying down on a cold table. You'll just have to relearn how to be you and you're going to be nicely surprised at how easy that's going to be.

And how uplifting to the spirit it is when we learn that not only *what* we say on the page, but *how* we say it—has immense value to others. That we've got pretty cool personalities, each and every one of us. That you've got countless numbers of potential "friends" waiting for you out there in Readerland—folks who are dying to meet *you* and not John Grisham #2 or Joyce Carol Oates the Recycled. *You*, mister. *You*, ma'am. Dying to hook up with you between the covers . . . (The covers of your book or magazine article, of course . . .)

Let us proceed.

The first step in overcoming this often-fatal condition is recognizing that you are infected.

Writer, Cure Thyself

Self-diagnosis is the crucial first step in curing the disease!

First, we need to understand the source and nature of the malady and how it manifests itself. And why, if untreated, the habit of affording overmuch respect to published writers will almost always lead to a steady stream of rejection letters.

How so? By influencing you into reverting to a voice that's really not your own because of a (mistaken!) feeling that your voice perhaps doesn't "measure up" to those boys and girls already on the bookshelves.

Your Critics

Let's look at who will be reading your work and passing judgment on it. Excluding your significant other, mother, father, teachers, roommates, or friends who pretend to be interested, the only audience that will count consists of two significant kinds of people. Editors and readers. *Paying* readers.

Let's look at each.

Readers

By readers, I mean those souls who plunk down their precious greenbacks or swap their prize goat or magic beans to buy your story, novel, article or four-hundred-page unauthorized bio of Pee-Wee Herman.

You create your readership in just about the same way as one creates a circle of friends or in the way a popular band creates a following. Just as all of us have people of our acquaintance who want to be around our sparkling and scintillating personalities, so does a writer's readership evolve. In music, for instance, the Rolling Stones will appeal to some and not to others who will only listen to interpretations of Mozart or who think the Stones are "so five minutes ago" and only pop for CD's with Britney Spears's midriff on the cover. It's like this in any artistic field. Lovers of Picasso may detest anything Norman Rockwell ever painted and consider Grandma Moses an example of all that has gone wrong in art. The astute artist in any field knows that he or she can't "be everything to everyone," and so cultivates his or her own particular and inimitable style, thereby appealing to some and not to others. That's fine. That's the way it should be. A boring world it would be otherwise, don't you think? Pretty drab and colorless. Think "Indiana in December . . ." or June, even.

Imitating others may be technically nice, but it doesn't get one very far down the yellow brick road of stardom. Only when one's own unique voice is listened to and utilized is there even the remotest chance for that elusive and much-sought-after national book tour.

Think about it. Picture two writers, both just beginning to learn their craft and send stuff out. One writer—we'll call him "Dusty F. Ski"—plunks his maximus glutamous in front of his Univac seven nights a week, diligently copying passages of Thomas Wolfe, just because one of Ski's teachers raved over Wolfe and declared him a genius.

He even wears an ice-cream suit and a Panama hat while he types. After six years of copious typing, he has captured just about every nuance and rhythm of Wolfe's prose and has become expert at EMPHASIS!!!! using CAPITAL LETTERS and MULTIPLE EXCLAMATION POINTS and QUESTION MARKS????!!!!! He has successfully transferred the techniques he's learned to his own writing, and he spends his spare time away from writing either in researching pop icons to cram into his stories or learning new email prose-writing strategems.

Imagine another writer, a block away. This second writer—we'll call her "Iyam D. Reelthang"—also cranks out stuff on her Univac. Only, she doesn't copy another writer and not only that—she won't even read her favorite authors while she's working on a story as she's found their style creeps into her own. Down at her day job in the stockroom at Penney's, she's known as the wittiest person on the first shift, and she's working hard at honing her sense of humor and getting that into her work.

Which writer do you think will be more likely to be inked to a big bucks advance and extensive book tour by St. Martin's Press?

(Hint: The answer to that is what we refer to as a "no-brainer.")

Dusty doesn't sound like Dusty; he sounds like Thomas Wolfe, warmed-over. He's a ventriloquist, not a writer. The rejections he gets back from editors are much like the famous one in which the editor wrote, "Dear Sir: Your material is both original and good. Unfortunately, the stuff that's good isn't original and the stuff that's original isn't good."

Don't let others say that about your work! If somebody reads your work and exclaims, "This sounds just like Georgette Heyer!" groan and get back to work and perform whatever exorcism is needed. Some priests can do this . . . Keep Georgette within the pages of her own books, while you get yourself within the pages of yours.

While Dusty's list of published credits are mostly "letters to the editor" in his local paper, Iyam is developing writer's cramp from signing copies of her bestseller and soliciting tips on how to overcome jet lag on her exhausting tour. Those of us as writers who separate our own personalities out from our prose may find ourselves being published now and then . . . but probably not in much besides fringe publications.

Iyam knew something Dusty never learned. There's only room for *one* writer with Thomas Wolfe's unusual voice. On the other hand, there *is* a place in the public's heart for an Iyam and her singular style.

'Tis the same with you.

There's a place waiting for you in Readerland. Editors are out there now, poised with checkbook in hand, hoping that today is the day they open a manuscript and a real, live person begins speaking from the page to them. A new, unique person with a voice they haven't heard before.

Your voice!

The world won't applaud a second William Faulkner, boys and girls. Especially a second-*rate* Faulkner . . . which is all any imitator can aspire to be. The reading audience can, however, be very receptive to the rollicking small-town tales of Jim Ray Poindexter from Bippus, Indiana. Eagerly open to the article Jim Ray delivers to *Gourmet Magazine* describing the cuisine delights of crawfish, delivered from the sensibilities of an observer with Jim's values and particular background that only he can bring to the writing desk. Ecstatic over the short story Mr. Poindexter has penned about the town drunk at Bippus, Indiana's Fourth of July barbecue.

Mr. P. is going to get his work published if he observes the principle behind Jules Renard's remark concerning his own struggle with the literature "masters" on his own shelves, that: "Whenever I apply myself to writing, literature comes between us."

Jim Ray's going to get published because he won't let literature come between his own personality and the page. The voice he respects the most is his own. As you should.

The world wants Jim Ray Poindexter from Bippus, Indiana's voice. The world wants *your* voice. From wherever you are.

Think that's not true? Look at the publishing success of a window-washer and an apartment-cleaner who wrote in a voice unlike any other in bookdom. He cleaned windows and apartments until an agent saw his work, recognized a writer who was proud of his voice (and rightly so) . . . and then, this writer just plain *cleaned up*!

I'm speaking of David Sedaris.

His first book, the best-selling *Barrel Fever*, is the funniest book I've ever read in my life . . . and I've read thousands and thousands and thousands of books. I've read Carl Sagan numbers of books.

Barrel Fever has the most hoots, hands-down.

Not so much for the content—he chooses almost boringly (in someone else's hands) ordinary topics to write about—a mother's smoking, a Christmas letter to family and friends, New Year's resolutions—but the *way* he writes about them, using his ultra-cool, cynical, wacky take on life and in his everyday language—resulted in a book that I read ten times straight, from cover to cover, and ended up falling off the couch every single time, convulsed with uncontrollable and unseemly giggles. Sedaris gave the world *his* take on life and he delivered it in *his* voice. That's what made his essays and stories cook.

Didn't hurt he had a wicked imagination! But then, so do you. You wouldn't be sitting here reading this if you didn't. Your imagination is what probably made you have to be a writer.

Let the world see it.

The goal isn't for you to be something to everybody at all. Use your personality on the page and chances are you'll end up like Sedaris where seventeen out of twenty love you, two can't stand you, and one finds you boring. If even ten out of twenty like the person they meet under your byline, those are best-seller numbers. Barry Bonds wishes he could hit .500! At least I think he does. He wouldn't agree to an interview so I could ask him.

I can live with those numbers.

I suspect you can, too!

The world wanted and embraced David Sedaris's work in large part because he let his personality shine through on the page.

Guess what? The world wants *your* voice just like it wanted his.

As do most editors.

Editors

Editors are people.

Really.

Okay. I've waited for five minutes for you to choke that last little bitter laugh out and get yourself under control . . .

Truly though, editors want to be your friend. The problem is, many of us writers don't do *our* part.

How's that, you say?

Editors are the same as most of your potential readers. They want to include you in their circle of friends. That's always their hope when they open your first submission to them, whether it be a query letter, an article, a short story, an autobiography or a novel. Whatever. Before they slip that dagger-shaped letter opener into the envelop bearing your street address and ZIP code, hope is alive in their hearts.

Hope that . . .

. . . this will be the writer with the different voice.

. . . this will be the writer to whom they warm to immediately.

. . . this will be the writer whose sentences will instantly affect one or more of their emotions. Make their blood pressure rise. Tickle their funny bone. Cause a blush. Bring forth a tear. Elicit a yearning sigh. Make 'em realize this writer has charisma.

In short, evoke the same kinds of responses we all get when we meet somebody special in person, somebody that fascinates us, a person who has that "chemistry" that makes others want to hang out with him or her.

Even someone that repels us. Any of y'all remember Howard Cosell? When he was broadcasting sports in his sepulchral tones, Howie was perhaps one of the most reviled personalities on the tube. He was also one of the most beloved. As many people hated him and threw objects across the room at some of his officious pronouncements as adored him for "telling it like it is." Didn't matter to the networks that large numbers of viewers considered Cosell odious to the max. The thing was, they tuned in. He had market value. He had a unique voice.

That individual voice editors yearn to discover.

What they don't want to see or experience when they open that envelop is, sadly, what they get ninety-nine out of one hundred times.

What author Tom Wolfe called "the beige voice."

The beige voice is the voice others've been trying to get you to write in since grammar school. You know, that "style" you see in legal briefs, newspaper journalism, business letters and memos, school reports and essays, and anything written by one government employee to another or in your average police report of a sundry crime.

Contemporary writer Meg Files refers to the same voice as her "public writing." Her "safe, madeup stories," as she refers to them in the beginning of her book, "Write From Life." She describes the same style of writing Wolfe has coined the "beige voice."

She writes: "My mother was an artist, and if I couldn't draw even a black cat on a moonless night, I could win her favor with clever poems and pretty descriptions. (In school . . .) My essays were charming, my book reports (of course) passionate. I knew how to do it in college, too. In creative writing classes, my sonnet and stories earned A's and the admiring comments—'This is the most . . . ' and, 'This is the best . . . '—from those I most admired.

"Oh, but the private writing. There, in my childhood diary and college journal, were the secrets; and there, in the poems I never handed in, were the yearnings; and there, in the scraps of stories, were the hurts and doubts. Now I know the experiences and emotions were not so unique as they seemed, nor was I so alone as I felt. But I sensed then, and understand now, *that this raw, messy, intense writing was the real stuff.*" [italics mine.]

"It wasn't that the public writing was dishonest. Rather, it was safe."

Later, Files goes on to say, "I kept writing and writing, never seeing the disparity between what I needed—to explore my own most personal material—and what I wanted—publication, success, admiration. I wrote entire books: Rejected, rejected, rejected. What was I doing wrong? I tried to write good, clean prose. And I tried to figure out what would sell. The only answer was *nothing,* at least nothing I wrote.

"Finally, I got mad. I wrote in my journal: *To hell with New York. I'm going to write the book I want to write and I'm going to make the prose as rich as I can, and I'm going to explore everything fully.*"

Then, she got published. She wrote her story and she wrote in her voice, not that "safe public voice."

Some maintain there is a time and place for the beige voice. I honestly don't think so. Neither does William Zinsser, author of some really nifty books on writing craft, Zinsser says, "If you work for an institution, whatever your job, whatever your level, be yourself when you write. You will stand out as a real person among the robots." He's talking about the beige voice used by many in business, government, academic, and other institutional settings, but his advice applies even more so to the professional writer. He's saying it exactly right: When you're yourself on the page, you're gonna stand out as a real person among the robots." The "robots" in this case being the folks in the mound of manuscripts piled high on any given editor's desk.

Zinsser wrote *On Writing Well,* one of the best books on nonfiction writing ever published. In it, he talks about all of those forms of writing that some feel are the place for the beige voice. Business, science and technology, sports and reporting, criticism, and education. He disagrees (and so do I), stating, "But just because people work for an institution, they don't have to write like one. Institutions can be warmed up. Administrators can be turned into human beings. Information can be imparted clearly and without pomposity. You only have to remember that readers identify with people, not with abstractions like *profitability,* or with Latinate nouns like *utilization* and *implementation,* or with inert constructions in which nobody can be visualized doing something: "pre-feasibility studies are in the paperwork stage."

Writing where nobody special is present.

The Root of Suppressed Voices

You may wonder why I've spent some time on our educational system when this is supposed to be a book on voice. The reason is, it's important, I think, that you understand and are aware of one of the primary reasons we find ourselves writing as we do.

It's what we're taught, by and large!

It's not your fault if you write with a beige or "public" voice. Not at all. If you do, it's most likely because you were a good, obedient student and paid attention and tried to do the right thing. How's an eighth-grader supposed to know what he or she is being given may not be the best advice? The answer is, you don't, most times. Gosh, at that age, it's hard enough to figure out the opposite sex, much less something as complicated as writing!

It's also not your fault if you feel reluctant to abandon that voice. After all, it took years and years to master it and for someone to now advise you to let it go may be hard to do. Most of us resist change. It's scary, to be honest! But, what may help is to realize that you're not going to learn an entirely new way of writing. You're only going to rediscover a way of writing you already know! One that's much easier.

I see stuff my own sixth-grader Mike brings home that I know is going to hurt him as a writer if he follows the models furnished. But, I'm a writer and involved in the "game" and can gently steer him away from at least some of the worst instruction he gets. No one else in his class has that advantage—having a parent slash writer driving them home from school. Which means the overwhelming majority of these kids are right now being "trained" to be beige writers. It may not be until college and then only if they get lucky and get a good writing instructor that they begin to break out of that mold.

The point is, you're not to blame and shouldn't beat yourself up for the state you may find yourself in. It's just not your fault! It's not only the schools who promote this kind of writing style. Most institutions—government, business, etc.—do their part to promulgate it as well.

Antidote for the Aristocratic Voice

But, hey! Help is here. You can overcome that voice you were taught to use and escape the tyranny of that style.

You know the "rules" of that style inside-out.

Always use complete sentences.

Never end a sentence with a preposition.

Use synonyms for "said" in dialogue tags.

A thousand and one other, dusty, musty rules.

Yuck.

As Tristine Rainer says in her excellent book on memoir writing, *Your Life as Story*, Tarcher/Putnam, 1997, Tom Wolfe's beige voice is a result of your listening to too many English and writing teachers pound it into your little pointy head to write something called "the King's English." As Rainer says flatly, these writers have learned to write the King's English, but since they aren't the King, it's a kind of ventriloquism.

Your voice has been stifled and warped and twisted until it fits into some kind of generic Jell-O mold.

Time for you to break the mold!

The editor ripping open that envelop wants to meet somebody new and exciting and *different,* just as the ordinary reader does. What he or she doesn't want to meet is another Stephen King or Lorrie Moore imitator. He's already got a Stephen King and Lorrie Moore friend in his circle. As well as a John Grisham and an Elmore Leonard and a Joyce Carol Oates pal. They're right behind him, on his bookshelf. No room there for John Grisham Jr.

This isn't to say that as a writer you shouldn't take advantage of what's hot or that you shouldn't write in a particular genre. Do so, but supply your own voice to the material. That will only make your submission stand out above all the rest who are trying to take advantage of the reading public's taste.

Cure for the Copycat

It's little wonder almost all writers suffer from an inferiority complex concerning their work. From Day One, we're told we're no good and never will be. Oh, not directly . . . although sometimes that happens . . . but by inference. All those dead authors our teachers speak of in authoritative, Charlton Heston-as-God tones. At first, it's Doc Seuss and Mark Twain, then when we get into junior high, the literary idols become Elizabeth Barrett Browning, Rudyard Kipling and Jack London, and by high school, Herman Melville, William Shakespeare and Geoffrey Chaucer take their places among the pantheon of English-teacher-designated gods. (In the really "hip" classes, perhaps the Sallinger stories and maybe a Carver tale or two make an appearance.) In college, the list really expands: Camus, Faulkner, Thackeray, Dostoyevsky and Barth, among many others, are floated out for our adulation. (Speaking of John Barth, about other writers he said, "I haven't read many of my contemporaries. They haven't read me either, and so we are even."). At each stage along the way, these writer ghosts are held up to be the demigods of literary worth and we're encouraged to emulate them in our own efforts.

Then, when we do, we're put down because we can't perfectly imitate their style. We're scorned because we can't out-Hemingway, the ol' ambulance driver and fish saga scribbler.

Well, who could? Besides the original? The teacher never seems to understand that he/she is dooming students to failure and steering 'em toward a goal that's impossible to achieve. That instead of encouraging her charges to copy the cadences of Steinbeck, they might be better served by being urged to listen to their own internal language rhythms and develop those. That future writers might learn something valuable they could use from literary history for their own prose—information such as the knowledge that it was only after Ernest Hemingway stopped trying to imitate Stephen Crane and break loose from Crane's influence that he was able to come up with his own wonderful minimalist style. Although, never entirely, which is possibly his biggest weakness. No doubt, the allegiance to *The Red Badge of Courage* guy that developed in Hemingway's psyche was initiated by some well-meaning teacher of his who thought Crane walked on water or fed the hordes with a single tin of sardines.

Removing the Rose-Colored Glasses

In one of my own short stories, "Rubber Band" which you can find in my collection *Monday's Meal,* the young boy protagonist's pederast/ alcoholic reform school counselor has gotten a book published. Here, in the story excerpts that follow, is a revelation that quite a few writers get about books once they've published one of the critters themselves.

From "Rubber Band" in *Monday's Meal*

He *[Maxwell Doone, the buggering counselor]* had quit being a writer the day his book was published. All his life (he said), he had believed the written word to be magic, to hold secrets that would explain things. He devoured books, searching for the revelation that would explain the mystery of life. It was in there, if not in one particular book, then in an accumulation of books. If he just read enough, everything would be clear and make sense.

But it never did, he said.

A bit later on . . .

He walked down to the bookstore to see his book, he said. He was real excited, in a feverish, agitated way. There it was, in the front window. Next to it, was a new edition of John Donne's poetry. He wondered at that, and then thought maybe the bookstore manager was trying to make the public think there was a connection between the two Donne's.

He said that was when it hit him. There his book was, next to one of the masters of literature, one of those who he had always believed to possess the mystery of what life was all about, and in that instant he knew there was no answer to any of it. Because he didn't have a clue. He knew no more then than he had when he first began to search, but he had a book, one of those places where others would search for meanings, just as he had.

What's not said, but implied, is that he's suddenly realized all his awe for the past masters of literature has been misplaced somewhat. Now, others will be looking at his book with the same rose-colored glasses that he formerly looked through at others' work. Overawe of their work . . . which leads to a desire to also emulate the *style* in which they wrote. It just seems to work out that way.

Don't wait until you have a book published to make the same discovery.

The counselor/author in my story made the same discovery as Gloria Steinem, who said, "Writing . . . keeps me from believing everything I read." This is a person with a healthy attitude toward those masters on the shelves, who also has a bit of faith in her own style! It shows in her work, don't you think?

The Ghost of Critics Past

Critics are like roaches. They come crawling out of the walls when the light goes off.

Many of us as writers have trouble finding our natural voices, not only because of those folks who've provided instruction, but also because of a host of others who've managed to lend a hand in squelching our individualities. We just can't hear ourselves think because of the din being made in our brains by all those past critics of our writing.

Your Personal Exorcism

We need to exorcise these demons.

Get out a piece of paper and write at the top of it, "My Writing Critics." Or, title it "Critic Nag Dudes."

Underneath that, begin a list of names.

Start with your parents.

Add your writing pals.

Then, most, if not all of your teachers from grade school up through graduate school.

Maybe your significant other. What the hey, *probably* your significant other . . .

Expand the list with the names of all the authors of writing "how-to" books.

Lengthen the list with the authors of all the articles in writing magazines you've read.

Pencil in the names of the folks in your writing club, especially the obnoxious one who sits to your left and never fails to find the many flaws in everyone else's manuscripts except his own.

Be sure to list the authors you've heard speak at writing conferences.

And the subjects of interviews with authors.

Editors who advise.

Fellow students, especially those who've been published.

Me. Yeah, me. You didn't think *I* was infallible, did you?

Keep this list for a week and keep adding names as you remember them. Somewhere on your list will be the names of all those folks who gave you advice on writing, or admonishments, or rules, or even praise.

Any time anyone spoke to you, in person, in print, or by any other means of communication about writing, they became your writing critic. Endowed with a loud, shrill, nagging voice. Think "Edith Bunker" and you'll recognize the sound. A voice that begins to screech the instant you sit down before your keyboard. A voice that is an amalgamation of all the hundreds, if not thousands of other such voices, vying for your ear and attention.

Controlling you, influencing you. Determining not only what you write about but how.

Keep adding to this list as names occur to you. At the end of this chapter I'll tell you what to do with it.

✦ ✦ ✦

- **Disclaimer:** This doesn't mean that every single bit of advice, that every rule, that every word of chastisement you've been given or encountered is wrong. Not at all. Much of what you've learned from others is valuable. Alas, much of it is slag and dross. Get rid of that and what you have left is the steel.

Make Your Own Rules

The trick is to figure out what's good for you and what's not. The key words in that sentence are "for you." How do you figure this out? As I said earlier, by trusting your own instincts. If it "feels" wrong, chances are it is. Your instincts are trying to warn you not to follow that rule or custom. How do your instincts know to do this?

Because you're a writer and that means you're a reader. That's where you've learned to write. By reading and reading and reading. All that reading hasn't been a waste of time. It's taught your inner intelligence what works and what doesn't. Learn to trust it more.

Let's look at just a few things you've been told.

Raise your hand if you've ever been told to "show, not tell."

Good advice. Sometimes. It may surprise you to be told that there are places in stories where the writer *should* tell and not show, however. The part of the advice, that, as Paul Harvey might say, is "the rest of the story." Another word for telling is *summary*. If, for instance, you have a scene involving a phone conversation, you shouldn't "show" the entire conversation. You only show the important part by including in dialogue the one or two sentences that are important to the story. And are interesting. The rest of the conversation, the "how are you," the "what you up to," the hellos and goodbyes . . . should be summarized. In general, the uninteresting parts of the story or article but the parts that are also necessary, shouldn't be shown but told.

That's one common example of a piece of advice routinely given by "experts" that requires you to fill in the rest of the advice this was abbreviated from (to provide a pithy saying), for it to be of value.

Another is to "write what you know." How many of you have heard that? Well, if you followed that advice, most us would have a bit of trouble in constructing a character who commits a murder. (At least, I *hope* most of us would . . .) Or design a story set in the year A.D. 3004 or one that takes place in 1823. Men wouldn't write stories told from a first-person female narrator's pov and vice versa. Thank goodness, Tim Sandlin didn't follow that particular advice, or we'd never have been able to experience his really cool novel, *Sorrow Floats*. Or Wally Lamb's *She's Come Undone*, both of which are written from a female point-of-view character. "Write what you can imagine and present convincingly" is better advice.

Forget as well, that advice some may have given you to come up with various and sundry synonyms for dialogue tag verbs. You know, that substitute list of words for the "said" in he/she/name said. You know, those words like replied, chortled, whispered, answered, shouted, explained, yelled, et al. Today, "said" in dialogue tags isn't even a word. It's become a form of punctuation, almost, and as such is invisible, which means the reader doesn't trip over it as he or she does with most other substitutions, which mostly have the effect of making the reader aware that someone is writing the dialogue.

Cut Out the Critics

This is the thing—listen up!—this is important! There is a virtual armada of folks out there whose only function in life is to make you feel inadequate as a writer.

Truth.

I know, I know . . . you've been told by dozens of people—even a couple of souls not related to you—that your writing is fantastic. If you hadn't, you wouldn't be here, yellow highlighter poised to mark the really important stuff. But . . . I'll wager that over the years you've been writing, the naysayers far outweigh those who've come bearing praise and backrubs.

Think about it.

I see you in the workshops I lead and in the classes I've been in

Exposing Critic Nag Dude

If you're still unsure if you have a Critic Nag Dude roosting alertly on your shoulder when you write, here's a list of symptoms to look for:

Critic Nag Dude is present if . . .

* **You find yourself consciously imitating writers you admire.** In my own case, I'm afflicted with "Faulkneritis." I love to read Faulkner, only I can't when I'm in the throes of creating a story. What will happen is I'll have two rapes, a lynching, six cases of incest, and somebody will have shoved a sharp stick into someone else's eye, probably his mentally-challenged sister's. And I'm still in the first paragraph! Which probably isn't exactly the way Faulkner writes, but I always seem to think he does. In your own case, you may have "Lorrie Moore-itis," for example. In your editing phase, you may find yourself going back and putting space breaks between the two or three paragraphs that don't already have one. If so, Critic Nag Dude is in the room.

* **You find yourself searching for alternatives to the word "said" in your dialogue tags or supplying helpful adverbs.** Somewhere along the line you've gotten praise when someone looked at your stuff and read, "I've blown up the nuclear reactor," Jimmy *screamed, glowingly.*

* **You place all your stories in New York City, Paris, London, or Tangiers. Even though you live in Montpelier, Vermont . . .** This is a telling symptom. It's a carryover from your inferiority complex as a writer. Not only have you been taught to feel inferior as a writer, you think where you live is a bohunk place, too. This isn't to say you shouldn't use your imagination and shouldn't write about places you haven't lived—if you can employ the setting convincingly enough that the reader believes that you are familiar with it, go right ahead. The point is, don't neglect your own hometown for a setting simply because you don't think it "exotic" enough for a sophisticated big city editor. Your brick ranch on Elm Street in Fort Wayne, Sioux City or Goober Creek is plenty exotic, believe me.

* **None of your characters—especially your protagonists—are anything like yourself. They all have glamorous professions and live exotic lives.** Your day job is in the field of plumbing or beauty shop work, but all your

protagonists are double agents with a license to kill, and they live in spacious, well-appointed apartments in Soho and date Miss September. Guess what? If you live in a basement apartment, put your character there. Readers will find the setting fascinating. Especially those readers who live in spacious, well-appointed apartments in Soho . . . If the only job you've had this past year was playing Santa at the local Sears' outlet, you've got a great vocation for your protagonist. Especially if you're an Orthodox Jew. David Sedaris's most popular story, "The Santaland Diaries" was an account of the time he got a job as a Christmas elf at Macy's. Writers too often ignore their own jobs when they know 'em cold, and more importantly, the jobs are not considered boring or mundane by others, but highly interesting. Use your own workplace! You'll be glad you did

- **You can diagram every single one of your sentences, and none of them are diagrammed easily, most filling an entire blackboard with multiple levels.** When rereading your day's work, you find you've somehow included a one- or two-word sentence, which causes your ulcer to flare up. You also don't want to go to the other extreme—where you only or mostly have one- or two-word sentences!

- **Someone says, "Your stuff sounds just like Stephen King's."** You feel proud of this and try to stifle the small, still voice inside that's shouting "Big, fat faker!"

- **You find yourself routinely using words in your prose or nonfiction writing that you'd never be caught using in ordinary conversation, or, if you did, your friends would say, "Huh? You swallow a dictionary or somethin'?".** You own a thesaurus and aren't afraid to use it. No one's ever told you there's no such thing as a synonym—there's only the one perfect word. Take the synonyms for *shame*. The difference in meaning between *mortification* and *embarrassment* can be vast.

◆ ◆ ◆

There are many other symptoms and if you stay with us here, you'll discover them all. Don't despair if you have one or even more of them. You're holding the cure in your hands.

myself. I've seen you in my mirror when I shave. Put your own name on the list. We're sometimes our own worst critic.

Now, to that list you've been making.

Take it to the kitchen sink or outside or somewhere where a small fire won't prove disastrous.

Hold it up by a corner and take out your Bic lighter. Set it on fire. Burn that puppy.

Watch your critics go up in smoke.

It's where they belong.

When you sit down to write from now on, if one of them should enter the room, scream at him or her to get out. Smack 'em up alongside their heads. At least, ask them politely to remain quiet unless they see you make a major mistake.

And mean it.

Let's take a step toward getting rid of Critic Nag Dude. Let's write him or her a letter.

A Poison-Pen letter

That's right. A letter that can be as angry as you want it to be. A letter telling Critic Nag Dude to back off—*you're* in charge of your writing destiny from this day hence.

Begin your letter with "Dear Ugly Critic Nag Dude" and end it with "Sincerely, Your Former Slave But No More, (Your name here).

What you put between the salutation and the ending can be as vitriolic or as formally polite as you wish, but get the point across that the addressee is never to enter the portal to your writing space again!

Here's the one I wrote (first draft):

Dear Maggot,

Your mother/father/favorite aunt/favorite uncle/favorite childhood doll/action figure wears combat boots. No, wait! That's another letter.

You stink. (That's better.)

If you wuz a drug, they'd stock you in the enema section. Even if you warn't a drug, they'd stock you there. (How 'bout them misspelled words, Critic Nag Dude? Hope you like 'em!)

They pick up the trash on Monday morning at our house. You're going to be out there on the curb, dude. Hope you enjoy your ride to your "final resting place." Ha ha!

Here's some wisdom for you to mull over on your ride to the dump, Critic Nag Dude. "The same things that make you laugh, make you cry." You used to laugh at my feeble attempts to write in the beige voice. Bet you're not laughing now, are you, scumbag?

You are hereby officially banished/excommunicated/exiled/sent to bed without your supper/driven out/evicted/cast out/ejected and otherwise forbidden to ever again enter my writing room without express permission, sir. If you sneak in without my permission, I will stuff a Dumpster up your nose and sic my son Mike's seemingly-mild-mannered-but-actually-viciously-ferocious-and-many-toothed beagle "Buddy" on you. And then, I will rent you out to the director of the next Rocky movie (*Rocky XCIVXXII, Rocky Meets Rambo*) as a sparring partner for Mr. Balboa.

Got it? Am I clear enough?

Good.

Begone, then.

I never want to see your ugly kisser around these here parts again, if you catch my drift, Your Ugliness.

Sincerely,

Mr. "I Am Not Kidding" Les Edgerton

CHAPTER THREE

You Want Me to Change My Entire Writing Style?

 In the long run, however little you talk or even think about it, the most durable thing in writing is style, and style is the most valuable investment a writer can make with his time.
—RAYMOND CHANDLER

Huh? *Change* my writing style?

Yep.

You betcha.

What you're doing now isn't working, is it? If it isn't (and chances are you wouldn't be reading this if it was . . .) then maybe you'll agree it's time for a change.

The good news is that you won't be changing to something new. You'll merely be applying a writing style you already know. And know far more intimately than that other style you've laboriously strained to achieve. The change will be painless and almost effortless. And . . . it'll be fun!

Not to mention rewarding.

Your chances of becoming published are going to increase dramatically!

Your first step is to rediscover your original voice. For that, we've got a handy-dandy exercise.

Handy-Dandy Exercise

1. Whip out three sheets of paper and a pen or a pencil. No computers, no typewriters! It's time to get basic and return to our roots as writers.

2. Get completely relaxed. Make your mind as blank as you can. (Hint: Try to think like a politician or day-old bread.) Get comfortable. Now, go back in time to when you were six years old. If you can't remember yourself at six (or maybe you're only five when you read this . . .), then go back to the earliest age you can remember. Once you're there, I want you to write a page describing an especially good time you had at that age. It might be a Christmas, it might be when your favorite pro baseball player came to see you at your sickbed and promised to hit a homer for you. Whatever. It's something that really happened that represented a joyful time for you. I also want you to write this description in the vocabulary of that six-year-old. Use the words you would have used then. This requires a silent time by yourself, to sit and try to remember what it was like to be that child and it's crucial you do your best to write in the "language" you possessed back then. Not the language you use today. It may help if you kept a diary or journal when you were a kid. If you did, revisit a few pages of that and it will help get you back to how you thought then and remember the language you used.

3. Next, I want you to do the same thing—write a page describing a delightful experience—only move ahead in time and describe an experience you had when you were a teenybopper. Also, in the words you would have used at that time in your life. If you're near my age, the words "groovy" and "cool" and "boss" will undoubtedly appear in the narrative . . . (Those were common words in the Neanderthal Era.)

4. And last, I want you to write a third page on a great experience you had as an adult, preferably recently. Use the language and vocabulary you now use.

5. That done, I want you to sit down with all three pages and begin to compare them. Take your time and really look at them for the differences. Notice anything? That perhaps the first papers were a bit fresher, even though the language was perhaps a bit more restricted? One thing you will hopefully notice, is that within these three papers, you'll begin to "hear" the one voice that's remained constant throughout your life, even though the vocabulary has changed. Look at the sentences and language that's peculiar to each piece. My guess is that those will be the shorter and simpler sentences and the sentences with few or no adverbs and adjectives. Strong verbs and nouns that say exactly what you mean. Direct and plain descriptions of emotions. I'd also guess that the third piece will contain more flowery language than the first one did. The ornate language probably increased in each paper, right? But, at the core of each piece, there will remain a portion of the writing that is clear, simple and direct. Shorn of ornateness and flowery prose. Pick out the sentences in each example that could fit into the piece written as a six-year-old and wouldn't have stood out. Those sentences stand out in all three examples as they're the ones that don't contain adverbs, multiple adjectives, ten-dollar words. That's *you*, boobie. When you identify that voice, grab hold of it like it was a life raft or a winning lottery ticket. That's the voice that's truly yours and the one you should take to the 'puter and begin writing your current work with. ■

Compare Your Voices

My bet is that if you let a friend read these papers, the voice of the six-year-old is the one she'll like the best.

I'll make another bet that you'll find your six-year-old piece will be sans adverbs and adjectives and the piece written from your current perspective will be loaded with them.

Tell you anything?

We do this exercise regularly in my Neighborhood Connections' classes (local, adult-ed classes here in Fort Wayne), and it's amazing how, without fail, the version folks write as their six-year-old selves always gets voted the best. The worst are always the last ones, written in the person's present language. It's always chockfull of adverbs and adjectives and abstractions—just the stuff of beigeness! From this exercise forward, the writing in class always gets better!

Read Your Work Aloud

One of the very best ways to see if you're writing in your "natural" voice is to read your work out loud to someone who knows you well. Someone like your significant other or a member of your writing group if you belong to one. Maybe even the entire group. Ask them if what you're reading "sounds like you." If they say it doesn't, ask them if they can identify the portions that don't. Those are the sections you need to rewrite.

Look at Old Work

Take out an old story or article you've written some time back. If it looks as if someone else wrote it . . . he did. Someone sitting in your chair and using the beige voice. Try rewriting the piece with the new-found knowledge you've gotten here.

Dialogue

In particular, when looking over older work, check out the dialogue you used. *Really* look at it. Speak it aloud. Does it sound natural? Isolate the words, sentences and phrases that aren't organic to you and rewrite that dialogue with your own, inimitable style.

Individual Words

Take a careful look at each word, both in your older articles, stories, and essays and in your current work. Look for words that you don't use normally. I'm not saying you should eschew all such words automatically, but try substituting the word you'd use in each case with the word you'd use in telling the same story to your best friend. Have someone who knows you well read both selections and tell you which example he or she finds more interesting. One of the clearest signs that a writer is attempting to be "writerly" to impress Critic Nag Dude is his use of words foreign to his normal vocabulary.

Get rid of 'em!

Here's something interesting about a writer's vocabulary. Somebody with too much time on his or her hands once sat down and counted every single word Hemingway used in the whole of his body of work. His essays, novels, nonfiction books—the whole lot. Know how many total words he used?

Eight thousand words.

Eight thousand words is about the total extent of the average sixth-grader's vocabulary.

Tell you something?

What it should tell you is that Hemingway was a pretty smart guy who was generally considered a fair-to-medium writer, and he hardly ever used a word like *ligula* to describe something tonguelike. He just said it was "tonguelike."

As should you.

Okay, someone interjects, "What about writers like Michael Ondaatje or Mario Vargas Llosa? Their prose is lush and rich. They shower you with their loquacity. What about them, huh, huh?"

Good question. The answer is that's *their voice*. Hemingway has a spare, journalistic voice and Michael and Mario don't. It would be a mistake for either of these guys (or you, if your own voice is lavish) to write as Hemingway or Carver did. Or for Hemingway to have tried to "lush up" his prose. Same with William James and Carlos Fuentes and any number of other, excellent writers. And that's all right. In fact, that's more than all right—it's the only way these guys should have written. That's their personality. Their readers who like that personality will find them, as will those who enjoy your personality, whatever that is. If yours is a verbose style, don't change it. In fact, whatever your style of talking or personality, that's the style that needs to be on the page.

Even more accurate than your style of talking is your style of *thinking*. If the voice in your head when you're musing over something uses a rich, complex language . . . then that's your voice. If it's a spare, no-nonsense voice, then that's your voice. Try to remain true to that voice in your work.

I would still cull as many adverbs and adjectives as I could! In most of the exercises within these pages, one of the objective is to pare down the prose, which seems to run counter to a richer style. It isn't, not really. Even a lush style needs some pruning.

Culture Comparisons

Do keep in mind that many of the writers whose prose is writ large and stuffed full of complexity come from a culture in which this is natural. Many of the Latin American writers, for instance, as well as Europeans, especially those with a Romance-root-based language grow up with a language that's rich in nuance. That makes their style "natural" to them. It's also why their material, however genius-like it may be, sometimes reads better in the original language than when translated to English. In the native language, it reads as it should; translated, it sometimes comes across to our ears as verbose or wordy, mainly because we're a culture used to blunt, Anglo-Saxon verbiage.

Just don't adopt a style that's not your own, whether that be spare or lush. Don't borrow, in other words, from a culture different from the one you were raised in.

Make sense?

Be true to yourself; that's the key.

Writing Autobiographically

One of the best ways to begin to recapture your own voice is to write autobiographically. The autobiographical voice demands that you write in none other than your own voice, more so than any other kind of writing. Just makes sense, doesn't it, that if your name is Betty O'Hara, you should be writing your personal saga in Betty O'Hara's voice and not in Anaïs Nin's. Same deal with your fiction, Betty . . . So, if you're having trouble getting into your own voice in your current short story or article on "The Dangers of Muscle Sprains While Hula Hooping," try warming up by writing a few paragraphs autobiographically. Pen a short account of the time you fell down on the buried coffee can when you were nine and gashed your kneecap and had to have sixty-two stitches for the bloody mess. Write it as if you were leaving an account of the incident to your kids. Then, go on to the story you're creating and keep that same voice going in it.

Even more useful for getting into your own voice is to write memoirographically. A memoir is much more narrowly focused than an autobiography. Autobiography spans an entire life, while memoir takes for granted that entire life and ignores most of it, concentrating on a single aspect of it. That's when your own, true voice really comes to life. The emotions you feel are just more intense. Memoir isn't life summary but more of a snapshot and writing a bit of your memoir before you get into the day's regular writing can greatly aid you in achieving your own individuality in the sentences you create when you go to your other material.

Take a look at a bit of Maxine Hong Kingston's memoir, "The Woman Warrior." In the following excerpt, she describes herself as a painfully shy schoolgirl beginning school in a new country (the U.S., in Stockton, California).

When I went to kindergarten and had to read English for the first time, I became silent. A dumbness—a shame— still cracks my voice in two, even when I want to say "hello" casually, or ask an easy question in front of the check-out counter, or ask directions of a bus driver. I stand frozen . . .

During the first silent year I spoke to no one at school, did not ask before going to the lavatory, and flunked kindergarten. My sister also said nothing for three years, silent in the playground and silent at lunch. There were other quiet

Chinese girls not of our family, but most of them got over it sooner than we did. I enjoyed the silence. At first it did not occur to me I was supposed to talk or to pass kindergarten. I talked at home and to one or two of the Chinese girls in class. I made motions and even made some jokes. I drank out of a tea saucer when the water spilled out of the cup, and everybody laughed, pointed at me, so I did it some more. I didn't know that Americans don't drink out of saucers . . .

It was when I found out I had to talk that school became a misery, that the silence became a misery. I did not speak and felt bad each time that I did not speak. I read aloud in first grade, though, and heard the barest whisper with little squeaks come out of my throat. "Louder," said the teacher, who scared the voice away again. The other Chinese girls did not talk either, so I knew the silence had to do with being a Chinese girl.

Think Kingston had any trouble finding or staying in her voice for the other material she may have been working on at the same time she was writing this? She didn't have any trouble simply because she was employing her own, very natural voice.

Write a bit of your memoir as a warmup before tackling the article or story or poem you're writing. Not only will it help you get into your own voice quickly, you may find you've ended up with a publishable memoir!

Can't beat that with a short stick!

Writing Letters . . .

Look over old letters you've written to friends. Chances are excellent that you used your "real" voice in those letters. And letters are a form of autobiography. You're usually relating something about yourself in them—your experiences, your intimate take on various situations or incidents, your feelings. Most of us don't attempt to write in any "writerly" style in our letters to loved ones or friends. We're just "us." Unless, oddly, we write a letter to a writer friend or a teacher. Sometimes in those, we lapse into a different style. The beige style.

When we sit in a coffee shop or a bar or some similar setting with a friend and just chew the fat or gossip or rap with them—we usually employ our own style. In those situations, we hardly ever pontificate or use elevated language. Again, we're just us. And again, our style of speaking is largely autobiographical in tone.

And . . . get this . . . *interesting.*

That's the heart of the voice we need to capture in our writing. It's that voice, the manifestation of our personalities, that attracts folks to us. It also repels other folks . . . and that's all right. Remember when I said a writer shouldn't try to be all things to all people?

Warts

Just about everything in this book is advice on how to get back to being you, to getting *your* voice on the page.

Minus the warts.

Although it's your voice editors and readers really want to hear, you may have a few glitches in your natural voice you'll want to be aware of and try to weed out. Usually, those take the form of little irritating mannerisms that even your best friend may be a bit tired of hearing.

Like the teenager who constantly interjects a "y'know?" after every six words he or she utters.

That's a wart.

Gotta cut those big, ol' uglies out of your prose.

The problem is, you may include irritating things like that in your normal speech so often that you're not even aware of them. If you suspect that may be the case, just ask a couple of acquaintances if they're aware of any such critters you're in love with and if so, to identify them for you.

If you happen to find yourself in possession of any, then type them out and post them above your computer. When you're done with the day's writing, check what you've written and see if any "y'know's" (or, your personal equivalent of such) have made an appearance. If so, position your cursor to the right of them and hit the backspace key until they disappear. Reread your material without the offending little buggers and if it reads just fine without them, you're done. If you find that taking them out leaves big, jagged, crater-like holes in the prose, then write something original and stick that into the hole(s). (Hint) "Y'know's" and the equivalent usually leave only pinhead-sized holes at best and usually no holes at all. You'll probably find you scarcely miss 'em.

What? You wanted something academic-sounding here? This isn't replicating DNA in an M.I.T. lab, folks. It's just writing. Don't make it harder than it is.

Get rid of the bad stuff and put good stuff in its place.

Minor Exception

Of course, if you have a teenaged boy in your story who's only in tentative possession of his three remaining brain cells and you want to create a believable character, by all means have him interject "y'know" after every six words of his dialogue.

I'd suggest making this character minor and killing him fairly soon on in the story. Or at least give him a horrible disease in which his voice box has to be removed surgically to save his life. Say, by the third paragraph . . .

Y'know . . .

In Conclusion

Just be yourself on the page (minus the warts) and you'll be happily surprised at the "friends" who begin to gather. Editor and reader friends . . .

CHAPTER FOUR

It's Okay to Be Yourself.
I Mean–It's REALLY OKAY!

Originality does not consist in saying what no one has ever said before, but in saying exactly what you think yourself.
—J.F. STEPHEN

The society we grow up in is responsible for many of our writing habits—some good and some not so good. What I mean by this is that we happen to find ourselves in a time and place and in a society in which it's considered important to follow the status quo. Many, if not most of us, are afraid to buck the "common wisdom" since being seen as a maverick is not usually a desirable label to acquire. In writing, especially. It's drummed into our brainpans that if we don't do this and that and that and this . . . bad things will happen. Mainly (as writers), that we won't get published if we drive off the established highway and choose our own routes.

(It may be important to note that this view isn't usually advanced by editors and buying readers—it's just everyone else who's appointed themselves an "expert" who promotes it.)

Some of this (wisdom) is undoubtedly good. It's probably sound advice to submit material in the accepted format to editors. No handwritten stories sent in on the backs of grocery bags to *The New Yorker,* for instance. Avoid "as" and "-ing" sentence constructions. Avoid run-on sentences. Forget writing many transitions between scenes. Lots of such advice makes sense and should be followed.

However, lots of advice and admonishments are pure *hooey*, which is a French word for crapola.

This just isn't in the field of writing. This attitude—of only doing what an authority figure has okayed—permeates nearly every aspect of the world we live in. More and more, we're losing much of our ability to think on our own. This used to be the province of teenagers, mostly; nowadays it seems to have pervaded the rest of us.

(I think that's true. I'm going to ask my wife for confirmation . . .)

As a culture, our ability to judge for ourselves has atrophied muchly and we rely more readily than even a short time ago in our history upon others to tell us it's "all right" to do something. Proof of that lies in the huge sums of money companies pay famous athletes to endorse their products.

Take Michael Jordan, for instance.

Companies paid him buckets o' bucks to spend forty-five seconds on the tube extolling their products in ads. Do you suppose that's because those CEO's simply thought ol' Mike's a really neat-o guy and they just wanted to make him rich? Or that they believed Mr. Jordan had spent years and years studying which breakfast cereals were the most nutritious, such scholarship taking place mostly on road trips spent in hotels that didn't get HBO? Not on your life! These were hard-nosed businesspeople and they were paying for a service that translated into a tenfold return on their investment. How's that, you say? Simple. These Armani- and Donna Karan-clad honchos know that the average American doesn't trust his or her own acumen to make even the simplest of decisions. They "need" someone they trust or admire, to tell them it's "all right" to buy a certain product, even breakfast cereal and tennis shoes. If that makes us sound like mindless sheep, well . . . baaaaa . . .

All this is just to let you know some of the reasons we find ourselves as writers following the herd on lots of things we're told. At times, we're somewhat unsure of our own intelligence and writing instincts and at least subconsciously feel we need an authority figure to grant us permission to do the things we should already be doing if we had more faith in ourselves. Sadly, many of us don't.

I Plead Guilty, Your Honor

That includes me. I'll give you a perfect example. For years and years, I was told in every single writing class—was advised in every single writing "how-to" book and article—that I had this left-brain thingy and this right-brain thingy and the "only" way to write, was to use the right-brain thingy and just get the story down. Go lickety-split and get in on the page, I was constantly told. Don't worry about misspelled words, syntax, grammar, punctuation. Especially don't stop if you don't have exactly the right word—just write like an ugly witch was chasing you down the Yellow Brick Writing Road and don't even look at what you're scribbling, but get it down, lickety-split. You can fix it later . . .

The only problem with that advice for me was I didn't work very well with that system of writing. All my instincts told me this was the wrong approach for my own prose. Rushing ahead, getting stuff down just felt wrong. What I wanted to do was find the perfect word for what I was trying to say before continuing. I had this uneasy feeling in my stomach that I'd forget to change it if I went on. Even if I marked it. I just wouldn't be able to recapture what I was feeling or "seeing" then. I got a feeling I ignored, but one I should have paid attention to. I'll bet you've experienced the same thing, at least occasionally. You know what you're doing is "by the book," but it just doesn't feel right.

Trust those feelings! Your wonderful, smart, cool, *learned* mind is telling you something important. Pay attention to it. The thing is, as a writer you're doubtlessly also an avid reader, and it's all that reading you've done that has truly taught you your writing instincts. Much of what you've read, and I suspect most of the stuff you've *liked*, has probably broken the so-called rules you may be trying to obey.

Forget the rules in those instances—at least question them as to their applicability—and follow your heart. If it turns out you were wrong, you'll probably figure that out when you reread it and prepare to rewrite it. Chances are greater, I think, that you'll discover you were right to pay attention to your instincts.

I didn't, because my thought was who was I to quibble with the "authorities?" I was just an unknown, unpublished, wannabe writer! And so I did my best to adhere to this method of writing. *My* instincts told me to stop when the right word wouldn't come easily, to wait until it did and keep searching until I got the only perfect word for that sentence. *My* instincts told me *not* to rush through the scene I was working on and just get to the next one, post-haste, but work with it until it was *exactly* what I was after. But, I couldn't do what my insides were pleading for me to do. Why? I already explained! No one in authority, i.e., a published, successful writer or a renowned teacher—had ever told me it was all right to do so. Whatever they said, I did. Mondo mistake.

Fortunately, I glommed onto a new writing book (and wish I could remember who wrote it so I could give him much-deserved credit), and this teacher gave the opposite advice of just about everybody else in the writer-advice field. His contrarian recommendation was for the writer to sit down and write each story as if it were the final draft. *Not* to rush through it with the right-brain thingy. Use the *good* paper, he further advised—the expensive, twenty-pound with the 25 percent rag content. Not the cheap typewriter stuff made from recycled beaver lodges. (This was in the pre-computer days when we used those artifacts you may have learned about in your study of ancient history, called "typewriters.") He admitted you'd still have to do a rewrite or two, but that you'd find you didn't have to do nearly as many rewrites as you used to. He also went on to demonstrate that when a writer just flies through the story, aiming to come back and "fix" it, the reality was that most of the time the writer couldn't even remember what it was he was going to fix, even if he'd starred, coded, or otherwise flagged the poor choice. The reasons the writer wanted to change it had disappeared from memory. Ever happen to you? (Maybe you just can't remember if it did, but I bet it has.)

I still remember the wonderful thrill I experienced reading this guy's advice. This was exactly the writing method my own instincts had always urged me to follow. With my left *and* right brain thingy fully engaged. Perhaps for many writers the common wisdom on this is the right way for them to write, but it sure wasn't for this Charles Dickens. I would have done what I wanted years before, but I was like most of us—a little sheep-like in my makeup. Didn't trust my own instincts. Needed a Michael Jordan of the writing game to tell me it was fine to buy the box of Wheaties.

Since that day, my writing has improved exponentially. I still perform rewrites, but whereas before it took ten to twenty revisions to get where I wanted to get with the story, now it takes one or two.

Well . . . maybe *three* for the really high-paying markets.

But no more. Three's the limit. Certainly not the double-digit numbers of rewrites I formerly did.

This is all just to illustrate how powerful writing teachers, gurus, editors, publishers, agents, etc. are, and how if we are to follow blindly what they tell us, we end up sacrificing our natural voices in trying to emulate some "standard" they're promulgating.

Your mama was right: Just be yourself, honey, and everyone will love you, pimples, bad haircut, gap teeth and all. Just be yourself, compassionate or ironic, flirtatious or embarrassed, imperfect and real; with *your* style, your tone, and *your* sense of humor. Write as you would to that little (big? huge? stupendous?) group of admirers who is really interested in what you have to say and laughs at your jokes. Loosen up, improvise, relish the sensuality of words. *Your* words, *your* language. Not language borrowed.

Remember this above all else: *Readers enter many (if not, most) pieces of writing not for the story or idea so much as they do to hear the author's voice and through it to enter his or her world. The principal appeal is the writer's distinctive voice.*

Join a writing group where you can read your work aloud to others who can (and will!) say to you, "*This* is your voice. Here, in this portion!" Once you've identified the parts of your work in which others hear your voice, return to those sections. Read them aloud and use them to put yourself in tune. With yourself.

If you can't (or don't want to!) join a writing group, tape yourself as you read your work. You'll hear instantly the sections that aren't written in your voice. Rewrite those until they are.

Clearing the Throat Exercise

One of the best ways to get to your own voice is to clear your throat, so to speak. Orally, you know how to do this. You just hack out the bad stuff in your throat with a "harrumph." To clear your writing voice, you can do something similar to rid yourself of the phlegm. Here's how:

Phlegm-ridding directions

1. Choose an article or a story you've written that you really like, and select what you feel is the best passage in it.
2. Got it picked? Good. Now . . . go through it and mark through every single adverb and adjective in it. No exceptions. Adverbs and adjectives are the hockers of your voice, believe it or not.
3. Read what you have left aloud.

◆ ◆ ◆

What you should notice is that whatever you wrote is still there and should be clear(er). What you should also notice is that the "pace" of the piece should be faster and it will probably have become writing more "alive." Then, if you want, go back and put back a few adjectives . . . but be sparing . . . and look for stronger adjectives than the ones you used before. Don't replace the adverbs. They bring bad karma and are rarely aligned with the planets.

Whaddya think?

This is an excellent way to begin your day's writing and ease yourself into your true voice. ■

Your Opinion Counts

One of the most beneficial things that can help you become the best writer you can be is to realize that no book, no authority, no teacher, no classic book example, should be absorbed unless it's ingested with a grain of salt. Seasoned with a healthy dose of cynicism. Turn on Hemingway's famous "bullshit detector." He's dead now and can't use it, so it's all right for you to. It's my hope that my own example here will do for you what that long-ago writing teacher did for me—open your eyes to the fact that your own writing instincts, even though they may go against the grain of the common mentality of the writing community—may be exactly what you need to be trusting and following. If you've read rabidly all your life, believe it or not, you know as much as just about anybody in the writing game. You may not be able to articulate it as well as some professors, but you don't have to. All you have to do is follow your gut. I give you permission to do so. In fact, I urge you to follow your own instincts, when push comes to shove or vice versa.

It'll save you a lot of time in your writing career and make your bank balance healthier.

Trust your instincts!

Trust your own voice.

It's a winner.

The following page is for you. Write your name in the blank provided. Then, tear it out and tape it above your writing desk. If you're the kind of person who doesn't like to deface books, then leave it there, but whenever a Critic Nag Dude perches his or her ugly self on your shoulder, turn to it and read it.

Out loud. In a belligerent, threatening voice.

Be Like Frank Sinatra

. . . and do it *your* way! With your voice.

Blues singer Jay Hawkins was like many writers at one point in his career. He knew music like engineers know cosines, but he just couldn't command an audience. He was much like many other singers, with nothing notable that stood out about his "sound." He wasn't putting his own personality into his voice, in plain language, as important in music as it is in writing. Kind of what Muzak is . . . He studied opera and then jazz and then moved on to the blues. In each of those music forms, he was

To: _____
(Your name goes here. I'd suggest a nice Caligula script.)

As a recognized writer and teacher, I hereby give you permission to use your own natural voice in your future writing.

Signed: *Les Edgerton*

---

just another anonymous singer, failing to build a following worth talking about. Then, one day, a mentor in the record biz suggested Hawkins stop singing and do what the executive knew he did well when he was "foolin' around"—and begin *screaming*. Yep. Screaming. I don't know if the exec heard him in the shower at the studio one day after a grueling sesh of La Bohéme or what, but the guy was slick enough to know that a classically-trained scream could mean gold, as in gold records. Nobody had the kind of guttural and sexy yowl that Hawkins possessed.

Thus was born a star, Screamin' Jay Hawkins.

"I didn't have the best voice for blues and R&B," he said. "But I could scream. I called on my opera training. I can scream soprano—like a woman."

He got popular because he got his own personality into his sound. If you tune into the local oldies radio station, you can still hear his songs played. Maybe you've heard his "I Put a Spell on You" which was a big hit in the fifties.

I'd like you to do something like Screamin' Jay Hawkins did.

Screamin' Jay Hawkins Exercise

Write a poison pen letter to Critic Nag Dude. Scream as loud at him in it as you want or can. Really tell him off! Rave, rant and bellow at the top of your pen or keyboard! Get downright nasty to the guy. He deserves it.

Or, if you're not the violent sort, pretend you're the leader of an Amish community and are composing an official *shun* letter to send to him. In case you aren't aware of the practice of shunning, when somebody commits a sin considered unpardonable in the Amish religion, he's allowed to remain in the society, but no one speaks to him or has any kind of intercourse with him. He becomes a nonentity.

Make Critic Nag Dude a nonentity.

You can even mail it off to him if you want. With the speed of the U.S. mails, it'll be years before it comes back. And when it does, the stamp you put on it will really be worth something!

Now, that's getting revenge on the pest! ■

CHAPTER FIVE

Here's Lookin' At You, Kid . . .
A New and Different Way of
Looking At Your Audience

 When I write, I aim in my mind not toward New York but toward a vague spot a little to the east of Kansas. I think of the books on library shelves, without their jackets, years old, and a countryish teen-aged boy finding them, and having them speak to him. The reviews, the stacks in Brentano's are just hurdles to get over, to place the books on that shelf.
—JOHN UPDIKE

While many of us have struggled to keep our own unique personalities from the page—using Wolfe's "beige voice" because we've been cursed with an inferiority complex by those influences we've been talking about—a flip side to that coin exists. Like most things in life, there's an opposite at work.

Nearly as many writers as are overawed by those authors on the library and bookstore shelves find themselves looking for ways to *oversimplify* their prose efforts. They go over the top to make their articles and stories "understandable" for their readers. Writing *down*, in other words, to the audience. The result of not showing enough respect for the reader's intelligence.

Which leads to . . . you guessed it . . . a departure from your own natural voice in a misguided effort to make what you're writing clearer.

Easily, one of the biggest problems I see in every class I teach among my students and perhaps the single toughest obstacle they'll need to overcome to achieve their natural voices is learning to trust readers' intelligence.

It may well be your own biggest flaw.

Not to worry. Help's on the way, I promise. A very easy "fix."

Inflated Ego Syndrome

Huh? I just found out I may have an inferiority complex and now you're telling me I may have a *superiority* complex?

Yep.

Very possible.

You may even be guilty of vacillating between the two extremes, depending on the audience you visualize or anticipate will be reading your stuff. Not trusting the reader to "get it" is actually the manifestation of the same problem

How So, Wiseguy?

I'm glad you asked!

A *superiority complex* arrives courtesy of those you interact with in your everyday life and how you've learned to view them.

Looking at it in another way, it's the same side of the inferiority complex coin. Because we may be intimidated by those who've been published, we may simply be transferring the condition we think we find ourselves in to our readers. This gets a little tricky, but the gist of what I mean is that even though we may be intimidated by those geniuses on the shelves, we kind of sense we at least know more about writing and literature than our potential customers. After all, we're *writers* . . . and they're not. Just makes sense that we're better read and more knowledgeable than the folks we're penning our stories and articles for, right?

Well, maybe. Maybe not.

The thing is, even if they're not, we have to assume they're as bright as we are and have had the same access to life and literature and all that as we ourselves have had. Some will have and others will not. Doesn't matter. By thinking too much about what our readers do or don't know, we become so focused on them that we lose our natural voice.

This is something we have to accept as truth if we want to get past writing down to our readers, i.e., "dumbing down the prose," and therefore adversely affecting our true voices. You'll find that pill isn't that bitter when swallowed. In fact, it's kind of liberating to realize you don't have to explain things in your stories to readers and can just get on with the fun of writing the story. Or article. Same thing happens with nonfiction writers. And poets. And advertising copywriters. No, scratch ad writers . . .

Let's look at some of the reasons this all comes about.

Writers' Isolation

I'll wager that most of you reading this book do something else to earn your daily bread. Which means that for most of your waking hours, you're among non-writers. That's probably true even if you're self-employed or stay at home with those small citizens roaming around the living room who bear your last name and a smaller version of your nose. If your main source of social contact happens to be your significant other, he or she probably isn't a writer either.

Further, most of the people you work in the office or on the assembly line with—or break bread at noon with—or meet in the coffee shop after work with—more than likely aren't writers—chances are they probably aren't *readers* either. Oh, sure, casual readers, but not readers to the depth you're a reader.

What does this mean to you as a writer?

Only this—it's easy to begin to think of your own potential readership as being comprised of the same kinds of folks you see at work or at play or bearing a strong resemblance to the family next door. Nonwriters and nonreaders or casual readers, mostly. Unless you lease a rent-controlled co-op in the Simon & Schuster building.

And why wouldn't you see your audience that way? After a while, it's only natural to imagine most people in the country itself are pretty much like the folks you see everyday.

Well, most folks are . . . but those aren't your readers, usually.

Your reader is yourself.

Write This Down!

I'll repeat: *Your reader is yourself.*

Or someone much like yourself.

Someone who shares your interests, knows just about the same things as you do, has close to the same intelligence, has a reading background and history similar to what you've had.

You may never meet him or her.

What I'm getting at is that *your* reader—at least, the sort of reader you *should* be writing for—isn't personally known to you and I doubt if you have much, if any personal contact with him or her, nor are you likely to.

How does this affect your writing style?

By getting out of your own natural voice to please someone else.

The answer?

Make yourself your intended reader. By writing to *you* as your reader, you get closer than at any other time to getting your real voice on the page. You write naturally.

You don't, for instance, include subtle "explanations" in your prose when you write to yourself.

What is somewhat derogatorily referred to by some as "dumbing down the prose." This is when you attempt to make what you're writing crystal-clear for a readership you may assume needs that info . . . because they're not you. We likely do this kind of thing because we make the people we see every day our assumed audience.

You and I both know that the folks you see every day are not dumb—not by any means, at least I hope not!—it's just that most of them are focused and interested in areas other than literature. Doesn't make 'em bad people. Doesn't make 'em dumb, either. Not at all. It just makes 'em *not* your readership. Makes 'em your friends and co-workers and wives or husbands or whatever. Nothing more. It doesn't make them the reader slash customer you're after. The problem is, because of who we mix with daily, we begin to assume the folks who will be reading our stuff are like those people.

Which means we begin to "write down" for that imagined audience. Mostly by providing "explanations" in a variety of ways to help out the imagined reader. A noble sentiment, but one that's detrimental to both your voice and to the overall quality of your work.

This gets us out of our voice because now we're trying to "explain" things to the reader, making it easier to slip back into the beige voice. Think about it. In "real life," if you feel you have to begin explaining something in the middle of a story—a term, some background you think necessary for the listener to understand the story—you slip out of that "natural" story-telling mode and tend to revert to a more formal diction. We might call it our "dictionary voice." Once you begin to think you have to explain something in your prose, the same thing happens.

It's just a mistake to do so in writing.

It shows. What happens in your desire not to appear elitist . . . is that you've just lifted your little finger off the teacup and stuck your nose up in the air! You've assumed your audience needs assistance, but they really don't. You simply have to trust that they'll get it, and if some don't (which is entirely possible), it really doesn't matter. Those few souls most likely aren't your audience anyway. Always keep in mind that as writers we can't "be something to everybody." If we have that mindset when we sit down to create a piece of work, we will very likely become "nothing to nobody."

Dang! Almost seems like we can't win, doesn't it? Relax. You can and you will. You can (win) if you figure out that this is what you're doing (writing to someone you don't know) and you will (win) if you just cease doing so. Once you recognize you've been guilty of writing down to your reader, it becomes a snap to quit doing so.

Think about it. How many times have you "simpled down" the story or article you're writing, chiefly because your experience "tells" you that you'll have to in order for others to "get it?"

More than once, I bet. *I'm* guilty of doing so. Not so much anymore, but at one time . . .

If you have, then you haven't been writing for your real reader. You've been writing for your acquaintances. Sorry, chum. That's what today's teenager might call, "your bad."

Examples

It would probably help if I gave you some examples of writing down to the reader, wouldn't it? Okay, then . . .

Over years of teaching beginning writing students, I've identified two basic areas in which tyros reveal that they're doing this writing down thing. (I shouldn't confine that to "newbies" as more than several of my students have been writing for a long time, are fairly polished writers, and still make many of these same mistakes. At the *beginning* of the class . . .) All correctable mistakes that hardly ever require complex surgical procedures. Just about all of the students I've been privileged to teach have corrected these problem areas by the end of a single class. It really doesn't take that much to fix the problems—recognizing the particular element for what it is and then just paying attention to the times it begins to creep in so you can cut it and toss it in the circular file. Getting you back to your natural, easy-flowing voice.

The two primary offenders lie in the writer's use of *backstory/setup at the beginnings of stories and articles* and *dialogue as an information dump.* The very same problems appear in nonfiction as in fiction when the author feels he or she has to lay out a bunch of "facts" or "circumstances" in the (usually) mistaken concept that the reader will need all this to get into the account. Just tell the story whether it's fiction or nonfiction!

Backstory/Setup

This is probably the most common way in which writers reveal they are writing down to the readers. Beginning stories and articles with too much background and/or setup. Writers include this (backstory/setup) in a mistaken assumption that if they don't bring the readers up-to-date, what follows (the story) will be hard or impossible for the reader to understand unless they are each fortunate enough to have an IQ of 3,684.

Not true!

Gonna show you what I mean by the use of an example from one of my own stories, "In the Zone" which was originally published in *High Plains Literary Review* and then chosen for Houghton Mifflin's "The Best American Mystery Stories 2001."

I'll give you *my* version first, the way it appeared in print. After that, I'll give you another version as it might have been written by a writer who thought the reader wouldn't "get it" without the assistance of a little backstory.

Here's an excerpt from "In the Zone" from *High Plains Literary Review* and *The Best American Mystery Stories 2001.*

> I told Manny the whole story. We were staying in, on a Saturday morning while everyone else went to the movie. Sat up at the front table, playing double sol and eating Keebler's Chocolate Chips and smoking tightrolls, Camels. Doing the prison day off thing.
>
> "I was hung up on her, bro," I said, trying to explain it to him. "She owned my ass."
>
> "I been there," he said and the way he said it I knew it was true.
>
> "We were broke up and I was taking out some other ladies," I went on. "One weekend, a Sunday, I must have had four different babes come over, different times, got laid each time. I was having a ball but it was crazy. No matter how much fun I was having, I still couldn't get Donna out

of my mind. I was "messed" (not the original word) up, man.

"Anyway, the last chick left about eleven that night and I went to bed. To sleep." Manny cracked up, leaned back in his chair and laughed with his head tilted back and his mouth wide open.

"I guess you weren't gonna pound your trouser worm," he said.

"I guess not. I was just getting asleep when the doorbell rang and I got up and it was Donna. 'I got to talk to you,' she said.

"Gosh (not the original word), Donna," I said. "I'm just about asleep. We're over, sugar. Why don't you just leave me alone. 'No,' she said, 'I've really got to talk to you.'

"Well," I said, "I'm just about asleep and if I don't go right back to bed I won't be able to. I oversleep and lose this job my P.O.'ll violate me.

" 'OK,' she said, pushing her way in. 'You go back to bed. I'll come with you and we'll talk in the morning. It's really important.' "

Okay. This is the very beginning of the story, from the git-go. Did you notice there was absolutely no backstory, absolutely no setup? We (readers) just plunge into the middle of a conversation between these two guys. I didn't start off with any explanation of who these guys are or where they were, but I think you "got it" from just a very few things that are delivered as the story goes on, that these are a couple of convicts in a prison and the narrator/protagonist is talking about a bad relationship he had. Don't even name the narrator! Yet. (His name is Jake if you're interested.)

I'm really proud of this story—it's my personal favorite. One of the reasons I take pride in it is because I trust the reader's intelligence. Believe me, I haven't always! Probably none of us who write do, at least in the beginning. That means if you're guilty of providing too much for the reader—not trusting his or her intelligence to "get it" without lots of help—then you're in the majority of us writer-types. But, hey! We're gonna fix that, right? You bet we are!

Let's take a close look at this story excerpt, and I'll try to show you how the readers' intelligence is respected by concrete examples. To begin with, I assume most of you reading this aren't ex-cons (as I am), nor have you probably had much experience with critters like me or the places we've been, such as in the joint. My readers are the same. Just about none of them have much experience or knowledge of this kind of life. Knowing that (and I did), it might have been tempting to bring the reader up to par on the situation before I jumped into the story proper. Only it wasn't. I didn't much care if the reader knew anything about prison life or criminals. It just didn't matter. Why? Because even if the reader didn't know much about any of this from personal experience, he or she did know about prisons and criminals and such from watching several dozens of movies and TV shows and from reading (hopefully!) hundreds of books about same. If I told the story and assumed he'd understand what was going on, I figured he'd get most of it. And I think the reader did. Didn't you when you read it? Even if you didn't know some or even all of the terms and didn't know the backstory, I'll bet you figured it out pretty well just from the context and the way it was presented, didn't you?

This is how you stay within your own voice. By assuming a reader who knows what you know and not being tempted to "fill in the blanks" for him or her.

Let's go through the example. It begins, "I told Manny the whole story." Without saying anything else, we know these are two people, and the narrator is going to tell a friend a story. The friend's name, "Manny" tells us a lot about him without anything else. He's probably Hispanic and because he's referred to as "Manny" instead of "Manuel," we probably get that he's not a professional person. This is usually a blue-collar nickname.

The last sentence in this brief, opening paragraph gives all the backstory necessary. "Doing the prison day off thing." With the few sentences that came before, we see these are two inmates and it's the weekend in the joint. Nothing about why they're there or, their crimes, (not important to the story) and nothing about their relationship. By virtue of the fact that Jake's telling a highly personal story to Manny, we know they're close friends and probably have been for some time.

Also, in this first paragraph is some material I could have been tempted to "explain." "Double sol" refers to the card game of double solitaire. That's not so much of a stretch to trust the reader'd get it, but the next one, "tightrolls" might have been. In prison, most of us couldn't afford real cigarettes, so the state furnished stuff in little gauze drawstring bags that looked like wheat chaff (and tasted worse), called "Hoosier tobacco," and papers, and we rolled our own. Tightrolls were a real treat. But, by following what might have been a confusing reference (tightrolls) by "Camels," I've furnished enough of a clue, I think. Without going into the kind of lengthy explanation I just did!

Then, the first bit of dialogue. *"I was hung up on her, bro,"* I said, *trying to explain it to him. "She owned my ass."* Lots of information here, but the reader has to bring something to the party, furnish a bit of the meat himself. (The author provides the skeleton; the reader the flesh. Stories are a participatory exercise in which both reader and writer do some of the work. Makes 'em more fun to read and certainly to write!) From this brief speech, we know Jake is talking about some girl and that she no doubt has caused him a problem. Else why would he be telling the story to Manny? Doesn't name her (Donna), but doesn't have to yet. Doesn't "explain" that he's talking about a lost love, his old girlfriend, none of that. Not needed. The reader will get it. He's already preambled this to Manny, but as the storyteller, I don't have to begin there when he does this as the context implies they've been talking for awhile. This bit also poses a kind of story question when it says, "trying to explain it to him." This shows that Jake hasn't really gotten a handle on what the experience meant to him and that by telling it, the implication is that maybe he'll come to that understanding. And, the reader subconsciously knows he's going to go through that experience right along with Jake and he'll receive the insight at the same time Jake does. This is the kind of thing that gets the reader into the fictive dream, suspending his disbelief.

When Manny replies, "I been there," this carries the bitterness of a soul mate, one who's been burned by fair female himself. *Shows* the reader these two guys have a bond, rather than *telling* them something. For instance, the narrator could have said something to show his friendship with Manny in an internal monologue like, "We were close." That's *telling*, not showing.

Jake then goes into a bit about how he was living the bachelor's dream . . . but Donna is still in his heart. He's got a real problem. A problem just about everyone has experienced, man or woman. Getting over a lost love.

I'll skip the rest of this for now, but look at it and see if you don't see other examples of where I trusted the reader's intelligence to get the picture simply by eavesdropping on this conversation, without any background/setup provided. By doing so, I was able to remain in my own voice throughout. I wrote to "me." I'm going to come back to this excerpt a bit later, when I talk about dialogue.

Here's how I *could* have written the previous excerpt:

> Pendleton Reformatory is one of Indiana's two maximum security prisons. The only difference between Pendleton and Michigan City—the other max prison—is that those convicted of a felony under the age of thirty were sent to Pendleton and those over thirty to Michigan City. I was in Pendleton, doing a two to five sentence for a variety of crimes. Strong-arm robbery, second-degree burglary, possession of narcotics with intent to sell . . . stuff like that. What had happened was I copped a plea bargain whereby I "confessed" to all my crimes, helping the cops clear up a bunch of cases they'd never be able to solve in a hundred years, and in exchange the prosecutor'd reduced everything to a single count of burglary.

Happens all the time. Only way the cops could clear up nine-tenths of the crimes on the book.

Anyway, here I was—one year down and one to go—only, as it turned out, I'd do a lot more time than I was figuring on at the time. It was a Saturday morning. Every other Saturday, half the cellblock got to go to a movie and the other half went out to the exercise yard. Or, stayed back in the cellhouse, watched TV in the rec room. This was in the days before inmates were allowed TVs in their cells like they are now and the only set available was a small black and white in the rec area.

Which is what I was doing. Skipped the movie—one of those twenty-year-old John Wayne epics they always showed—along with Manny DeJesus, a dude I'd partnered up with when I first came in. A guy I'd become closer to than a brother.

Manny and I were sitting at one of the picnic tables in the TV area, munching on a bag of Keebler's chocolate chip cookies, playing double solitaire and rolling cigarettes.

Get the picture? You should, since I've just laid it all out in minute detail. Not nearly as much fun to read though, is it? After reading the published version and then this, isn't your intelligence insulted maybe a tiny bit by the "revised" version? Especially after reading the first?

My point.

Assume that your reader is a pretty smart cookie and you'll remain within your voice because you'll be writing to someone like yourself. Or even . . . *yourself.*

Dialogue

One way to check your work to see if you're not respecting your reader's intelligence is to check the dialogue you give your characters in both fiction and nonfiction exchanges. Determine if you're providing the kind of dialogue that moves the story along or if you're using at least some of it mostly as an "info dump" for the reader's benefit.

This gets you out of your own voice just as providing backstory/ setup as explanation does.

Looking again at the example from "In the Zone," let's see how that works:

"Gosh, Donna," I said. "I'm just about asleep. We're over, sugar."

That's the way Jake talks in real life. He and Donna have a history, so he doesn't say (for benefit of the reader), "Gosh, Donna. Our relationship is over, sugar. We're not together, anymore." That would be using dialogue for an info dump. Not trusting the reader's intelligence to "get it."

In the next paragraph, Jake says, *"I oversleep and my P.O. 'll violate me."*

Again, I don't explain what a "P.O." is. I trust the reader to get that this refers to his "parole officer." I also don't explain that "violate" means that his P.O. will rescind Jake's parole status and send him back to prison. I just let Jake talk the way he would. Donna knows what a P.O. is, and she knows what "violate" in this context means. Therefore, he wouldn't explain either term to her in real life, and if such an explanation appeared here, it would only be there because I wanted to make sure the reader understood it. Another information dump. Another way to say that I think my reader's apt to have the brainpower of a Shetland pony.

This is what Jake *might* have said if I hadn't trusted the reader's smarts:

"I was just about asleep, Donna. You know me. If I get waked up, I can't get back to sleep. I'll be awake half the night and I might oversleep in the morning and I've got to be at work at seven o'clock. Sharp. If I'm late, you know my boss is a prick and hates me and is just looking for an excuse to call my parole officer so he'll violate my parole for being late to the job and send me back to the prison at Pendleton."

See how I got out of my voice to give you all this information? Went from informal to formal? That's precisely what happens when you begin using dialogue for an information dump. Your language changes almost automatically because you're straining to deliver dialogue that isn't natural to your reader. In effect, your character has to "think" now before he or she speaks, and the result is contrived and unnatural. And, far, *far* away from your own effortless voice!

To overcome this tendency if you have it, you merely need to assume your reader to be a person much like yourself. Someone with your background and experiences and who's read the same books you have.

When you write for a reader like yourself—your twin—you begin writing for a reader who doesn't have to have much explained to him. Doesn't require backstory/setup or doesn't need to be fed information via characters' dialogue. After all, your reader knows the same things you do and you get to "talk" to him or her in the same kind of shorthand you do when you think to yourself or talk to an old, close friend or relative.

In *your* voice.

Nonfiction

Think this only applies to fiction?

Nah.

Let me give you an example of how writing for someone other than a reader like yourself can affect your writing style when you're writing nonfiction:

This is from Lucy Grealy's sobering memoir, *Autobiography of a Face*, an account of her overcoming her facial disfigurement caused by childhood cancer. It starts out like this:

> My friend Stephen and I used to do pony parties together. The festivities took place on the well-tended lawns of the vast suburban communities that had sprung up around Diamond D Stables in the rural acres of Rockland County. Mrs. Daniels, the owner of Diamond D, took advantage of the opportunity and readily dispatched a couple of ponies for birthday parties. In the early years Mrs. Daniels used to

attend the parties with us, something Stephen and I dreaded. She fancied herself a sort of Mrs. Roy Rogers and dressed in embarrassing accordance: fringed shirts, oversized belt buckles, ramshackle hats.

Okay. Here's the deal. Grealy wrote this for a reader she obviously imagined having much the same background and knowledge she possessed. How do I know that? That's easy. From the sentence that begins: *She fancied herself a sort of Mrs. Roy Rogers.* She doesn't explain who "Mrs. Roy Rogers" is, although I know for a fact there are quite a few people, under, say, the age of thirty-nine or so who don't have a clue who she's referring to. I tested this out, asking my twelve-year-old son Mike if he could tell me who Mrs. Roy Rogers was. Now, if I'd asked him who "Tré Cool" was, he would have given me one of those "I can't believe my dad is so five minutes ago" looks, and said, "Dad. Tré Cool is *only* the drummer for Green Day. You know, the group that had the tunes "Geek Stink Breath" and "Brain Stew" I'm always playing."

But . . . asking him about Mrs. Roy Rogers predictably got me one of his famous blank stares. The same kind of look I usually get if I ask if he's cleaned his room yet or brushed his teeth or done his homework.

For those of you, who, like my son, may not be familiar with the name, "Mrs. Roy Rogers," she was the late Dale Evans, wife of the oater and TV star back in the forties and fifties. An American pop culture icon, in her day.

I knew who Mrs. Roy Rogers was—after all, I've been around since God was a little boy—but I'm pretty sure many of Grealy's readers were like Mike and didn't have the slightest intimation to whom she was referring.

Did she stop to provide an explanation?

No ma'am! No sir! She assumed a reader like herself. For those "in the know" the way Grealy presented her name—"Mrs. Roy Rogers" instead of "Dale Evans"—was humorous. There's a lot going on here. Referring to her as "Mrs. Roy Rogers" instead of Dale Evans requires the reader to *really* be aware of who she was, as well as make a subtle statement about American society at the time. Women then were largely considered second bananas to their husbands and she's making a clever statement here. Also, by using Dale Evans as Mrs. Daniels' role model, she's showing the reader what era the scene took place in. A lesser writer would have furnished the year or decade, but Grealy is a superb writer who knows that the best writing leaves some work for the reader to do. She gives the "clue" to all this—status of women, the year of the scene— via the reference and this is what good writing is all about. Allowing the reader the delight of figuring stuff out for herself.

If Grealy had been trying to overexplain for a reader, she might have written a different sentence. Something like, *She fancied herself a sort of Dale Evans—the one-time famous wife of Roy Rogers, the famous "Singing Cowboy" movie and TV star of the '50's—and dressed in embarrassing accordance with that former pop icon: fringed shirts, oversized belt buckles, ramshackle hats.*

But Grealy wrote the book for a person like herself, a reader who knows as well as she does who Mrs. Roy Rogers was and also her image in our culture at one time.

It's just plain exciting to come upon a book and an author like this. One who doesn't overexplain to her reader and who remains fully within her own voice by refusing to do so.

All you have to do is follow Grealy's example and the readers of your work will react the same way upon encountering your writing. Just assume they'll get it.

Will some of the readers of Grealy's memoir be lost when they encounter the reference to Mrs. Roy Rogers? Be totally clueless as to who she's talking about?

Without a doubt.

Should she care?

Nope.

Why?

Because . . . a writer can't be everything to everyone. However . . . I'll bet they become her readers. As will those who read your prose become yours, even if they don't understand all the references. Why? Because you've given them the ultimate compliment a writer can give to a reader.

You've told them you think they're pretty smart.

Know anyone who can resist that?

Trust the Reader's Intelligence

Assuming your reader to be a person much like yourself and writing accordingly is what writing teachers and writing texts are referring to when they urge you to "trust the reader's intelligence."

At this point, we've illustrated how very easy (and common!) it is to fall into one of two traps in our writing styles. One trap being the tendency to use elevated language, ten-dollar words, etc., which comes from an inner uneasiness that we just don't measure up to those published authors on the bookshelves. The reverse snare, in which we do the opposite—overexplicate our writing—stems from the supposition that our audience is comprised of those with less awareness than ourselves.

Dumbing down our writing results in work that kind of automatically lapses into that "bureaucratic" style of writing we've been trained to use. Which means . . . you guessed it! . . . we're now out of our voices and into vapid, generic ones.

Not good!

How to avoid it? Write for yourself.

We've also seen how we can bounce back and forth between the two stances when we sit down and begin to type our manuscripts.

The "cure" I've advised in both instances has been to be yourself on the page and write for yourself.

The Big "But"

But—there's always a "but" isn't there?—the perhaps obvious question that arises from that advice is, "Wait a minute. Do you mean that all the characters I create in my stories or articles speak in my voice and, use the language I'd use in ordinary conversation with my friends? Am

I expected to make every character in my book an extension of my own personality? In other words, are you saying that each character in my story or article be *me*? Look like me, speak in my voice, react only the way *I* would in situations?"

Good question! Shows you're thinking.

And the answer is a resounding *No*!

'Course not.

It'd be a pretty bland story if all the characters sounded the same. It'd be a snooze of an article if all those making an appearance were alike.

"So then . . ." you say . . . and I interrupt to finish your thought for you, " . . . how do I create a character totally unlike myself and still remain within my own voice?"

I'm glad you asked that!

By stealing from the pros.

Actor pros.

A great example of how to put your own personality into characters different from yourself is right in front of us. I'm talking about the people you watch nightly on the tube.

Actors

Successful actors—that is, actors who actually get gigs and make a living from their craft—make marvelous use of their own individualities in creating the roles they play on the screen. You can use the same technique to create the roles you "play" on the page.

It's an easy approach to master. All you're going to do is reach within yourself for the quality you need to bring to the creation of your characters. Let's say you've thought up a really neat character whom you see as having an addiction to heroin and it's that "flaw" that makes her memorable. Only problem is . . . you've never had a smack jones your own fine, law-abiding self! That thought sobers you up the minute it occurs to you and you reluctantly try to imagine another character, one with characteristics you can relate to.

Stop!

Think back. Remember that period in your life when you were a chain-smoker and had a permanent yellow stain on your fingers from the Camels you inhaled? Or when you couldn't live without at least half a pint of Häagen-Dazs Chocolate-Chocolate-Chip per calendar day?

There you go. That's where you go, what you draw on. You just put yourself back into the place you were at at one time with your own addiction. Exaggerate that a bit and voila! you're cooking up a terrific heroin addict (no pun intended).

You just draw from related experiences from your own life. Doesn't matter if the connection is a bit tenacious. Look for the connection from your own background or experience to the character you're creating or the situation you're writing about and use it.

If you're writing a magazine article on adoption from the adoptee's pov and you've never actually been adopted yourself (far as you know!), you probably still have a personal experience you can draw upon to get inside the adoptee's skin and create a memorable, emotional article. Maybe your parents forced you to go to science camp the summer you were ten. For the first two days, you cried and cried in your bunk each night, and then the counselor talked to you and suddenly everything was all right. Go back to that experience and remember how you felt when you're creating the scene where little Jimmy leaves the foster home for the home of his new permanent parents. It's not the same thing, sure, but it's close enough to work and allow you to render a scene that carries the verisimilitude of truth to it.

Actors do this all the time.

As can you.

One of the many examples in literature of a writer assuming a character vastly different from himself and carrying it off convincingly, is the first-person Delores in Wally Lamb's best-seller, *She's Come Undone*. Look at just one paragraph from the novel, where Lamb writes as a ten-and-a-half-year-old girl.

> I was on the brown plaid sofa, watching TV and Scotch-taping my bangs to my forehead because Jeanette said that

kept them from drying frizzy. Across the room on the Barca-lounger, my mother was having her nervous breakdown.

Do you doubt for a moment that this isn't a young girl talking to us here? And, I'm reasonably certain Lamb is neither ten years old nor is he a girl. But . . . he's *been* ten years old at one time and he's also an astute observer of human beings in their behavior. From his own experience, he's able to create a believable character that on the surface appears to be quite unlike his own, and he makes us believe that character is real.

The "trick" isn't to go outside the self, but rather to go deep inside for what already resides there, bringing to the writing desk the same techniques that talented actors employ. And how to do this?

One way I've discovered, is by using an exercise I've "borrowed" from my friend, writer and creative writing teacher Jane Bradley. Okay, okay, so I didn't borrow it; I stole it. (Bear in mind that bad writers *borrow*; good writers *steal* . . .)

Another Handy-Dandy Exercise

Here's what I'd like to ask you to do:

1. On the list provided next, pick out a character. (Or, if you'd rather, use a character you've created in the story you're currently writing.)

CHARACTER LIST

Rookie policewoman	Hooker	Baptist preacher
Elementary schoolteacher	Barber	Arson investigator
Teenaged Amish boy	Deaf girl	CPA
Cabdriver	Priest	Heroin junkie
Nail technician	Actress	Major league pitcher
Blind man	Gymnast	German shepherd
Alien from Xanatu 12	Wino	Serial murderer
Professional shoplifter	History professor	African-American girl
Mother of seven girls	Adopted boy	Child molester

Criminal court judge	City planner	AIDs sufferer
One-hundred-year-old man	Circus clown	Surgical nurse
Dogcatcher	Travel agent	Banker
Thirty-year-old mama's boy	Parakeet	Electrician
Sudanese man or woman on first day in the U.S.	Rock star	Marine PFC (private first citizen)
Stunt man in porno movies	Baker	Double amputee
Editorial writer	Twin (boy)	City mayor
Ex-convict	Newborn baby	Comedian

2. Now, take a drive or walk around your own city, town, farmland, industrial wasteland, whatever.

3. As you drive, take in the scenery through the eyes of the character you've chosen and take notes. Better (so you don't pose a danger driving) take a tape recorder and record the things you see through that character's eyes! If you can't drive—or are too elderly, too young, or don't have access to a vehicle or lost your license in your desire to emulate Dylan Thomas with demon rum—then take a bus or walk.

4. When you return home, write a description of what you've just witnessed *through your character's eyes*, but with this condition. You're to write the description for your character's *peer*. If, for example, you've chosen the character of the ex-con, perhaps what you noticed was businesses that seemed ripe for burglaries. Write what you noted as if it were for a fellow practicing felon. As you both practice the same "profession," you won't "write down" to him or her, explaining terms or "trade techniques" you're both familiar with. This will help you get in the habit of assuming your reader is a person much like yourself, one of our primary goals in this chapter. ∎

Use This! You'll Be Glad You Did

Use this exercise when you're creating your story or article characters. You'll be delighted at how much more "real" your fiction and nonfiction folks become on the page!

You've seen how this works in fiction. Here's how it works in nonfiction.

Nonfiction

Not only is it a great exercise for fiction writers, but it's just as useful for nonfiction work. Many of you who pen magazine articles or write nonfiction books often begin by writing about areas you know intimately—professions, hobbies, places, personal passions or causes, etc. After a time, the well begins to run dry on the topics you know well—you've exhausted your knowledge on the subject—or, you've run out of places to submit your work to. After all, if your abiding passion is "vacationing in Bermuda," you may have had a good run selling articles on the joys of browsing duty-free shops on Front Street in Hamilton and the best sunbathing beaches to head for, but there are only so many airline and travel magazines. After some time has passed, sure, you can sell new, updated articles to these same outlets, but in the meantime you still have to pay your coal bill for that half ton of #2 bituminous that's heating your cabin in Fargo where you work and play among the antelope.

You look for other subjects to write about. Natch.

It occurs to you that the reading public might just be receptive to a piece on the life of a game warden. Just yesterday, you were driving west out on U.S. 94 toward Valley City, N.D., and you noticed a game warden had pulled over a car towing a fishing boat. As you drove by you saw the warden reaching into the boat and pulling out what looked like a string of midget smallmouth bass. That got you to wondering about what the day-to-day life of a game warden might be like . . . and with your finely-tuned magazine article writer's mind, you knew right then that if something like that interested you then it would also interest others. The subscribers of *Fur, Fish and Game Monthly*, for instance.

You whip your Lexus around and head back for Fargo to begin research on game wardenry.

Here's where Jane's exercise can help.

After you've done your research and looked up everything you could on the profession—perhaps followed a game warden around for a day or two as part of that—you're ready to write your query letter.

First, take a drive out in the countryside, and look at the scenery flashing by with a game warden's perspective.

Near a small woods, you see a pickup truck parked beside it. Before, you may not have even noticed it. Now . . . in your "game warden" persona, you wonder if the owner of that truck isn't maybe a poacher, especially since you know deer season doesn't begin for another week. If you were really a game warden, you'd probably pull over and go investigate. A sense of danger rises within you and you notice your hands begin to sweat slightly. If it *is* a poacher, he'll probably be armed (most deer hunters—legal and illegal—are, since throwing rocks at the animals usually leads to a low success rate) and since he'd be involved in the commission of a crime . . . *dangerous.*

Yo.

That's the kind of thing you can take back to your typewriter when you begin writing your article. The kind of experiential immersion that can give your work invaluable verisimilitude you wouldn't achieve otherwise.

Maybe even a different and more exciting angle on the article you're trying to create!

Instead of a piece titled, "How a Game Warden Spends His Day," the keys begin flying on your Smith-Corona or Gateway as you furiously type out the lead paragraph of a query letter suggesting an article you've retitled, "Peril in the Scrub Pines: A Game Warden Encounters a Possible Poacher."

See how this works? Cool, huh?

♦ ♦ ♦

Jane invented this very effective exercise for getting into a character's skin while retaining the writer's own voice, during a motor trip with her young daughter Susan. She passed it on to me years ago and I've used it both in my own writing and in teaching craft to others and it's proved over and over again to be a dynamite, practical strategy.

Her version was that she and Susan would take turns describing the scene they were then experiencing . . . but through the eyes of another character, one assigned by the other player in the game. The reality is, everybody in the world will see the same scene in a different way. Their point of view will be influenced by a myriad of factors. Among those might be their profession or occupation, their sex, their background and personal history and experience, their education, their upbringing, their religion, their nationality, their age . . . dozens, if not hundreds of elements affect what a particular individual "sees" in a scene and what remains invisible to them.

And this is precisely what you need to do when you are molding your characters and writing from their point of view! Their point of view . . . but also with your voice coming through, simply because you're ensconced in that perspective and can now better write it as "you."

Too often, we simply don't realize this basic fact. We take our characters through the plot twists and turns, events and scenes of the situations we've placed them in, but often from our own, personal vantage point. Which can't be the same as the character's! This is one of the chief reasons the characters in some stories seem much the same.

Jane's exercise allows the writer/creator to filter the world through her character's eyes, not her own. Although, not entirely through the character's eyes. The next part of the exercise is where the player in this "game" does much the same as an actor does in creating a role such as Jason Alexander's portrayal of George Costanza. By not only approaching the scene via the perspective of the character you've been assigned by your opponent in the game (or by yourself for the scene you're writing), but also (this is important!) *filtering that perspective through yourself,* i.e., taking full advantage of the writer's own personality. Filtering the scene through your own persona is what is required to provide the "authority" needed to make the character come alive. Doing so makes both the character and the experience "true."

It also then gets delivered in your voice and that only makes the character more believable and natural. You're now "familiar" with and "comfortable" inside the skin of the character and can therefore be "you" when writing it, even though before you took this step you may not have been.

The Iceberg Theory

Utilizing the technique shown here in this exercise for getting inside your character's skin, is somewhat related to what Hemingway talked about in his "iceberg theory." For those who are unfamiliar with that, what Papa was referring to was how you create quality stories. In his view (and mine), a good story was a participatory exercise in which both the writer and the reader took active part. When the writer does everything for the reader—furnishes everything ("dumbing down the prose," for example)—then it becomes a passive and therefore, boring activity. Readers who read lots of such books become Nielsen families. Such writers are rarely published. The writer should provide the "bones" or skeleton of the story and the reader furnishes the flesh, so to speak.

Like an iceberg, a "good" story only shows one-tenth of what lies below. Nine-tenths of an iceberg is submerged (and not visible), and that's the real power of an iceberg. Not what you see, but what you don't see. What's implied by what you see. And the same is true of a quality story.

By getting inside the skin of the character you're putting on the page, you are more apt to employ the "shorthand" that someone in that profession or circumstance would use in both your dialogue and backstory/setup.

Getting closer to your own voice by doing so. Why? Because you're not packing in extraneous language in an effort to furnish explanations for the reader, but are simply telling the story. When you do that, you're in a natural writing state and your own voice will take over.

Going another step, that is how research for a short story, an article, a novel, or a nonfiction book should properly be used. Sparingly. Just because the writer spent three months holed up in the library researching every possible known fact about whales, doesn't mean he should use every single bit of minutiae gleaned in his sequel-opus to "Moby Dick." Just the fact that the writer has researched and painstakingly learned all this will show through in the story by virtue of the knowledge he's gained, even if none of the information learned is directly included in the story or article. This is what we mean by verisimilitude. A kind of quiet authority is attained that lends the aura of truth to the piece being written.

The very same thing happens when we write to a "reader much like ourselves" as the above exercise requires. Even though some of the terms and references may be unfamiliar to some readers, it doesn't matter. Most of it will be clear from the context in which it's used and even if it's not, one of the pleasures of reading is to learn something new. Stories and articles that allow the reader to participate actively (as they do in such cases) end up teaching us something we didn't know before, and we improve our knowledge and general intelligence. And we get that new knowledge not by being told, but by figuring it out ourselves from the clues the intelligent writer has given us.

And the other pleasure the reader gains is making a new friend and that is accomplished when you use your own voice, revealing your own, unique personality.

Wonderful You

Before we leave this chapter, I'd like to ask you to think about something.

For the vast majority of us writers, there's always going to be someone who can write "funnier" than we can, if humor is our forte.

There is always going to be a writer who writes "deeper" than we do, if we aim for so-called "literary" prose.

Someone out there is capable of writing a sadder scene than we can.

At least one writer is going to be better at coming up with clever beginnings and endings, and even more memorable character names.

Someone will possibly write a better romance or a western or an article on New Zealand or a poem or a how-to book than you may.

The point being, no matter what you write, there's a good chance that someone else may do the same thing better.

There's only one thing another writer can't do better than you.

And, it only happens to be the most important thing a writer can possess.

Yourself.

Your voice.

They can't get *your* personality on *their* page. And, since a personal voice is the single most important component of writing and the single most important element leading to success, no matter how good the competition may be, you've got an edge on them by simply being you.

That's a true thing.

CHAPTER SIX

The Elements of Personality or "Voice"

What I am trying to achieve is a voice sitting by a fireplace telling you a story on a winter's evening.—TRUMAN CAPOTE

That's it. That's what we're all about with this book. To help you do the same thing Truman Capote aims for—that "voice sitting by a fireplace telling you a story on a winter's evening."

Although . . . that voice need not be a quiet voice. It can be a howl emanating from the exile, the angry voice of a writer who has been treated unfairly by the world, the voice of a lover, the cynical voice of one who sees the world differently. There are a thousand different voices you might possess. The important thing is that the voice be yours and no one else's. Your natural voice, whatever form that takes.

One of the ways we can begin to get your personality on the page is by understanding the elements that go into voice. Once we understand those elements, we can then go to work on "fixing" them so that we attain that pleasurable *publishable* sound on the page. The voice of a friend. Sitting by a fireplace . . .

Tone

The most vital element in the writer's voice is the *tone* you tell the story or write the article in. Tone is a musical term and is, indeed, the "sound" or music of our voices along with the rhythm, which we'll get to in a bit. It's also a mood.

Tone can take many forms. It can be ironic, sad, matter-of-fact, melodramatic, understated or muted, boisterous, droll, excitable, serious, disrespectful . . . in short, tone echoes any number of *emotional stances directed at the material by the author.*

Allow me to repeat that: *Tone echoes the emotional stance directed at the material by the author.*

It's the tone of the writing in a particular piece that allows the writer the most flexibility in her voice. We all, to paraphrase Walt Whitman, "are large and contain multitudes." We have many voices within us and each of those voices evolve over time.

Tone is what allows us variety in our voice. As well as a variety of voices. Why Frank Baum could be both the Tin Man and Dorothy and make us believe they were both different and unique characters in *The Wizard of Oz.*

Here are some examples of that diversity in the following examples of my own work. All of the stories are from my collection, *Monday's Meal.* After each example, I'll include a short description of the tone I employed in each.

From "Blue Skies"

What I did was I just kept sitting on the bed in my clothes and dialing room service for drinks, and smoking cigarettes one after another down to the filters until dawn and I had drunk myself around to being sober, and then I went back down in the French Quarter with its streets left black and glistening by the street cleaners and did some more drinking in the white New Orleans morning sunlight. Drinking in the French Quarter in the early morning, after a night of booze, I found to be a unique and strangely delicious feeling. Like some Parisian a hundred years ago sitting with his raw umber and linseed oil before a virgin linen canvas, idly sniffing his armpits and working his wrist to loosen it

Waiting for the perfect north light before he begins.

* (Contemplative, serious tone)

Contemplative, because of the somewhat elevated and abstract language used and the musing nature of the content.

From "I Shoulda Seen a Credit Arranger"

A thousand to one longshot, I figured; the odds on Sam "The Bam" McMurtney finding me here, clear out in Fat City, but when Tommy LeClerc waltzed right up to me, I knew my goose was ready to be a Thanksgiving Day feature. Tommy was quick, had some street smarts, but he was only in Double A Ball compared to Sam.

(Breezy, colloquial tone)

Because of the vernacular and loose, easy conversational tone.

From "Telemarketing"

There was this big ol' yellow dog they were chasing out in the parking lot when I first noticed them. The girl I'd seen before, but the man was a stranger. Back and forth they ran after the mutt and then a stray comes from around our building and the fight was on.

"Jim," I said, "come and see."

That's when the man steps in between both dogs and grabs each by the scruff of the neck and throws them apart, drop-kicking the stray in the slats. It was some athletic feat I can't begin to describe, like Bruce Lee or something. Jim watched for about thirty seconds and then wiped his hands on his apron and went back to the grill. I stayed glued to the spot until they got a collar on the yellow dog and led him back to their shop.

(Confidential, friend to friend tone)

Akin to the example from "I Shoulda Seen a Credit Arranger," but a more intimate voice, like a neighbor chatting over the back fence.

From "Phone Call"

> Remembering that afternoon at the café, Grandma, Inez, Billy Watson the sheriff, me sucking on a Dr Pepper, all sitting at a back booth with the poster of Lone Star Beer, crackling, loose, yellow-dried gum showing from the corners where it was working free. Remembering Inez, black and huge, opening my Dr Pepper with her teeth, the cap thunking off, her wiping the bottle lip on her white apron and handing it across to me and Grandma saying for the thousandth time, Don't do that, Inez. You'll have that boy doing that.

Stream-of-Consciousness

Eavesdropping on the narrator's fragments of thoughts and associations that roam from description to emotion to action. This is also a writing technique, but a technique that inspires an almost hypnotic state for the reader. As such, although not technically a "tone," it still qualifies because it satisfies that one requirement of music (from which tone derives) and that of setting a mood, from the rhythm and percussion as one image leads to another, seemingly unrelated, but all fitting together as a whole, kind of like a discordant jazz riff as the words strike the ear and taken singly are "heard" as separate, unrelated snatches of music, but at the end come together as an entity. I think it a part of tone.

From "Dream Flyer"

> They never bust cock fights—least-ways I never heard of it before—hell, half the spectators is always cops—but here I was, in the Orleans Paris Jail and here I would sit my butt another ten days. Twenty down, ten to go.
>
> I'm not one to bellyache, but it just ain't fair, this roust. I was just there, as a sort of observer of the human melodra-

maticus, not betting or nothing, and the judge sentenced me anyway. I might have had a lousy five bucks or so down, but that was it. A hundred, tops. Hell, some'a these players light their Cubans with a C-note!

I even brought up my college education to the honorable barrister, but that didn't cut no grass.

"Your Honorable," I says, "I've got nearly a full semester in right here at our own Delgado J.C. and woulda finished up pret near the top'a my class, only there was that ruckus at the Saint's game you mighta read about, landed me in the clink right before mid-terms and that washed my higher edification right down the spigot. And," I tacked on, "I only made a general comment about our famous quarterback, which I might add, half the town agrees with, having witnessed with their own two eyeballs ol' Junebug Taylor out and about the party trail powdering his nose over to Pat O'Brien's before the home games, and besides, I never laid a glove on the other guy as he had me down and tromping about on my rib crate before I knew which end was sideways, and it wasn't my fault twenty or thirty other hotheads jumped in and began mixing it up and got the security guys involved in stuff that wasn't none'a their bidness."

(Familiar, somewhat "offended" tone in which the speaker feels an injustice but isn't overly-wrought up over it.)

He's a bit resigned to being misunderstood and that's the tone he brings to the narrative. Good-humored resignation to his lot in life.

◆ ◆ ◆

I used these examples because they're all stories from the same writer (moi), but each uses a vastly different tone. Each one employs a different emotional stance toward what it's telling the reader, and each employs a vernacular unique to the character. Yet . . . all written by the same person.

Just as I contain multitudes (of voices) within me, so do you.

Tone is where you get to have a lot of fun with writing and get to unloose all the Sybils running around inside! You've probably all led at least three lives, ala the movie of that name, so why not use 'em!

Other Examples

Let's look at some other examples of tone from other writers. The following is an excerpt from crime writer Elmore Leonard's, *Killshot,* which just happens to be my favorite of his many books. Mr. Leonard is generally considered a master at providing realistic tough guy dialogue in his stories to create believable characters. The tone he uses in creating his dialogue is particularly strong and identifiable with his work. It's "wise-guy" smart-mouthed, clipped, and carries within it a slightly-weary, "been there, seen that" view of the "hard streets" Leonard writes so convincingly about.

From Elmore Leonard's Novel *Killshot*

The Blackbird lay in his bed staring at the ceiling, at the cracks making highways and rivers. The stains were lakes, big ones.

"I can't hear you, Chief."

"I'm thinking you're low."

"All right, gimme a number."

"I like twenty thousand."

"You're drunk. I'll call you back."

"I'm thinking this guy staying at a hotel, he's from here, no?"

"What difference is it where he's from?"

"You mean what difference is it to *me.* I think it's somebody you don't want to look in the face."

The voice on the phone said, "Hey, Chief! F*** you. I'll get somebody else."

This guy was a punk, he had to talk like that. It was okay. The Blackbird knew what this guy and his people thought of him. Half-breed tough guy one time from Montreal, maybe a little crazy, they gave the dirty jobs to. If you took the jobs, you took the way they spoke to you. You spoke back, if you could get away with it, if they needed you. It wasn't social, it was business.

I love this book! Elmore Leonard can come sit by my fireplace any time he wants and tell me stories. How about you?

Listen carefully to the tone. How do these two characters talk to each other?

Short, clipped, cynical tones. Doesn't that describe what you just read? These are guys who've seen every antisocial thing there is to see and have committed violent acts all their lives. Their lives are based on intimidation and every line they deliver carries a veiled threat with it. It's just the way they both see life. Black and white. Might equals right. The tone Leonard uses here is implied savageness, barely held in check, just below the surface of the water, breaking the skin of that water every so often to give us a glimpse of brutality lurking, letting us know it can be unleashed at any second for the slightest of reasons.

David Mamet is another writer who employs a similar tone in many of his plays and movies. In fact, reading the dialogue in quality stage plays and screenplays is a good way to help develop your own dialogue style.

Elmore Leonard uses the same tone throughout *Killshot*, but particularly relies on it when giving his characters their dialogue. Contrast the way Leonard uses his lip-curled delivery to paint his criminal characters with the way Mario Vargas Llosa creates some very different characters in his magic realism novels.

An altogether different voice as you'll see. What Leonard accomplishes with dialogue, Llosa does equally well with description. Llosa uses description for his character's portrayal the way Leonard uses dialogue. Again, the tone of Llosa's voice is crucial in delivering the reader to the emotional state Llosa wants you to be in. Through dialogue, description, narrative summary, and all of the other elements involved.

Remember, tone is another way of describing the *mood* of a piece, just as it does in music. The tone transports you to an emotional place as a reader. This example is from Mario Vargas Llosa's novel *Aunt Julia and the Scriptwriter.*

> On one of those sunny spring mornings in Lima when the geraniums are an even brighter red, the roses more fragrant, and the bougainvilleas curlier as they awaken, a famous physician of the city, Dr. Alberto de Quinteros— broad forehead, aquiline nose, penetrating gaze, the very soul of rectitude and goodness—opened his eyes in his vast mansion in San Isidro and stretched his limbs. Through the curtains he could see the sun shedding its golden light on the lawn of the carefully tended grounds enclosed by hedges of evergreen shrubs, the bright blue sky, the cheery flowers, and felt that sense of well-being that comes from eight hours of restorative sleep and a clear conscience.

I love this book, too. But, what a difference in voices! Llosa uses the languid, poetical tone of the Latin American writer; flowery, lush notes that drift away from his flügelhorn. Indeed, if the tones of authors' voices could be compared to musical instruments (and they can!), then Leonard's might be likened to a percussion instrument while Llosa's would be a French horn or flügelhorn. One (Leonard) writes with the blunt, direct words of the Anglo-Saxon, while Llosa gets at his narrative in the softer, glancing manner of those writing in a Romance language, obliquely. Anglo-Saxon words used by one writer for directness; Latin-based language employed by another for a kind of poetry.

Two entirely different tones; both fine writers. Both sell lots of books and to different audiences. The tone each uses in his voice is a big reason readers of both are attracted to them.

The same way you'll attract *your* readers with *your* own individual voice. By paying attention to and capturing the right tone for the material you're working with. The following exercise will help you do just that, as the more you're aware of tone and recognize it when you

see it used skillfully, the easier you'll be able to create the tone you
need at the time for whatever it is you're writing.

Tone Exercise

The next thing you pick up to read—novel, article, short story, poem—
simply make yourself aware of the emotional stance the author is applying in the piece. When you lay the material down, try to identify the
tone used with a single word or short, descriptive phrase. For instance,
if I've just finished reading the following—

> Please allow me to introduce myself. I'm a man of poverty
> and taste. My name is Steve Reeves. What you can gather
> from this name, I do not know. Little, I suspect. The Oglala
> Sioux would at least wait until the rite of passage into man-
> hood before bestowing the proper sobriquet. I guess that
> really wouldn't work nowadays. There'd be too many guys
> driving beer delivery trucks named *Hits with Thunder* or
> *Arm like a Rocket*. All the computer guys driving Porsches
> and living in million-dollar houses would be known as *Pim-
> ply Nerd* or *He who Snivels at the Wind*. The closest I have
> to such a name is "College Boy." My dad likes to call me
> that.
>
> (Beginning of Stephan Jaramillo's novel *Going Postal*)

then I might describe Jaramillos' tone as "smart-alecky."
Or, I might read—

> When my grandfather died he had a pair of my mother's
> panties in his pocket; white cotton, soft-worn from my
> mother's three-year-old girlish round butt. There in the
> pocket, he could reach, rub the smooth fabric between his
> thumb and finger when feeling thoughtful, worried, afraid.
>
> (Beginning of Jane Bradley's novel *Living Doll*)

—and the words "darkly confessional" might pop into my mind as the way I'd describe Bradley's tone.)

See how it works?

What will happen after you've done this a few times, is you'll begin to instantly be aware of the author's tone. In works of quality, the same tone will prevail throughout, in most cases.

Which should tell you graphically just how important maintaining consistency of tone is. As well as assist you in being more and more aware of the tone you yourself use.

Now that you see how tone works, the second part of this exercise will help you build up your own "tone" muscles.

Situation: Mickey, man in his twenties, wants to get a date with Minnie, a young lady of his own age who he just met briefly a week ago at a Starbucks. He goes to Club Wild Times where he knows she'll be this evening from overhearing her conversation with a girlfriend when they were at the coffee shop.

What I'd like to ask you to do is to write a scene based on this situation with two different tones. The first with Mickey as a serious suitor who's more than a bit unsure of himself with the ladies. The tone would be one of "fear." The second, with Mickey as a sophisticated "player" who has loads of confidence in his charm and sex appeal. This time, the tone will be "confidence." In both cases, have Minnie give him a hard time. You can have her grant him a date, but only after she's played hard to get. Or, if you're feeling particularly puckish, you can have her turn him down in both pieces! You could also vary this by writing one version from Mickey's pov and the second version from Minnie's. Or even from a third party's. Focus on establishing a different tone in each version and have fun with it.

When you're done, you'll have proof before you that you too "contain multitudes" as do I and Walt Whitman! Many, many tones and many, many voices, all of which are useful tools in your writer's toolkit. ■

Setting the Mood

Since tone is really a mood that comes from the author's emotional stance toward his or her material . . . and since as human beans from the third planet from the sun our moods change almost daily (some of us more tortured souls may change minute by minute, according to my wife . . .), then we need to be aware of that internal emotional influence when creating our stories and articles. We may, for instance, begin a novel in a sarcastic frame of mind, and the narrative we start out with reflects this. Perhaps something in our personal lives has led to this emotion. Then, the next day we sit down to continue the work, but we find ourselves with an entirely different mood. Maybe today we're ecstatic because of something that happened the previous evening. For instance, perhaps for once your significant other didn't set off the smoke alarm while cooking supper. Something like that can lead to joyous abandonment and leaping and dancing in some households . . .

(Not mine. I'm talking about a friend's . . .)

And affect the mood we take to the writing desk, which in turn affects the tone of what we're trying to write.

What do we do? Do we begin the novel over each day, writing with the tone that reflects our "real-life" mood that day? Throw away the article we're penning and start anew? Deep-six ten of the first fourteen lines of the poem we began last night?

Well, you could, but if you do that, you're probably doomed to any number of false starts, as your emotional makeup from day-to-day will likely vary significantly from the preceding day's. Unless you're under heavy medication or a member of the president's cabinet . . .

The best way to recapture the tone you've established in the beginning is simply to read as much of the previous work as it takes to get you back into that mood. That may be as little as a single page or you may need to read more. Read just as much as it takes to deliver you back to the tone of the work.

There are also some other ways to do this.

Music

Another "trick" that works to get into the emotional stance we want for a particular piece of writing is by using music. For instance, when I was writing "Blue Skies," I always played the same album. Miles Davis's *Sketches of Spain*. Not only that, I only played one of the cuts from the album, the one titled "Concierto de Aranjuez." Each time, each writing session while writing the story, which took about a week to write. I came to my writing table in a different mood almost every day I worked on the story as I happened to be going through a particularly rocky personal period in my life, but no matter how I was feeling that day, a few minutes of listening to Miles hit the high C he does in that tune (the rumor is, he hit such a high C that he split his lip and it began to bleed), I was able to regain the emotional state I needed to work on the story in.

In fact, I can name the song, singer, or whatever, I was listening to at the time, for just about every story I've written. For example, this is what I had on the Victrola for each of the following stories:

"The Jazz Player"	Sonny Rollins's "The Bridge"
"Hard Times"	Willie Nelson's "Greatest Hits"
"Credit Arranger"	Louis Prima's "Collector's Series"
"My Idea of a Nice Thing"	Various country-and-western drinking songs
"Dream Flyer"	Roger Miller's "Vol. 3 Critique Collection"

. . . and so on. It's wild—whenever I pick up one of my old stories, I instantly "hear" the music I was playing at the time I was writing it in my noggin! If you happen to have a copy of my collection, see if you can guess what tunes or artist I was listening to when writing it. Might be easier than you suspect!

I use music for this reason all the time and if you haven't discovered this little "trick," by all means try it and I think you'll be happily surprised at how easily and quickly you can go to the emotional landscape you need. Music is emotionally powerful and can help you get the tone you want in your writing voice that's likewise emotionally effective.

Hang around. There are more "tricks". . . .

Pictures

Another little "trick" you might find useful in getting to the emotional state you need to be in to recapture the tone you need, is to look at pictures or artifacts that you know from past experience will trigger a certain mood within you. The mood that helps you capture the ideal mood or tone of voice for what you're writing.

A photograph may do it for you. Let's say you're writing an article or story or poem that you want a wistful sort of nostalgic tone to. Let's say you're working on a poem written by a voice that was angst-ridden. (It's okay—angst is a good thing to be ridden by, lots of times.) When you began the poem yesterday, you were in just that kind of mood and it was easy to write from that emotion. Last night, though, Ed McMahon showed up on your doorstep with a television crew and one of those huge cardboard checks, and this morning, after nine cups of coffee to shake loose the champagne hangover, you've decided you still want to write poetry—especially *this* poem as you just know it's going to be an important one—but it's danged-awful-hard to recapture the same level of angst you were ridden with yesterday.

Get out that photo of yourself from the summer of '89 when you had all your hair still and see if that doesn't bring you down a bit to where you can finish the poem. Bet it will.

If you've got *any* artifacts from a past experience that you know will evoke an emotional memory that matches the emotion you're trying to get your writing tone . . . get them out.

Paintings sometimes work for me, when I'm trying to recapture a tone. I like to set some of my stories in the time of my youth and to "get back there," my favorite ploy is to get out the copy I have of *Gas*, Edward Hopper's famous painting. For some reason, this particular painting really does it for me in transporting me back to another era!

You may have such a painting in your own life that represents an emotion for you. Use it!

Vocabulary

Although tone is the most important component of voice, the element that is responsible for more writers being "writerly" is the vocabulary they utilize in their writing. While the tone can be true to your own unique voice—a lackadaisical or even "lazy" selection of the words chosen can drive your personality right on out of the piece at a speed, which, if you were driving on the open highway, would result in a ticket and mandatory attendance at a series of safe driving classes.

As you might guess, a lot of substitutions in our word choices take place when we rewrite our material.

Here's a common example of what happens. A student of mine recently wrote this sentence in the story she was working on in class: A scream *spewed* out of her throat. (Offending word in italics.) She used the word "spewed" in a praise-worthy effort to come up with original language, but it failed. "Spewed" is an action reserved for lava emissions from volcanoes or Texas tea erupting from oil wells, but not for screams, as a rule. Just doesn't describe the way a scream comes out of one's throat very accurately at all. In her original version, the writer had written, "A scream *tore* from her throat." I'd written in my comments that that was a clichéd way of describing a scream, and she then came up with "spewed." An honest effort, but unfortunately, misguided. She looked more for a word to impress (what being "writerly" is all about), than for a word to be clear and original. She got the original part right, but kind of fell down on the clear requirement that goes into a good word choice. And, being clear is the first obligation of writing. Well . . . the *co*-first requirement. Being *interesting* is just as important.

Anyway, this student got it right on the next try when she came up with: She screamed.

Says it all. Without being writerly. Doesn't get in the way of the prose and doesn't draw attention to itself. Simply and clearly describes what this character did. *She screamed.* This cuts the wordiness and simply tells what the character did. And the story goes on, uninterrupted.

The rewriting period is the prime time for the Roget to come off the bookshelf and make an appearance next to our computer, and that's when we're in the most danger of departing from our own language. During rewriting periods are the times when we really need to pay attention to what George Bernard Shaw meant when he said, "In literature, the ambition of the novice is to acquire the literary language; the struggle of the adept is to get rid of it."

I'm not saying it's never a good idea to consult a thesaurus. I'm just suggesting that you be careful! Try not to choose substitutes that are too foreign to your usual vocabulary, that's all. That doesn't mean you should eschew every word you're not already familiar with, but simply become familiar with that word before you substitute it for a word you *are* comfortable with. If you're not confident with it from personal usage, that fact will become evident to the reader. A word foreign to you will come across that way to the reader, sounding strained or forced and therefore not in your voice.

Find the substitute that makes you think, "Aha! That's *exactly* the word that describes this the very best!"

Let's try the following exercise to see if we're mucking up our prose with a borrowed vocabulary.

Vocabulary Exercise

Read the following paragraph, and see how many words you can identify as the author's attempt to be "writerly." Some will be obvious and others not so apparent.

Since my chance of finding Cox is infinitesimal, I had to ferret out E.J. Watson. That's what I'm pondering when the door explodes open like thunder in the wind, bangs closed again with a man backed up against it, as the Marco men heave back, groaning like banshees in a graveyard. Hand hid

in his baggy coat's right pocket, the man is contemplating
nobody but me. Picked me out through the window, and
picked out his own vantage point as well. He knows that
every single able-bodied man in this small settlement would
be here in Collier's store, abandoning the womenfolk to huddle where they could.

Here's the same passage, with the "writerly" words or phrases in
italics:

> Since my chance of finding Cox is *infinitesimal,* I had to
> *ferret out* E.J. Watson. That's what I'm *pondering* when the
> door *explodes open like thunder* in the wind, bangs closed
> again with a man backed up against it, as the Marco men
> heave back, *groaning like banshees in a graveyard.* Hand hid
> in his baggy coat's right pocket, the man is *contemplating*
> nobody but me. Picked me out through the window, and
> picked out his own vantage point as well. He knows that
> every *single able-bodied* man in this small settlement would
> be here in Collier's store, *abandoning* the *womenfolk* to hud-
> dle where they could.

Now, look at how the author actually wrote this paragraph. This is
from Peter Matthiessen's novel, "Killing Mister Watson."

> Since my chance of finding Cox is small, I had to locate
> E.J. Watson. That's what I'm thinking when the door bangs
> open in the wind, bangs closed again with a man backed up
> against it, as the Marco men heave back, groaning like cattle.
> Hand hid in his baggy coat's right pocket, the man is watch-
> ing nobody but me. Picked me out through the window,
> and picked out his own vantage point as well. He knows
> that every man in this small settlement would be here in

Collier's store, leaving the women to huddle where they could.

The difference is clear. As is the language Matthiessen chooses.

Now, try the same thing with your own work. Look over a sample paragraph of something you've written and consider finished, and see how many words or phrases you might identify as being writerly or culled from a thesaurus.

I hope there aren't many, but if there are, you know what to do with them now. Find the clearest, simplest word or phrase you can—staying away from clichés, naturally—and always look for an original way to say what you want to say. Matthiessen chose originality when he wrote: *groaning like cattle.* Simple, clear language, but presented originally. Use *your* vocabulary, and you'll find that *your* voice has appeared on the page! ∎

Imagery

This has to do with the various images you choose to use in your writing. The metaphors and similes and other techniques with which we describe the world of our stories and articles.

The imagery we provide in our work will only be consistent with our natural voice when we draw from our own world and experience to provide it.

This also means to draw from the world of our characters, keeping the imagery we use organic to it. In my story, "Hard Times," a tale about an impoverished country woman in the Ozarks, a deputy sheriff makes this observation to his boss, Faustis, after they'd arrested the woman's no-good husband:

> "Asshole didn't look like he weighed more'n a hunert ten, hunert twenny pounds," said one of the deputies at the jail an hour later. "Li'l ole scrawny arms, bout as big round as your Slim Jim, Faustis."

I could have had the deputy say, " . . . bout as big round as one of your number two pencils, Faustis," but if I had, it might have conveyed the image and it might even have been funny and clever, but it wouldn't have been in my character's frame of reference. They may use number two pencils, but they probably wouldn't ever think of them in that way. But . . . "Slim Jim's" *are* an item they do know well and using that for the deputy's comparison keeps it within their "world," i.e., organic.

Draw and create your images from the world of your story or article.

◆ ◆ ◆

Mark Mathabane, in his autobiography, "Kaffir Boy," writes about his growing up in South Africa, and gives us this image of his home in the village he grew up in:

> It was similar to the dozen or so shacks strewn irregularly, *like lumps on a leper* (italics mine), upon the cracked green- less piece of ground named yard number thirty-five.

"Like lumps on a leper" isn't an image most of us are at all familiar with, but it *is* organic to Mathabane and his world where they see real-life lepers with their attendant lumps on their bodies every day. Therefore, an organic image to the world he's describing. He could have said instead, " . . . like warts on a toad," or something like that, but that would have been an *American* image, not a South African one. Besides being organic to the world he's recreating for the reader, touches like this add powerful verisimilitude to the story, making the world come alive for us as we're immersed in images from that world's environment and from that character's pov. It works, as we see in a nonfiction form like autobiography; it works just as well in all other forms of nonfiction as well as it obviously does in fiction.

◆ ◆ ◆

Look at this nonfiction example from an essay contributed by Ted

LoRusso to Bruce Griffin Henderson's droll collection of comments from waitpersons, titled *Waiting*.

> "A major pet peeve is when people want things changed. People who come to a restaurant and say, 'I want the salmon you have, but can you do it without the sauce, and with a piece of bread?' It's the *Five Easy Pieces* syndrome."

He goes on to develop the image further.

> "That's a scene I have more than anything, because I'm *not* on his side. I want to tell him to go back in the kitchen and put a hocker on that bread and spread it around."

Outtasight! What a terrific image and perfect for the world of restaurant servers. He's, of course, referring to the classic restaurant scene with Jack Nicholson and the stubborn waitress. Since it's a well-known image from the restaurant world, it's an organic image, as opposed to a metaphor from another environment. Instead of that, LoRusso could easily have said:

> "It's the same old story where the guy climbs in the taxi and says, 'I want to go to the airport, but I don't want you to follow the speed limit, and I want you to take Sixth Street instead of Wayland Boulevard, and can you let me sit up front with you?' "

Perhaps the image gets across LoRusso's point, but it isn't an image organic to the world of restaurants, which is what the book is about, and therefore isn't going to work nearly as well.

Look for ways you can express images in an original way, but use images that are natural to the character's or story's or article's particular world. Try your darndest to avoid generic comparisons that fit loosely at best or can be used in any number of situations and aren't particular to the one you're writing, or images drawn awkwardly from another milieu, no matter how clever they may seem to be.

Let's take a look at one of my buddy Jane Bradley's stories for some wonderful examples of a writer whose story images are poetic and descriptive, but never take you out of the range of her experience, but remain inclusive of that experience. Her "experience" was growing up poor and Southern, part of her childhood spent in the country and part in the city. She also had a mother who went to prison and was one of Nashville's biggest drug dealers. The following selection is from her collection titled, *Power Lines*. Note the portion underlined.

> "Yeah," Billy Ruth said. As she watched her momma set out the fried chicken, sliced tomatoes, and white bread, she remembered walking in the garden with her daddy and watching him bend down to pick a ripe tomato. He would pull a shaker from his hip pocket and salt the tomato each time he took a bite. Then he would wipe his hands on the large white handkerchief he always carried, and he would move on through the garden. Whenever she told this memory, her relatives said she was too young to remember. But she could see him in the garden from hearing it said, or from standing there next to him and looking up at the tall dark man who ate fresh whole tomatoes *as neatly as deer picking bark off a tree*, whether she had witnessed it, or imagined it, she knew it was true.
>
> (From "Twirling")

Jane's images incorporate her experience as a little rural Southern girl and the result is a voice that can only be hers. She doesn't make the mistake of creating images from outside of herself, thinking them to be more exotic. What *is* exotic is an image created organically and one that could only be Jane Bradley's and from her own unique background and life experience.

Bradley's life experience also includes an advanced formal education with several graduate degrees. She doesn't talk in the language she possessed as that little girl—example, the word "witnessed" belongs to the educated adult, but the image of a "deer picking bark off a tree" is one she observed as that little girl. She *does,* as Whitman tells us, "contain multitudes," and it is from those voices within her that she creates her prose.

✦ ✦ ✦

Here's one that's from a book my son, Mike, and I co-wrote last year when he was eleven—a spoof on the "types" found in youth baseball. The book recently sold to Diamond Communications and should hit the shelves this year.

The title we came up with is: *How to Survive Little League Coaches, Parents and Teammates.* The following example is from a chapter on a "parent-type."

The Critic

This is the Siskel and/or Ebert of the baseball world. His (or her: moms aren't exempt) passion in life is to review his son's performance on the diamond. Before, during, and after the game. Or practice. He doesn't miss many practices. Not nearly as many as his son would like him to.

He doesn't miss many of his son's mistakes, either. More accurately, he doesn't miss *any.* He can even find some no one else can, including the coach, fellow teammates, and his son himself.

If this is your dad, when you run to the car, flushed with the rosy glow of a 3 for 4 afternoon, you're on your way to a pop exam as to why you flied out to deep center on that one at-bat.

Even when you do good, you'll discover you did bad.

"I know you caught that fly," he'll say on the (long) ride home. "But you caught it sideways. I'm *so* disappointed in you! Not fingers up. You think Ken Griffey Jr. catches flies sideways? Yeah, right. If Ken Griffey Jr. caught flies that way, he wouldn't be in the majors.

He'd be on a girls' softball team is where he'd be. You want to end up on a girls' softball team?"

Don't reply, "Well, if the pay's good and you won't be around, then yeah, maybe. Would they be *cute* girls?" If you have to ask, "Why not?" then you haven't been paying attention here. That kind of answer will get you the same reaction from Pops it did that time you asked for a raise in your allowance and he said, "You think money grows on trees around here?" and you answered, "Not on any in our back yard."

Don't go there. Just nod your head seriously and say, "Sir! Yessir! No excuse, sir!" This is what he wants to hear. And, for gosh sakes! Get your fingers up next time. Even if the ball's so low you have to dig a hole to get under it for that "fingers up."

Just start digging.

Look at the situation this way. It could be lots worse. Dad could also be your coach.

Oh.

He is?

My.

Oh, my. ∎

We wrote this from the sensibility of a couple of guys, one of which has coached youth baseball for the past seven years and the other one (the shorter one) has played the game for the same period. The portion I underlined is a direct quote from Mike in response to a comment I made concerning his request for a bigger allowance.

✦ ✦ ✦

Listen to another friend of mine from our time together in the MFA program at Vermont College. Writer Fran Gordon is a New York girl who's on the cutting edge of what's happening there (in the center of the universe, as she'd see it . . .). Her first novel, a brilliant, semi-autobiographical account, titled "Paisley Girl," traces her experience with a rare, painful and usually fatal form of mast-cell leukemia, collo-quially called "paisley" by the way it spirals itself visibly on the skin.

Here, the narrator/protagonist describes the effect she receives from
pain medication.

> The cocaine solution never lasts longer than twenty
> minutes—about the time it takes for the ice in Doc's post-
> op highball to melt—then pain comes screaming like a car
> crash.

Her comparisons come forth from the images in her world. "Post-
op highballs" and "car crashes," both of which are common artifacts
of her world. Can't you just see the Yellow cab on Forty-Second Street,
caroming through traffic and smacking into a limo? Fran hosts big-
time literary readings with such luminaries as Norman Mailer and all
the biggies in the world of letters, and highballs are a constant part of
the scenery.

She might have opted for this, instead:

The cocaine solution never lasts longer than twenty minutes—about
the time it takes water to boil—then pain comes pouncing down like
a hawk after a rabbit.

Workable descriptions . . . perhaps . . . at least the first one, but
they don't work nearly as well because the first one is generic in makeup
and the second one isn't even close to being inclusive to the world of
the character and of the setting.

Whatever *your* world(s)—and of the world of the piece you're engaged in writing—make your images natural to that world.

◆ ◆ ◆

Listen to a nonfiction writer, the humorist Dave Barry. Mr. Barry
grew up in New York City and has the Big Apple "take" on anything
west of the New Jersey eastern-most state line. Especially toward the
Midwest. This is from his essay about teaching his young son to fish,
titled "The Lure of the Wild" from the book, *Dave Barry's Greatest
Hits.*

Nevertheless, Robert and Uncle Joe and I did manage to land a fish, the kind veteran anglers call a "bluegill." It was three to four ounces of well-contained fury, and it fought *like a frozen bagel.* [Italics mine.]

Barry's images almost always derive from his background as a cynical New Yorker and vocation as a "Big-City Newspaper Journalist," the stance he usually writes from. Organic images and not images from abroad ("abroad" meaning somewhere else, like Metairie, Louisiana), so to speak. "Frozen bagels" are a part of his experience, and one of the reasons his images work so well is that they're natural to him as an individual and not strained as they might be if lifted from a foreign life-experience, borrowed, let's say, from a place like the aforementioned Metairie, Louisiana.

Instead of comparing the bluegill's struggle to a frozen bagel, he might have written, " . . . like a frozen po-boy."

But he didn't.

You shouldn't either.

◆ ◆ ◆

From a writer with an entirely different background, let's take a look at an excerpt from Phyllis Barber's *And the Desert Shall Bloom*, her nonfiction account (novelistically-written) about the building of the Hoover Dam. Barber is a Mormon who grew up on a farm in Utah and later in Las Vegas.

First her shoulders convulsed, then she laughed out loud until tears rolled through the fine dust on her cheeks. Then she had a coughing fit which, when it ended, had somehow cleared the car of its congestion and stale resentment. *Everyone leaned forward like horses toward evening hay* and strained for glimpses of the river and their new home. [Italics mine]

The image, of course, derives from her farm background, an experience she brings to the images she creates. As I bet you will, after reading this chapter!

✦ ✦ ✦

Finally, I'd like to share something special with you. The following passage is from the first novel of Lynette Brasfield, a former student of mine. The novel's titled "Nature Lessons" and is forthcoming in 2003 from St. Martin's Press. You get an advance peek at an author I think the world is going to find tremendously exciting.

"Nature Lessons" is set primarily in South Africa and is written in the first person. Some chapters are from the pov of the narrator, Kate, as a child growing up in the sixties, and some are from her pov as an adult who in 1995 returns from the States to South Africa to search for her missing mentally-ill mother. Watch how Brasfield weaves the two cultures and time frames together, combining images from each into a tapestry that shows the world of each, but relates to the other as well.

> Beneath me, the box—which contained sheets, a clay chameleon, an owl, and a wooden hippopotamus—began to crumple, inch by slow inch. Like my life, I thought. Perhaps I'd slip gradually off the edge and dissolve into a puddle of unhappiness on the hardwood floor. In time, I'd evaporate upward, leaving only my clothes behind. When my ex-fiancé Simon arrived on Monday to pick up the last of his things, he'd find my empty Levis, red sweater, and scuffed tennis shoes huddled within a circle of packing crates and wardrobe boxes.

In the previous excerpt, the author uses artifacts—a "clay chameleon, an owl, and a wooden hippopotamus":—to evoke the character's African origins as she packs up her Ohio home. Brasfield then uses a magical, dream-like image—"In time, I'd evaporate upwards"—to transition seamlessly from Kate's present, ordinary life in the States—

represented by her "empty Levis, red sweater, and scuffed tennis shoes"—into memories of her South African childhood (see the following paragraph). Note how the circle of crates and wardrobe boxes—mundane objects—are used to offer a visual image common to magical ceremonies all over the world, from Stonehenge to the kraals of Africa. This is masterful writing. An individual voice. Hers.

Watch for this author!

◆ ◆ ◆

Drawing from your own experience is what will provide the power in your own similes. If you grew up on a farm fifteen miles outside of Des Moines, your metaphors may likely include references to chickens and home-made biscuits. If you spent your youth in the foothills of Brooklyn, your figurative language will be much more effective if it's created around stickball games or "doing the dozens."

One more thing to watch for in both your vocabulary and the imagery you employ in your nonfiction and fiction writing: the use of clichés. Nothing is more apt to get you further from your own voice than these little critters, simply because clichés are always borrowed language and not your own. Someone else came up with the words or phrases years or eons ago and others turned them into clichés by overusing them. It's easy to rely on them—they're everywhere and on the tip of most of our tongues, but using them is actually a form of laziness. Go beyond the easy and search out the original and you'll be firmly entrenched in your own voice. The voice that makes editors jump up and down in excitement when they encounter it!

If you come up with really good and original language then your phrases and clever descriptions will become clichés. It's the ultimate compliment!

Look at how English author Nick Hornby creates an original image, when there are piles of clichés doubtlessly lying around his writing space that he could more easily snatch a few from. From *How to be Good* by Nick Hornby, this is a scene in which Hornby's narrator is describing how blaisé her life is:

> *That is another chamber of my heart that shows no electri-*
> *cal activity—the chamber that used to flicker into life* when
> I saw a film that moved me, or read a book that inspired
> me, or listened to music that made me want to cry. [Italics
> mine.]

Wow! Instead of using one of those weary descriptions that great, gray mobs of other writers would use to show an emotional state, Hornby reaches beyond staleness and carves up imaginative lines. And yet with simple, everyday language. *Clear* language. He could easily have said: *I felt no perspiration on the palms of my hands, no quickening of my heartbeat*—as I did when I saw a film that moved me . . . etc., etc., blah, blah, blah. Notice I said he could have come up with something like that *easily,* and that's the key word. Using stale, trite, overworked descriptions is always easy. It's tougher to come up with your own language than it is to just pluck the nearest, handy cliché floating by in the air. Tougher, but much, much *gooder* if you want to create your own voice with your own language.

Here's an exercise you can use to excise the images that are foreign to the world you've created on the page. When completing this exercise, I trust it's as clear as the morning after a Santa Ana blows through that you should reach beyond the easy, the clichéd, and come up with your own creative images and language.

Exercising Alien Images Exercise

I'll give you three situations. In each of them, create a line or three that gives a metaphor or simile or image that could only "work" within the parameters of that environment and that environment only. You can write it in any tense you choose and in first-, second-, or third-person. To help you get started, I'll provide an example of how you might have written it.

1. You're writing a story from the pov of a nun teaching a history

class in a parochial high school in Kentucky. The situation is, she's just caught Brenda cheating on an exam.

My example: "Brenda! I saw that! You're just like your Uncle Jake was when he sat in this class—always trying to hunt with the neighbor's dogs instead of your own lazy hounds!"

2. You're writing an article about lawn care for a magazine. You've interviewed dozens of experts and are focusing on some common mistakes lawn-care nuts make in caring for their pride and joy patch of Bermuda bent.

My example: Dr. Greenleaf also cautions us not to apply nitrogen in the spring. It greens lawns up, sure, but at the expense of later burnout when the August sun arrives. Kind of like overfeeding steroids to the tomato plants—you get basketball-sized 'maters but they're all rotten on the bottom after they fall from limbs that couldn't afford the price of their drug habit, so-to-speak. (This may be a tad too "cutesy" but . . . I couldn't resist . . .)

3. You're penning your autobiography. You grew up on the hardscrabble, mean streets of Gobbler's Knob, Michigan (population 303), and you're describing a Little League experience from your childhood.

My example: I stretched as high as I could to snag Joey's line drive. It soared just above my out-stretched glove, just like my Frisbee tosses usually did to Pepé, our family's attack-trained Chihuahua who had the reach of a . . . what? . . . a short chipmunk? ∎

Try this exercise, and then carry it to your work. Test it when you've written it to see if it's an image that's organic to the world on the page and one the characters would feel at home with. Simply be aware of your images—that they're not borrowed from places or situations alien to the world on your page. Use what you know in creating your images. You've already done the research . . . by living! Also, by being able to realistically imagine the story or article world you're putting on the page. The proper images—images born of that world only—will create a stronger fictive dream in your stories and a much more authoritative voice to your nonfiction. Use the metaphors and similes and other imagery techniques that spring forth from yourself and aren't borrowed (no matter how funny, interesting, or pathos-inducing they may be), and your own voice will emerge. A strong, *particular* voice!

Rhythm

The last component of a writer's voice is the rhythm he or she uses. This is the drummer or the bass player of the voice "quartet." The timekeeper of your band.

In the case of writing, the rhythm is the gait at which we desire the reader to proceed to turn the pages.

Rhythm is how we pace our writing.

Here's a simple formula to use in that pacing:

1. *Use short sentences to speed up the pace.*

2. *Use long sentences to slow it down.*

Further, you can make the reading go quicker or slow it down by making your paragraphs shorter or longer. Also, the length of individual words strung together helps control the pacing. Short sentences with short words equals a fast read; long sentences with long words slows it down.

The same applies to other units such as chapters.

It's also important to realize we all have an internal timing sense within ourselves that's unique to us. You have such a sense and I have such a sense. Work to develop it. It's the cadence you use in various conversations. I'll bet you speak with one rhythm to your boss and another to a person you just met and are attracted to. Different rhythms—but rhythms that are yours, individually, depending on the situation.

For instance, you may jabber nonstop and at a high pitch when you're telling your best friend about that fabulous new nightspot you just discovered. Later, that same day, you might speak with a slower, more measured rhythm when explaining to your physics prof how you aim to go about completing that semester project. Both delivered in *your* voice—both different rhythms. Bring to the writing arena those pacing abilities you already "own" and are expert.

Take a look at a story or article you're currently working on.

Test to see if you've achieved the rhythm you want by reading it aloud. If you've meant to write a breezy, flip kind of paragraph and you read it aloud and no matter how you try, it sounds forced and slow, then you've missed the rhythm. Rewrite it and try to "hear" the "beat" of the words you want in your mind as you write.

After you rewrite it, see if you stumble or trip over any of the words or phrases. If you do, you've merely gotten away from your rhythm. Try creating verbally, aloud, for a sentence or two until it "feels" right again. Write down the sentence(s) you just created that way and begin anew from that point in your rewrite.

Guess what? You're getting closer and closer to your own voice. Kinda neat, isn't it!

◆ ◆ ◆

Let's take a look at how to create your own beat or rhythm. Following are a couple of selections from Octavia Butler's fantastic book, *Kindred*. See which one you feel reads faster.

But for three days I didn't see Rufus. Nor did anything happen to bring on the dizziness that would tell me I was going home at last. I helped Sarah as well as I could. She seemed to warm up to me a little and she was patient with my ignorance of cooking. She taught me and saw to it that I ate better. No more cornmeal mush once she realized I didn't like it. ("Why didn't you say something?" she asked me.) Under her direction, I spent God knows how long beating biscuit dough with a hatchet on a well-worn tree stump. ("Not so hard! You aint' driving nails. Regular, like this . . .") I cleaned and plucked a chicken, prepared vegetables, kneaded bread dough, and when Sarah was weary of me, helped Carrie and the other house servants with their work.

◆ ◆ ◆

He hit me.

It was a first, and so unexpected that I stumbled backward and fell.

And it was a mistake. It was the breaking of an unspoken agreement between us—a very basic agreement—and he knew it.

I got up slowly, watching him with anger and betrayal.

"Get in the house and stay there," he said.

I turned my back and went to the cookhouse, deliberately disobeying. I could hear one of the traders say, "You ought to sell that one too. Troublemaker!"

At the cookhouse, I heated water, got it warm, not hot. Then I took a basin of it up to the attic. It was hot there and empty except for the pallets and my bag in its corner. I went over to it, washed my knife in antiseptic, and hooked the drawstring of my bag over my shoulder.

And in the warm water I cut my wrists.

That was pretty easy, wasn't it? (I trust you picked the second excerpt as the fastest-reading . . .) Would it surprise you to discover that the second selection is ten words longer?

Both voices are Butler's. One just has a somewhat different "beat" to it. Imagine you're a drummer and you need to capture several different beats on it. The band you're playing with swings into a light, catchy tune and being as you're the timekeeper for your group, you want to give them something light and airy to follow.

So . . . you drum this: *Ta-dah-dah . . . dah-dah-ta-dah-dah-dah!* Short, punchy beat. More of a staccato.

The next song is a leisurely ballad. You change the beat to a slower one: *Ta . . . dah . . . dah . . . dah . . . dah . . . Ta . . . dah . . . dah . . . dah . . . dah . . .* Long, drawn-out beat. Long thumps with space (time) between each.

How do you do that in writing?

One way to get the staccato, is to break actions up. Give each action its own sentence. Also, write more sentence fragments. Cut out adverbs and adjectives. Use the shortest words you can. Shorten everything you can, even the length of paragraphs. Especially shorten paragraphs! Use short lists and parallel structure. Each technique gives the effect of speeding up the read.

For instance:

> He hit the man. He screamed. His head whipped back. Hit him again. Again. Harder. The blows came faster. Blood flew. He panted with exertion. The man moaned.

To slow the same material down—give it the measured, steady thump of the bass drum—write longer sentences. Write complete sentences and use longer words. Include more adjectives and adverbs. Combine actions. The more actions you combine in a sentence, the slower it feels. Slow the scene with the character's thoughts, impressions. Paint the scenery. Include metaphors or similes. Give lists in series, not in sentences. "The bird opens its wings, stretches them, flies . . ."

Now, write a passage using the same material as above. It might look something like this:

> He hit the intruder with everything he had . . . brought everything he had to the job, including the proverbial kitchen sink. It hurt his entire arm. He bet the guy felt like he'd been hit by that ol' sink! The instant he felt his fist on the fleshy part of his face, he heard him begin to scream. It went on forever, one of those frozen screams of pain and terror. He drew back his fist again and came forward with all his weight behind the blow. The man's head—he could see him for an instant clearly from the light of a car that passed just then outside—whipped back savagely and the blood flew in a fine spray and he began pounding his knuck-

les into his face as they both fell forward, him on top of the man, straddling him, striking over and over and over and over again, until he found himself so fatigued he could scarcely raise his arm for another blow.

See?

Rhythm is also related to breath control. Read your work aloud. In longish passages, especially, see if you find yourself running short on breath before the natural pauses—the commas, semicolons, em dashes, end-of-sentence punctuation, etc. If you find this to be the case, your "natural" rhythm is being violated. Rewrite the sentence until you can read it easily without straining your lungs. This will get the rhythm of your writing in tune with the rhythm of your body. If nothing else, doing this will help you when you go on your book tour and at readings—you won't find yourself having to pause to suck in air at unnatural places in your delivery!

Everything you do to be "you" increases the likelihood your voice emerges on the page. Including getting in touch with your natural body rhythm. Makes sense, doesn't it?

Kind of a yoga thing . . . In fact, some writers find attending yoga classes helps tremendously in getting the rhythm they want in their writing.

Attaining your own natural rhythm in what you're writing— adapting it, of course, for the situation or scene you're creating— communicates itself almost physically to the reader. Write your prose with your own internal rhythm and the reader will be lulled even more into the fictive dream of the story or the world of the article.

For an interesting discourse on rhythm, check out what Dr. Robert O. Greer has to say in chapter eleven. In his opinion, rhythm is the single most important element of a writer's voice.

For an exercise that will help train you to recognize the elements of style, I've "borrowed" the basic framework of the following exercise from Pam Painter's and Anne Bernays' excellent book, "What If?"

Recognizing the Elements of Style Exercise

Part I

Read the following passages by William Faulkner, Sherman Alexie, Judith Krantz, Tracy Kidder, John le Carré, Larry Niven, and Stephen King, paying attention to what makes them distinctive.

Sanctuary | WILLIAM FAULKNER

In the pavilion a band in the horizon blue of the army played Massenet and Scriabine, and Berlioz like a thin coating of tortured Tschaikovsky on a slice of stale bread, while the twilight dissolved in wet gleams from the branches, on to the pavilion and the somber toadstools of umbrellas. Rich and resonant the brasses crashed and died in the thick green twilight, rolling over them in rich sad waves. Temple yawned behind her hand, then she took out a compact and opened it upon a face in miniature sullen and discontented and sad. Beside her her father sat, his hands crossed on the head of his stick, the rigid bar of his moustache beaded with moisture like frosted silver. She closed the compact and from beneath her smart new hat she seemed to follow with her eyes the waves of music, to dissolve into the dying brasses, across the pool and the opposite semicircle of trees where at sombre intervals the dead tranquil queens in stained marble mused, and on into the sky lying prone and vanquished in the embrace of the season of rain and death.

✦ ✦ ✦

The Lone Ranger and Tonto Fistfight in Heaven | SHERMAN ALEXIE

Rosemary MorningDove gave birth to a boy today and seeing as how it was nearly Christmas and she kept telling everyone she was still a virgin even though Frank Many Horses said it was his we all just figured it was an accident. Anyhow she gave birth to him but he came out all blue and they couldn't get him to breathe for a long time but he finally did and Rosemary MorningDove named him _____ which is unpronounceable in Indian and English but it means: *He Who Crawls Silently Through the Grass with a Small Bow and One Bad Arrow Hunting for Enough Deer to Feed the Whole Tribe.*

We just call him James.

◆ ◆ ◆

Scruples Two | JUDITH KRANTZ

They'd gone to Dominick's, the dark, smoky, cramped, uncomfortable, undistinguished grill without a sign over its door that was one of the best-kept secrets in Hollywood. Dom's served only a short list of basic steaks and chops, although on rare days a favorite customer could get grilled chicken. Its limp tablecloths were authentically red and white checked, you had to pay cash or have a house account, they wouldn't take a reservation unless you were a regular, you left there with your hair smelling of cooking, wondering why you'd gone, but every night a number of the power players in Hollywood congregated at Dom's, where there were no civilians to be seen. Like the Polo Lounge, it was a place at which you were guaranteed to be noticed, and when Maggie and Vito had dinner there three days in a row, nobody, not even Dom, thought anything of it. You couldn't carry on anything you shouldn't at Dom's because it was a part of the industry, and you couldn't carry on with Maggie MacGregor for the same institutional reason.

◆ ◆ ◆

Home Town | TRACY KIDDER

One day when he was ten years old, Tommy O'Connor's Little League baseball coach made him the starting pitcher. A signal honor, but then Tommy couldn't get anyone out. He walked the first batter, and from their lawn chairs on the sidelines the parents called, "Make him be a hitter, Tommy." So he threw an easy one right over the plate and the batter nailed it. His teammates in the field behind him did as they'd been taught: they talked it up, they chattered, squeaky voices calling, "Hum chuck, Tommy. No batter, no batter. Hum it in there, Tommy baby." He threw harder and walked the next two batters. He eased up and the next kid hit it over *everything*. Many games of Little League reach this kind of impasse. Five runs in, the bases loaded once again, and still nobody out, the fielders grumbling, the parents looking on in silence, all except for one, someone else's father, who cares more about a good ball game than his neighbor's son, and shouts, "Get him outta there, for Christ's sake!" Tommy stood on the mound, staring at his shoes.

✦ ✦ ✦

The Russia House | JOHN LE CARRÉ

Why do I keep coming back to her, I wondered. To visit the scene of the crime! To seek, for the thousandth time, her absolution? Or do I visit her as we visit our old schools, trying to understand what happened to our youth?

Hannah is still a beautiful woman, which is a consolation. The greying and the broadening have yet to come. When I catch her face backlit, and glimpse her valiant, vulnerable smile, I see her as I saw her twenty years ago, and tell myself I have not ruined her after all. "She's all right. Look at her. She's smiling and undamaged. It's Derek, not you, who kicks her around."

But I am never sure. Never sure at all.

✦ ✦ ✦

Rainbow Mars | LARRY NIVEN

+ 390 Atomic Era. Svetz was nearly home, but the snake was waking up.

Gravity pulled outward from the center of the extension cage as it was pulled toward present time. The view through the wall was a jitter of color and motion. Svetz lay on his back and looked up at the snake. A filter helmet showed only as a faint golden glow around its head. It wouldn't strangle on post-Industrial air, and it couldn't bite him through the inflated bubble.

A ripple ran down the feathers along its spine, a gaudy flurry of color, nine meters from head to tip of tail. It seemed to take forever. Tiny rainbow-colored wings fluttered at its neck. Its eyes opened.

The natives of -550 Automic Era would have carved his heart out without losing that same look of dispassionate arrogance.

Svetz raised the needle rifle.

✦ ✦ ✦

Carrie | STEPHEN KING

The last of Buddy's control broke and he began to scream hysterically, his eyes bulging, his long hair seeming to puff into a grotesque helmet around his bloody, soot-smudged face as the root of each strand stiffened and stood on end. Blood poured from his mouth in freshets and drenched the collar of his parka; he tried to skid backward, hooking into the snow with his hands again and sliding his buttocks as the thing came toward him. IT had no eyes. Its eyes were gone, eaten out of its face by God knew what squirming things. *And he could smell it, oh God he could smell it and the smell was like rotting tomatoes, the smell was death.*

✦ ✦ ✦

Part II

Now, read the following unidentified passages by the same writers. Then match up these unidentified passages with the appropriate writer, and in each case make a list of as many of the elements of voice that you relied on for your answer.

A_____: She thought of herself racing around her thirty-foot-square dressing room, practically caroming off its lavender silk walls, barefoot on the ivory carpet, banging herself black and blue on the Lucite accessory island in her haste to find the few indispensable clothes among the hundreds and hundreds of garments, so many of them never worn, that hung on the long racks. Of course, she told herself wrathfully, if the girls hadn't taken an apartment together in West Hollywood, claiming that they were too accustomed to their independence to move into her house, she could have supervised the way in which they did their shopping bags, to make sure they didn't cheat, as they both most certainly had.

B_____: From 50 Ante Automatic to the present was a thirty minute trip. Ra Chen's call to the Zoo must have come less than thirty minutes ago. Weird, how an emergency could telescope time.

Unless that was a side effect of the paradox. Unless the paradox had chopped away Zeera's extension cage and left her stranded in the past, or cast off into an alternate world line, or . . .

There had never been a temporal paradox.

Math was no help. The mathematics of time travel was riddled with singularities.

Last year somebody had tried to do a topological analysis of the path of an extension cage. He had proved not only that time travel was impossible, but that you couldn't travel faster than light either. Ra Chen had leaked the news to Space on the off chance that their hyperdrive ships would stop working.

C_____: He leaped, blind reflexes taking over, and this time the bullet was closer, clipping leather off one shoe and turning his left foot instantly numb. He turned crazily on his hands and knees, like a small child playing I Witness at a birthday party. Blood from his mouth now mixed with the snot running freely from his nose; one of his broken ribs had nicked a lung. Blood ran down his cheek from the hole in his head where his ear had been. Frosty air jetted from his nose. His breath came in whistling sobs.

D_____: The trooper smiled a little, but it was a hard smile. You know the kind.

"However," he said. "I think we can make some kind of arrangement so none of this has to go on your record."

"How much is it going to cost me?" I asked.

"How much do you have?"

"About a hundred bucks."

"Well," the trooper said. "I don't want to leave you with nothing. Let's say the fine is ninety-nine dollars."

I gave him all the money, though, four twenties, a ten, eight dollar bills, and two hundred pennies in a sandwich bag.

"Hey," I said. "Take it all. That extra dollar is a tip, you know? Your service has been excellent."

E_____: The last trumpet-shaped bloom had fallen from the heaven-tree at the corner of the jail yard. They lay thick, viscid underfoot, sweet and oversweet in the nostrils with a sweetness surfeitive and moribund, and at night now the ragged shadow of full-fledged leaves pulsed upon the barred window in shabby rise and fall. The window was in the general room, the white-washed walls of which were stained with dirty hands, scribbled and scratched over with names and dates and blasphemous and obscene doggerel in pencil or nail or knife-blade. Nightly the negro murderer leaned there, his face checkered by the shadow of the grating in the restless interstices of leaves, singing in chorus with those along the fence below.

F_____: How convenient, I thought, for him and me, if I could have pointed to some great crime that haunted him, some act of cowardice or omission. But Ned had shown me his entire life, secret annexes and all, medical history, money, women, wives, children. And it was small stuff all the way. No big bang, no big crime. No big anything—which may have been the explanation of him. Was it for want of a greater sea that he had repeatedly wrecked himself against life's little rocks, challenging his Maker to come up with something bigger or stop bothering him? Would he be so headlong when faced with greater odds?

G_____: Samson was a pioneer of sorts, or else he was like a seed on the wind. He may have been the first—certainly he was one of the first—to bring crack to Northampton. You couldn't buy it here when he arrived. But it was easy enough to travel down to Holyoke or Springfield, in a cab or a bus or the car of one of his new friends, and carry back some rocks. And his favorite kind of crack pipe was everywhere for the taking in the parking lots, in the form of car radio antennas. You broke one off and turned it into what was called a straight shooter.

Samson had always made friends easily. Soon new friends here had given him a nickname: Sammy. Then a fateful encounter occurred. He was riding a bus back from the mall in Hadley. He had his eyes closed but wasn't asleep. He felt a hand shaking him by the shoulder, and a female voice with a Hispanic accent said he was going to miss his stop. Samson opened his eyes and found himself looking at a short and buxom woman. "This is Hampshire Heights," Samson told her. "This isn't my stop."

"Yes, it is," she said. "You wanta have some coffee?"

◆ ◆ ◆

You should have gotten most of these matched up, even if you'd never read some of these authors before. Try this from time to time with other authors to "sharpen" your eye for tone.

Here are the answers:

A. Judith Krantz

B. Larry Niven

C. Stephen King

D. Sherman Alexie

E. William Faulkner

F. John le Carré

G. Tracy Kidder

How'd you do? If you didn't get them all, don't worry. I'll bet a dime to a bottle of Pouilly-Fuissé, 1994, that you got at least half of them right.

This is a good exercise to do from time to time, to sharpen your recognition and awareness of voice. If you begin to recognize another writer's voice more and more easily, it'll become less and less difficult to be consistent with your own. Every once in awhile, pull down a stack of your favorite books and have a friend read you selected passages from each (so you don't see which book she's reading from) and try to guess who wrote it. More and more, you'll be able to recognize the author of the piece.

And steal from 'em. Not their voices—yours is the only voice you should be using—but by paying attention to those writers and how they incorporated the elements of voice into their work, look at how they did so. For example, you might be reading Octavio Butler's "Kindred" and notice there are places in the novel where you can't turn the pages fast enough. Other places where you linger over the prose. See what she does to control the pace you find yourself reading at. In the parts where you're racing to read, you'll probably note she's used short, pithy sentences with strong nouns and verbs and little other verbiage. She's probably ended the chapter on a cliff-hanger—an excellent "trick" to keep that reader who's lying in bed go on to the next chapter instead of laying the book down and turning off the light . . . Take what she's done to your own writing and use it for those passages you want to speed up for the reader. When you get to those places where the read slows down, break it down how she achieves that.

Steal her techniques.

Steal the techniques of any writer who does something to control the pace of the story or article.

It'll only help you in creating your own individual voice.

To arrive at that stage in your own writing that Walt Whitman talks about when he says, "Dismiss what insults your own soul, and your very flesh shall be a great poem."

CHAPTER SEVEN

Strategies for Getting and Keeping Your Voice on the Page

 Waaalll, you can up and call me Speedo, but my reee-al name is Miiisss-ter Ear-ll.
—FROM "SPEEDO," A HIT SONG BY THE CADILLACS IN THE 1950s.

Who are *we* when we write? Are we Speedo, or are we Mister Earl? Perhaps we start out as Mister Earl and end up as Speedo. Maybe they'll write a song about us, too . . .

In this chapter, we'll explore some methods you can use to get your own voice on the page as you begin writing. A little later on in the chapter and perhaps even more importantly, we'll look at some ways to keep your voice from sneaking away and disappearing during revision(s).

The narrator's voice—whichever of your own inclusive voices you've chosen for that—should remain constant throughout the particular piece. The characters, however, can vary . . . and should. Their characters' voices are only limited by your imagination and ability to be convincing to the reader with them.

Not only in fiction, but also in nonfiction. Making the folks who people your essays, bios, articles, and how-to's unique in their language, descriptions and actions, and narrating the work in your own voice, will only make what you're writing that much more appetizing to the reader. *As* important, it can transform what might potentially be a dry subject into an article or a book that appeals to a much wider audience than just those looking for information on the subject.

For a worthy example, John McPhee's nonfiction book on the Merchant Marine, *Looking for a Ship*, appeals to many more thousands of readers than just those who are interested in rust-bucket oil tankers plying the Great Lakes and the Panama Canal because he invests himself in the prose—uses his own highly-distinctive voice in the telling.

Here's a couple of passages from that book to illustrate what I mean:

> On the bridge, before day, Calvin King's presence at the wheel is signed by the glow of his cigarette. Calvin seems to live on smoke. He stands steady, and seems not to notice any motion but the ship's heading. One assumes that if the ship were going down he would continue to inform the mate, in his slow Carolinian voice, "Three-four-one, three-four-one," until his drawl became a gargle.
>
> and—
>
> The door opened. Chester Dauksevich came in, wearing a Mets cap and smoking a Salem in a holder. The guayabera of the day was adorned with filigree.
>
> Ten minutes to go and Andy's eyes were still flickering toward the door. Dauksevich, in response to a question, said that his high-school class was 1950 and he went to the Massachusetts Maritime Academy. Landy asked him how shipping was in the fifties.
>
> Dauksevich said, "It sucked."
>
> The telephone rang at one-thirty-one. MaLinda was calling from Maine. Yes, Andy had the ship: the Stell Lykes.

Dauksevich and Abbate signed on to night-mate her in Charleston. The various men present started to leave, telling Andy to say hello to this person or that on the Stella.

Dauksevich, surprisingly, said, "Where you going?"

"West coast of South America," Andy said.

Dauksevich said, "Don't get the clap."

Makes you want to read him, doesn't it!

Start Out on the Right Foot . . .

Before you even begin writing . . .

The first step is to match one of the several voices you already possess to *what the material calls for.*

How do you figure out which voice to use?

By taking into account several factors. First, how do you emotionally feel about what you're about to write? Is it a tragic story from your own life that you want to express—either in a story or as nonfiction—so others can see what you experienced and come away with empathy for what you went through and perhaps learn how to deal with a similar situation for themselves? Is it a subject you think is hilarious and should be presented that way? Or is it an article that calls for a tone of somberness or one in which you want the reader to take some action on after reading it? There are at least a dozen or more different emotional approaches you could probably take for any one piece of writing. Choose the one that bests suits how you really feel about it. This is the first requirement to make it yours and in *your* own delicious voice. The emotion behind the prose will be heartfelt and honest and will come through that way on the page.

Learn to trust your instincts when you try to decide which of your voices the material calls for. Here's a couple of ways to help you more easily tune into those instincts.

Passion, My Friend: Passion!

Ordinary people ("ordinary" meaning those unfortunates who aren't lucky enough to be writers . . .) select the right voice for material naturally all the time, without thinking about it. By simply going with their emotional stance toward the subject. One of the most visible pieces of evidence for that can be found in your local newspaper for great examples of how people instinctively choose the best voice to use for the material they're working with.

In . . .

The "Letters to the Editor" Section . . .

Yup. That's a great place to observe examples of how to best choose a voice for what you've chosen to work with. At any given time, raging emotional debates are going on in just about every burg in the land. Furors over politics, religion, education, crime, and every other conceivable subject are featured daily.

Pick up your local paper and read some of those letters. What should become evident is self-instructive in how to choose your voice. *Most* of the writers write from a strong belief in whatever point they're making and that's their primary consideration when they sit down to pen their letters. Passion for what they want to get across is their primary consideration. The technical quality of the writing itself varies widely, but I'll bet that even the more crudely-written letters get read. Why? Because of the passion the writer brings to the project.

Now. Notice I said "most" of these writers write from obvious and deep, honest fervor. There will be another kind of letter published at least occasionally if you read them for a few days. A letter from someone who is perhaps also passionate about his or her subject, but who has a different agenda. The writer who wants to be thought of as erudite or learned or scholarly or wise. The writer who has "thesauritis," for instance, or uses professional jargon, or whose basic aim seems to be chiefly to impress the readers. Don't your eyes kind of glaze over when you encounter one of those? Do you even finish the letter? If you do, aren't there parts of the letter at least, where the author has ignored Harry Crews' self-imposed dictum for his own writing to try to "leave out the parts people skip?" The author may have passion for his or her subject, but with this kind of prose style it's often hard to tell.

That's the voice you *don't* want to opt for!

Here's a great example of what I'm talking about (written passionately and in the writer's natural voice):

From: *The Journal-Gazette* (Fort Wayne, Indiana), Wednesday Aug. 21, 2002, Letters to the Editor, "Impatient Drivers Endanger Road Crews"

When was the last time you went to work and were randomly cussed out, flipped off or charged at by vehicles just for doing your job? Not lately I bet. My husband is on a road crew at one of the county's biggest construction jobs this season. Not only is his job dangerous by nature, motorists with absolutely no patience or common decency for someone trying to do their job make an already difficult situation that much more dangerous.

Earlier this summer, a flagman was clipped by a car, knocking the worker to the ground, when a motorist lost patience and floored it when it was his turn to go. The last time you were hit by a car did you get up and go back to work? This guy did.

These men and women are husbands, fathers, grandparents, sisters, brothers, wives—our loved ones. Have the courtesy to treat them with the respect you would like to be treated.

Although they follow safety procedures, no orange vest, safety cone or barrier is going to save them from a driver with road rage or another yapping away on a cell phone.

Signed: *Leah Felger*

Isn't that delicious writing? Plain, unvarnished language that speaks with a passion about something that matters intensely to Felger. Look at her word choices, words like "cussed out," "yapping," and "flipped off." She uses her own natural, *interesting* expressions, and the result is that, even if we're not particularly interested in highway construction workers' safety issues, we'll read this because of the passion and the prose style she brings to her subject.

In *her* voice . . . A voice that emanated from how she felt about her subject. Your first guideline to use when carving a publishable piece out of the material you've chosen to work with!

There's another factor that works against a writer using his or her own voice as it pertains to the passion brought to the project.

Censorship

Censorship has been with us since, well . . . forever. It's the nature of both individuals and groups to want to suppress what the opposition has to say. We're fortunate in this country in that we have laws guaranteeing freedom of speech, but that freedom exists only if each generation fights to preserve it. The way censorship works is that if allowed to, it dulls your passion for a subject or cause by the threat of reprisals, both real and imagined. By doing so, it also subverts the unrestrained and natural voice you were most likely to employ before you realized you needed to couch your language. It works against your passion by applying a muzzle to it and by doing so, it alters your voice.

These days, a particularly dangerous kind of censorship exists in the movement they call "political correctness" (PC). A movement I'm personally very much against. As Stanley Banks, Kansas City playwright and poet, says of censorship in general, "We will begin to see dull art which has no freshness of vision. Certain points of view will be silenced. When that happens our society will be threatened without a bomb being blasted."

Kathleen M. Sullivan, a professor of law at Harvard Law School, in talking about the PC issue says, "As [U.S. Supreme Court] Justice Thurgood Marshall once put it, the problem with a 'sword of Damocles is that it *hangs*—not that it drops.'" And that's what we as writers who wish to express ourselves with both our own thoughts and our own voices need to be acutely aware of.

Gordon Weaver, one of our most creative writers and author of *Count a Lonely Cadence,* among other novels, says flatly, "Censorship from without is bad for the language, bad for those who speak or write it; self-imposed censorship, whatever the motive, is worse. If you won't say what you think, you run the risk of losing the powers of both speech and thought. I suspect we'll be safe just as long as we refuse to accept censorship for *anyone.*" Weaver says, "If the king is naked, we're all (including the king) better served if someone says so."

Weaver goes on to describe the situation he sees becoming prevalent in higher education, which he feels is the newest bully on the (censorship) block, and whom he feels is the worst enemy of free speech of all. "There is a greater danger, it seems to me, when the censors come from the ranks of the presumably 'enlightened.' It is not surprising that a number of college and university communities nurture factions who wish to control free speech; it is unsettling when more sophisticated citizens (faculty) add their clout to movements desiring to police our utterance in the interests of what one minority or another deems politically correct."

We unfortunately learn about censorship at a very early age and it serves to append the natural language of many of us. As free speech advocate Nat Hentoff, author of *Free Speech for Me—But Not for Thee: How the American Left and Right Relentlessly Censor Each Other,* feels that in too many cases, publishers, school boards, and principals remove or change material for students rather than face the wrath of militant parent groups. Seeing authorities suppress ideas in some cases, and being in a school in which books keep disappearing, gives a graphic lesson to students, Hentoff feels, in that they may have doubts that theirs is a country of intellectual freedom.

Don't allow censorship—both real and imagined—keep you from either your honest thoughts being expressed nor the voice you express them with. Okay . . . I'm off my soapbox now, but you should be aware of how censorship in movements such as the PC movement may work to keep you from really being you on the page.

Form

Another element to consider when determining what voice you should use for the material, is the *form* you plan to write it in. Much of the time, this is predetermined. If, for example, you're creating an article for a specific magazine, your prior research and knowledge of the publication pretty much tells you what kind of voice and tone it requires if you expect the article to be accepted.

But, what if you've got an issue or a story burning in your brain or heart you simply must get out—write about—and you're not sure how best to present it and along with that, aren't quite sure what voice to bring to the keyboard?

In this case—experiment!

Try it first as a poem.

If that seems ill-suited, then try it in the form of a short story.

If that fails, then try it as something else—a bit of memoir, a factual article, even one of those "letters to the editor!"

It'll be a rare occasion when you have to resort to this, but if the material does prove especially baffling as to which voice you need to use to shape it with, this isn't a bad tactic to figure that out with.

Play the voice out of the hand you've been dealt or have decided to stick with through the coming raises.

Colloquial Voice or Not?

A colloquial voice is one that is generally considered overly-informal, idiomatic, "everyday" language, slangy, etc.

Keep in mind, however, that you're not after a strictly colloquial voice. At times, yes, it is properly colloquial. But what you should be aiming for is a writer's voice. Not a "writerly" voice, but a writer's voice. A voice that's just a bit above your normal colloquial voice, but a good ways below the "writerly" beige voice. Better, perhaps, is a "conversational" voice.

The voice that loves and respects language and its many nuances and moods and meanings. Not so much the language you normally speak, but the language with which you normally *think* with, depending on the situation.

The voice the material you're shaping calls for. Which will be a voice you already have. You just have to think about it before proceeding with the particular piece you're working on and bring out the appropriate of the many voices you're capable of.

Believe it or not, we all have different ways of expressing ourselves, depending on the situation. As different as they may be, they're all "us." Take a simple greeting, for example.

If I'm meeting a buddy from work at a bar, and I saunter up to him and he's got a stranger with him who introduces to me, I may grin and say something like, "Hey, mon. Nice t'meetcha. Whassup?" (I may also change my greeting slightly depending upon the sex of the party being introduced or other factors!)

However, if I'm at a formal dinner party, and someone has just introduced me to the governor of the state, I may smile and say something like, "I'm very pleased and honored to meet you, sir."

Both times, I'm "me," even though both language choices are quite different.

I'm sure you do the same things, don't you? This is what we need to do in our writing. Match whatever of the many voices you already possess to what the material calls for. That makes it a different voice, but still yours.

Got the Voice You Want Now? Good! Next . . .

Whatever voice you decide is best, write it on a slip of paper, post it above where you work, and stay true to it. Most of the time, if you find yourself slipping into a different voice than the one you determined best fit the material, then stop, go back to the point where you began to break away from that voice and start over at that place.

An exception would be if you began with one voice in mind and then as you wrote another voice strongly presented itself as being a better choice. If that happens, just begin again. However, to avoid numerous restarts, spend some time before you begin writing to make as sure as you can that this is the voice you want to tell the story or pen the article or whatever kind of piece it is with.

The more you do this, the less often you'll find yourself switching voices. After only a few times of consciously preselecting the voice you want to employ for the material, you'll find your ability to make the right choices increases quickly.

Next Step. Prewriting . . .

Okay. You've determined the voice you want to bring to the writing project. Before you begin actually writing, you may want to "warm up" a bit by getting into that voice.

You can do this in several ways. Here are some suggestions:

1. Write a quick (short) letter to your best friend about the content or gist of your material. Use the voice and tone you decided on—angry, witty, sad, bemused—whatever. Don't make this too long—a page at most.
2. Write a short poem. Two-three stanzas.
3. Do some "clustering." This is an ancient writing trick, in which you basically free-associate words. Write down four words you associate with your material and then, without thinking overmuch, just free-associate and write down the word that occurs, drawing a line and circling each word. Don't do more than three words per each of your four original ones.

Keep the sheet of paper you've compiled the previous exercise on handy. You'll find that once you've written something like this, all kinds of ideas for the piece will come rushing forth, almost magically. As you write the article, poem, or story, ideas and images unleashed by your prewriting exercise will appear before your amazed eyes! Trust me. They really do!

One More Prewriting Activity . . .

There's another action you can take before sitting down before your keyboard or parchment.

Read something.

Anything.

A brief section from an article, a story, a "how-to" writing book, a poem. Try to make it something related to what you want to begin working on, although that isn't always necessary. Ideas come from the oddest, seemingly-unrelated sources. Just the act of reading someone else's work will quite often jog your own creative juices and get you raring to go.

Don't make it a longish passage—you don't want such reading to take the place of avoiding writing the way we sometimes do when we spend time sharpening pencils that don't really need sharpening . . . (especially when we do all our writing on a computer!) . . . now do we? I don't think that will happen, though. I almost always read a snatch of something each morning before I begin to write and I've found I can't spend too much time in that exercise as I find not too far into the pursuit that my own "idea factory" has been stirred out of slumber and is panting to get to my own workspace.

Here's another hint to help keep your creative flow churning. When I hit a wall, I find I can climb over it by taking a short, five-minute break and reading something by someone else. I think it's just because I relax for a minute in concentrating on what someone else has written, and it gives my brain cells time to recharge.

Get Physical!

One other thing I find works also for me and may for you. In clement weather, I go outside and shoot a few baskets at the hoop my son, Mike, and I have in our backyard. (In winter weather, I do a few jumping jacks in the kitchen, but that's not quite as much fun!) At that time, I also play a psychological "trick" on myself, something akin to delaying the eating of a special meal or treat I've been waiting for with great anticipation or in delaying the act of sex.

Ha! Got your attention, didn't I?

What I mean is that like some of you perhaps do, I've sometimes purposely held off the activity I'm anxious to pursue until the desire to do so reaches the breaking point.

Here's an example.

I'm writing a memoir along with this book, and I just finished David Mamet's exquisite book of reminiscence, "The Cabin." In fact, I read bits of it each morning these days, before I begin my own writing.

Anyway, a passage I'd read the night before really struck something in me and I couldn't wait to do something similar in my own writing. I jumped out of bed this morning and couldn't wait to get to the Gateway. Didn't even want to brush my teeth, I was so anxious.

But, I didn't brush my teeth *or* go to my desk. Instead, I went outside and spent ten excruciating minutes shooting hook shots. Then, I brushed my teeth. Slowly. All the while, I kept thinking about the ideas Mamet's book had presented to me and with each passing second, the desire grew and grew to write. Also, the original ideas the reading had brought forth from my imagination's soil were growing shoots and new branches by the minute! By the time I put my toothbrush away, it was all I could do to keep from running into my writing room! The head of steam I built up lasted me well past my usual writing time, which most times amounts to about two hours before I take my first break. I couldn't stop and didn't get up from my chair until nearly noon.

What ideas did Mamet generate in my feverish brain? Simply his attention to detail. Too often, I find myself painting my prose with broad strokes, and reading him reminded me of that. I saw where I could add depth to the stories I was telling in my memoir to make them come more alive.

I do this often. Delay my gratification. Might work for you, too. It's worth a try, don't you think?

Time to Write . . .

Okay. You've figured out the voice you want to use, and you've begun to write the piece.

There are two ways to write first drafts.

One is to forge straight ahead and write from beginning to end, nonstop, and don't pause for anything. Lots of people write like this, and it works well for them.

The other approach is to write more carefully, stopping to find the precise word or phrase or whatever before moving on. Other people write like this and it works as well for those folks.

Use whatever method feels comfortable to you.

The Compromise Method

This may be the one that works best for you . . .

With this method, you plunge ahead, but take a few seconds to jot down a note alongside a word that you feel isn't right, or a scene, or whatever—maybe star it and/or write the note in bold type so it doesn't get forgotten—a note to yourself that you need to change this in the rewrite. Include enough detail in the note so you'll easily remember why you wanted to make a change.

Here's an example of how you can do just that.

I wrote this paragraph in the first draft of my short story, "Blue Skies":

First Draft Version of "Blue Skies"

> Elise is not tardy; she is late. At a quarter of five I open the door and she comes in with a rush of ***need to show her expensively-dressed by specific items of clothing that fashionable women were wearing at this period. Thinking not only of clothing, but expensive perfume, stuff like that. Need to find specific brand names.

That was the note I included in the draft before I went on to write the rest of the story. I also had a couple of other such notes later on. This may seem like a lot of detail, but you need to remember when you're providing these little reminders for yourself that it may be awhile before you rewrite it and we all have a tendency to forget what was on our minds at the time. Make your notes in these instances just as detailed as you need to recapture what you had in mind at the time. Don't just say, for instance, "research clothes." Won't be enough even two weeks later. You'll have forgotten in the interim.

The story I was writing here had come to me entire (well . . . almost!), one of those rare fictions that God kind of drops in your lap and you're just the stenographer, getting down what's being dictated to you. Wish there were more days like that! I knew what it was going to be about, and I didn't want to lose my momentum in writing it, nor "forget" the story before I could get it down. Usually, I stop when I don't have the right word or phrase or whatever, but in this case, I knew that might be a mistake. Here's what I came up with from the note to myself:

Rewritten Version of "Blue Skies"

Elise is not tardy; she is late. At a quarter of five I open the door and she comes in with a rush of Royal Secret perfume, dressed in a pinstripe and a hat and Ferragamo shoes, all different shades of gray. A hat! I don't remark on her little pillbox thing I've seen on women all over New Orleans since I drove up from Houma.

And that's how I'd suggest you get through the first draft if you're like I was in that situation—not wanting to lose my momentum to find the right material before going on as was my usual wont.

Let me reemphasize that you really should take the time to make a note that will be clear enough to you days or even weeks (or longer!) later. It's easy to forget what you had in mind at the time, so make sure you include enough detail in the note!

The Rewrite

Okay. Let's say you've corrected all you can during the initial writing of the piece as you were writing it, and now it's time to go over it again. No matter how careful and thorough you were during this first draft, be assured you need to rewrite it at least once.

Many times, we create first drafts of our stories, books, and articles that are very close to our own voice . . . but end up taking it out or corrupting it in the rewriting stages.

You may, for instance, have agreed with many other writers, that the best way for you to write is to turn off your left brain and just go with the creative flow of the right side. Get the stuff down; just write! The result is oftentimes a voice that is clearly yours, simply because you've turned off your internal editor.

That accomplished, you sit down to begin the arduous and often daunting task of rewriting the material. You turn off the right side of the brain and fully engage the left. It's when the editor side of us enters our writing areas that we can easily stray into that oft-mentioned and infamous beige voice. The voice of learned mediocrity . . .

The first rough draft was for *us*. Our eyes only. We could (and did) put down anything we wanted, damn the consequences! No one but us was going to read it.

But now . . . this stuff is going to go out into the world. Others are going to read it. Judge it. Tell us if we're worthy of being called "writers."

This is when temptation hits the hardest. When doubts creep in— am I really good enough? Do I sound like a dummy? Will the editor(s) I want to send this to think I'm hopeless and suggest I take up another trade, one that preferably doesn't involve the use of the English language for success? Perhaps consider becoming a brain surgeon instead or the president of a small-to-medium country. All these and other, equally-damaging thoughts begin to enter your consciousness. And why shouldn't they? After all, you've just let down the gate and let loose your internal editor. Critic Nag Dude has just been given full permission to enter the room! And he's smacking his lips with glee, rubbing his hands together ala Snidely Whiplash.

Well, let him into the room, but gently and also firmly remind him he's a guest and has to obey the rules.

Which are:

1. Don't put language into your mouth that isn't your own.
2. Don't become imitative of other writers because you've suddenly lost faith in your own voice. Just because Critic Nag Dude is a second-rate Snidely Whiplash doesn't mean you have to let him convince you to try to become a second-rate Judith Krantz. Don't join his pathetic club!
3. Remind Critic Nag Dude that at best he's only second-in-command here. *You're* the editor-in-chief!

The "trick" in rewriting is actually quite simple. Improve the language, striving for originality, but remain within yourself and your voice. Don't, for instance, come across the word "beautiful," see that it's too generic a word for what you mean to convey, make a knee-jerk reactionary reach for the thesaurus for a "better" word, and then use the first alternative that sounds "okay." Roll it around on your tongue, say the sentence it's in aloud, see if it "feels" perfect to you. If it doesn't . . . keep looking until you find one that does.

Do that with everything you want to change.

Choice Within Your Voice

If I'm writing characters in those same situations as the social examples given earlier (meeting the governor, etc.), I would not only assign them similar language, but I'd also probably choose different forms of the same verbs and different adjectives to describe their actions and the setting. Notice, for example, where I used "grin" in the first example, and "smile" in the second?

Both simple words that say clearly what the action is, but "grin" is a casual way of describing it and "smile" is a slightly more formal version of the same thing. That's the kind of language choices you make and still remain within your own voice.

The thing is, I'm quite capable (as, I'm sure, are you) of being many different people with many different voices, and all of the various voices are still me no matter how diverse they may be. I decide which of those richly varied voices to use depending on the material, the situation, the character, and so on.

I do it naturally, just as I do in "real-life" situations. In real life, if I'm at a formal dinner party and meet a distinguished guest, I don't sit there and think for a moment that "I better get into my formal diction here." Nor do I do something akin to that in an informal situation, such as an after-work bar. I just automatically do it.

We should do the same with our stories and articles. We get into the "skin" of our characters—perhaps by using Jane Bradley's exercise in an earlier chapter—and it becomes natural to "talk," act, and react like that character on the page.

When rewriting—this applies to both fiction and nonfiction—look carefully at how your characters speak and think or how your nonfiction narrator comes across. How and why they make their choices of reaction and/or action. If you find they all sound eerily similar, it's time to make 'em real people. Turn loose all your Sybils, and find the one who fits the character you've created the best. Step onto the stage in that role.

Draw on all of your personal experience, education, knowledge, and observation to accomplish realistic voices for your characters.

This is fun, kiddo!

To decide which of your voices need to be used, look carefully at the material you want to shape. Is it a story you want to write in a snappy, wise-cracking voice? Then, use that voice you use when you're hanging with the gang and "doing the dozens." Does your article call for a serious, informative voice? Use that voice you bring forth when you're explaining how the copier works to that new employee. These are examples that admittedly may not apply to your experience, but the point is to look at the material, decide what voice is called for to present it the most convincingly, and then go to your own experience to find the one that fits the best.

Look at just two voices I used my own self for two different stories (both from the collection *Monday's Meal*):

This first excerpt is from my short story, "A Shortness of Breath." In this story, an allegory, I wanted to use an archaic prose style, one that is stilted, a bit pompous and wordy. I think I succeeded. You be the judge.

From "A Shortness of Breath"

All events prior to John Sykes' father's funeral were useless prologue, unessential except for comparisons, and few remained who cared to expend time in such pursuits. What was there to say? That John Sykes was a young man with active hormones, quick to show strong white teeth to the young ladies, first on the dance floor, first to head for the back row of cars with a giggling girl in tow? That he was like any twenty-year-old Louisiana country boy who enjoyed snagging a six-pound largemouth, shining for frogs, pushing a pirogue through a bayou in a gator hunt?

This is a story about a rural Louisiana man.

◆ ◆ ◆

Now. Listen to the sound of the voice in another of my stories, "Dream Flyer," which is also about a rural Louisiana man who now lives in New Orleans. I think you'll see a different voice altogether.

It's a different character and as such, demands a different voice. Both of which are within my experience to provide. Both are within my multifaceted "writer's voice," and it is from one of those voices that I (and you!) am able to draw upon to provide a different character's voice.

From "Dream Flyer"

Well, there is some squirrely folks in jail, and I've met a couple of 'em, but the Dream Flyer, he's an original-diginal if I ever come across one, with both cheeks fulla walnuts and pecans.

Least he was. Yesterday was the day they was supposed to extinguish him and they even let me go to a conference room and listen on the radio for when it happened. All the stations had remotes there since it was such a big deal and one of those days the governor hadn't accepted a bribe—slow news day is what they call it—and I guess the turnkey thought me 'n Dream Cookie was bosom sidekicks since we celled together awhile, and so I got to go up and listen with Whitey and the other moron guards. Beats laying around in your six-by-ten, winking at your trouser worm and teaching it to sit up.

◆ ◆ ◆

Schizophrenia Iss Goot, Munchkin!

Both voices are me and I think you'll agree both voices are vastly different. That's all right—it's perfectly legal to be schizophrenic when writing! In fact, that's one definition of intelligence—the ease, quickness and skill of one's ability to adapt to multiple environments. For me, as a writer, my "environment" is the world I'm creating at the moment. The particular story or article or scene or character I'm writing.

In my own life, I've found myself in such disparate situations as being surrounded by pissed-off bikers who'd just found out the disturbing news that I'd sold 'em some watered-down coke . . . and a month later, standing next to a fine-looking woman in a bookstore trying to get a date with her just after finding out she was a top executive with the hottest rock radio station in town (New Orleans) and had graduated from Smith College. I emerged successful in both instances, escaping with my life from the bikers in the first, and going with the lady as her guest to a Michael Jackson concert in Dallas in the second. Do you suppose I used the same language with each?

You've had equally-dissimilar circumstances arise in your own life if you're normal, and have (I hope!) handled each of them by slipping into the appropriate persona called for at the time and place. This is pretty much what we do when we create our characters on the page. Draw upon that finely-tuned skill we use in varied social situations.

Make sense?

For a final illustration of yet another and even more different voice I've used in a story, look at this selection from my story "Princess." The narrator-protagonist, Princess, is a young, wealthy Uptown (New Orleans area of "old" money) girl who, in this excerpt, thought she had just seen her ex. Now, I'm not a woman, I grew up in Texas and Indiana, not New Orleans, and I haven't been wealthy since I was a young kid, and that wasn't my money—it was my grandmother's. However, I have been around all those folks and did live in New Orleans for a long time, and I have a memory that works well. I can also imagine what it might be like to be this character and in her voice.

Even though I'm male, I have a distaff side. All of us contain both sexes as well as many other personas within ourselves. That means I probably have enough to capture Princess's personality and thought processes and manner of speaking on the page. The voice of Princess . . . but also the voice of Les Edgerton. You judge if I was able to carry that off in the following.

From "Princess"

> Boy, did a chill go through me! I hadn't seen Evan since the annulment. Once, I thought I did, right after I got back from my Aunt Desderada's (Dee Dee), in Virginia, at PJs on Magazine. They have the best coffee in New Orleans. Everybody goes there.
>
> I had just come out, after buying some dark roast, and I saw the back of this man's head. He was standing outside PJs with his back to me, and my little heart just jumped up in my mouth! He turned and I thought I'd faint, but it wasn't him. Even so, I dropped the coffee and the package broke. I had to go back and buy another. That was just like Evan. Even when he wasn't there, he was causing me grief!
>
> My momma told me right from the start that I shouldn't go out with him. His family wasn't right. He'd been born in New Orleans, but both his parents were from up north, Chicago. Well, his daddy was from Chicago, but his momma! She was from Cleveland! Have you ever heard of anyone being from Cleveland? I can't imagine anyone ever admitting it! But she did. She was even proud of it.

All of these selections weren't to impress you with my virtuosity as a writer (well, maybe a little . . .), but more to illustrate how a single writer can and should be able to achieve different voices and still remain true to himself on the page.

Trouble-shooting

Let's say you've written a first draft and have even rewritten your story or article a couple of times and there's that one pesky scene that just isn't working. Odds are, it's because you've failed to write it in your own voice, no matter how hard you've tried. It doesn't feel "true," but you can't quite put your finger on what's wrong with it.

What may help is submerging yourself even deeper into the scene.

Here's an exercise I think you'll find helpful in those instances. This one is taken (with a few small changes) from Tristine Rainer's excellent book on memoir-writing, *Your Life as Story: Discovering the "New Autobiography" and Writing Memoir as Literature*, Tarcher/Putnam, 1997. By the way, if you're writing a memoir or autobiography, glom onto this book!

The same technique shown below also applies to your nonfiction writing. As you probably already know, the best nonfiction is written using fictive techniques these days!

Sensory Exercise

1. Pull up on your screen that troublesome scene you're presently writing or rewriting. If you really want this to be cool and ultra-helpful, begin with a scene you're not sure of just yet. One that you perhaps know the general outline of, but aren't sure how to construct it. Or, one you've already written, but for some reason that you can't quite put your finger on, isn't *there* quite yet.

2. Begin with Bradley's exercise. See the environment through your character's eyes briefly to get a "feel" for that character. Even take a short drive if that helps, rather than just gazing out your tastefully-and-functionally-well-designed-writing-workshop-window.

3. When you get back, go to your writing area and get rid of any possible distractions. Unplug the phone or turn the ringer off, snip the little wires to your doorbell (just kidding! sort of . . .), tell everyone in the house you are not to be disturbed. Don't use your computer for this exercise. Use a pen or pencil.

4. Begin by relaxing your body and mind. Systematically tighten and relax all your muscles, then take a deep breath, hold it—then release it completely, releasing all the tension.

5. Close your eyes, and take another deep breath. Release the tension. Allow your breathing to become deep and regular. When you feel relaxed, allow the setting of the scene you're trying to write to come to you. Put yourself in the place of the character whose scene it is. Is it a wide open expanse or are you confined in some way? Are you moving, sitting, standing? Who's there with you? See all these things. Feel yourself becoming emerged in the scene? Good.

6. Now, begin to accumulate more information by asking yourself the questions listed below. Each time you think, "I don't know for sure," relax and invent an answer. Don't worry about being "right." Simply and quickly jot down on your paper the first thing that comes to you, so long as it feels plausible.

Ask yourself:

What is it I see before me?

What is it I feel?

What do I hear?

What do I smell?

What do I taste?

What's the light like?

What is it that I want?

What do I think?

What's my primary emotion right now?

Write the answers in the present tense. Don't think about your answers, but just jot down whatever comes to you. Use your imagination in the "dream" you're having.

At this point, the scene you're imagining is probably like watching a series of pictures in a photo album, full of detail but without movement. Now. Add movement! Turn it into a movie. See and feel yourself move a part of your body. If you can, actually move as you would have in the scene as your character.

7. Then, ask yourself these questions, writing down the first thing that occurs to you. Don't think about it, just write.

What happens next?

What do you do?

What do you think or say?

What do the other characters in the scene do or say?

What's changed? What's different now from when the scene began?

8. Using your notes from the previous question, write the scene quickly without censoring it or worrying if it's "right" or not. Just write the thing! ■

You can even go back and do the same thing with all the other characters involved in the scene and answer the same questions from each character's point of view. Do that and their actions, reactions, and dialogue will be right on the money, honey. You'll find you've delivered a scene that rings true and it's all because you've "become" the character and are now writing in your own voice as the character.

If you've been successful (and I'll bet you were!), you will probably have ended up with a pretty powerful scene. It may still require some editing, but I'll wager not as much as it ordinarily does when you've written such a scene.

You can use this technique when originally crafting the scene and you can also use it later, when you're rewriting those scenes that now seem "dead" or artificial and where your own voice seems to elude you.

Take a break right here and try it!

CHAPTER EIGHT

The Link Between Material and Voice . . . And Why You Should Break It

 The ideal reader of my novels is a lapsed Catholic and failed musician, shortsighted, color-blind, auditorily biased, who has read the books that I have read. He should also be about my age.—ANTHONY BURGESS

It's more than a coincidence that Burgess is a lapsed Catholic, failed musician, shortsighted, color-blind, a bit hard of hearing, and so forth . . .

Burgess is not writing for a "market" so much as he's creating fictional worlds for an individual. The fact that there are many who fit this description of the reader he writes for is the reason his publisher can place an "s" at the end of "reader." A big "S"!

Even though Burgess sees only that lapsed Catholic . . .

With that attitude, his work appeals to a lot more folks than "failed musicians."

Go figure.

The problem is, many of us attack our writing careers bass-ackwards.

We sometimes mistakenly look to see what is "hot"—commercially or artistically—when we decide what to write about, rather than the issues that truly drive our need to write. Many times, in looking to see what's hot, we also emulate the voices of those whose work is on the best-seller lists. That's a major mistake!

The best advice I've ever gotten, which you've also probably heard somewhere, but which I'll pass on in case you haven't, is to write the book or story or article or poem you wish someone else had written . . . but hadn't. So *you* have to write it!

Then, once it's written, look for a market.

But . . . write it first, and write it for *you* as the target reader.

Writing, of course, in *your* voice.

What Interests You . . . Will Interest Others!

If you write articles, look for things to write about that interest you. If they interest you, then chances are probably pretty good there are plenty of others who will share that passion . . . and if so, there's a market for it.

Writing material with yourself in mind as the target reader will mean that you'll be more apt to write it in your own voice. Meaning your article or query will have a much more individual "feel" to someone else reading it, and it will stand out from the rest. You'll have gotten your personality on the page and most others who might be submitting the same article probably won't.

Let me give you an example of how that works.

Several years ago, I had a bustling "mini" writing career going, penning lots of magazine articles. Rather than try to figure out what was "hot" at the moment—which I knew was a losing proposition, as about the minute I figured out what that was, it was probably already changing—instead, I just tried to keep my eyes and ears open, and if something piqued my own curiosity, I figured others would be likewise interested.

At the time, I owned a thriving hair salon (Bold Strokes Hair Designers) that saw lots of people come through the doors every day. People from all walks of life, from dentists to school custodians to strippers in clubs to ministers. Every imaginable profession, vocation, or lifestyle you can imagine congregates in a hair salon! A rich source of ideas for material.

One day, I overheard a male client of one of my staff state, while he was climbing out of her chair, that when he left Bold Strokes he was going to visit one of his customers to straighten him out on a misconception this guy had about lawn care. My ears perked up at the word "misconception," and I rushed over to him and began peppering him with questions.

As it turned out, the man had a lawn services business and had a regular customer who wanted him to apply nitrogen to his lawn to "green" it up.

"What's the misconception?" I asked, not knowing diddly about lawn care. In fact, not only didn't I know squat about lawn care, I carefully avoided walking near my own lawn mower parked in my garage, lest I found myself pushing it. Thankfully, my wife, Mary, enjoyed mowing, so I didn't have to!

Anyway, according to this gentleman, one shouldn't apply nitrogen in the spring to lawns. It greened 'em up all right, but it was the wrong time of the year to do so as it also burned up lawns. The proper time to apply nitrogen and several other fertilizers was in the late fall or winter. However, he confided, there was more than one lawn care company who routinely did apply nitrogen to their customers' lawns in the spring. It was dramatic in the lush green that sprang up, almost immediately. He felt himself a more ethical businessman and was on his way to explain to his client why it was a bad idea to slap this particular fertilizer on the guy's lawn in mid-April.

"That's wild," I said, when he was done explaining. "Are there many more such misconceptions about lawn care?"

There were a lot, he said. That's when I really got excited.

"Are there ten?" I asked

"There's probably several dozen," was his reply. "At least."

Bingo.

I knew that if there were at least ten common misconceptions about this subject—lawn care—then I had a sound article idea on my hands. There are at least several people in just about every town who have lawns and actually care about how the lawns look and their health and all that stuff.

And, most importantly, what he told me was interesting. Even though I wasn't a lawn person. I kinda dug the fact that there were all these people out there toasting their lawns.

I ended up interviewing him and getting leads to other sources and in two days had my article. It was fun doing the research, and it was fun learning about the more than twenty common misconceptions I unearthed, and it was fun writing the article.

In my voice. The voice I'd use in relating the information to a friend.

Then I looked for a place to sell it.

And how I found a magazine to take it is interesting in itself. Every year, I purchase two reference books; (current year's) *Novel & Short Story Writer's Market* and (current year's) *Writer's Market*, both from the publisher of the book you hold in your hands. And I always read the interviews and tips sprinkled throughout both books. They've been a huge help to my writing career, more times than I can count. I suddenly recalled an article from a couple of editions back in *Writer's Market*, in which the editor of *Kiwanis Magazine* said that their best-selling article of all time had been one on lawn care. Which made sense. Their readership is composed of the kinds of subscribers who would not only have lawns but would take some serious pride in them. Those kinds of weird people . . .

Since I'd read that article a couple of years earlier, I thought perhaps enough time had gone by since its appearance. The magazine might be in the market for another article on the subject.

I was right. They loved the idea and bought the article! I got interested in something . . . figured if I, of all people—me, who hated maintaining a lawn—could find this stuff engaging, then there should be others who would be as well.

I could probably have developed the idea into a book, but I simply wasn't *that* interested in the subject. I had plenty of enthusiasm for an article, but for something the length of a book, I needed a hotter button pushed.

It's possible to research the markets and find out what publishers are buying and even be successful doing so, but I suggest it's even easier to find something *you're* interested in, write your material based on that . . . and then seek out someone to buy it. If it trips *your* excitement button, it's bound to trip others.

And, you'll be more apt to write it in your own, individual voice, rather than the voice you may (usually, mistakenly) think your audience wants. For those who are only after the content (just the facts, ma'am), voice won't matter as much, but to reach a wider audience you'll need to put your personality on the page. Even those who are only after the info the article promises will find the read much more engaging and interesting if you put yourself into it (your voice), and they will look for your byline again. Sometimes, they'll even come across your name affixed to an article they normally wouldn't read, or recognize your style when encountering it in such an article, and will continue reading because of the pleasant experience they've already had.

If you don't think that's so, look at a couple of our best-selling nonfiction writers, Tracy Kidder and John McPhee. These guys, and a few more, have completely revolutionized the nonfiction book and article biz.

How?

Simple. By being themselves on the page. Using their own voice, which personalizes the material. Tracy Kidder has written about all kinds of things, lots of them on subjects you wouldn't have thought all that interesting. He makes them interesting by being interested himself and conveying that interest by speaking to the reader in his own, way-cool voice. He says, "You can write about *anything,* and if you write well enough, even the reader with no intrinsic interest in the subject will become involved."

John McPhee does the same thing. A review in *The Christian Science Monitor* once said about his books that "John McPhee ought to be a bore. With a bore's persistence, he seizes a subject, shakes loose a cloud of more detail than we ever imagined we would care to hear on any subject—yet somehow he makes the whole procedure curiously fascinating."

Why? Because McPhee found it fascinating himself and got the excitement he felt across to the reader by telling it in John McPhee's voice.

✦ ✦ ✦

In his classic book *How to Write a Book Proposal,* agent Michael Larsen has these interesting comments concerning the writer's voice:

> Although style is more important in a literary biography than in a how-to book, the more pleasurable any book is to read, the better its reviews and the more word-of-mouth recommendations it generates.
>
> Make how you write as important as what you write about. Make style as important as content.

Get *your* personality on the page. That's what counts.

CHAPTER NINE

Undue Influences–Tuning Out the Masters

 The four greatest novelists the world has ever known—Balzac, Dickens, Tolstoy, and Dostoyevsky—wrote their respective languages very badly.—W. SOMERSET MAUGHAM

The weaknesses we find in our prose are usually a result of an unconscious imitation of those writers we (over)respect the most. The writer we think of when the word "genius" is applied behind his or her name, such as " . . . Joyce Carol Oates, *the genius.*" We, too, want to be known as geniuses, at least to our immediate circle of acquaintances, so it's just natural to want to emulate somebody we think is already that neat thing—a writing exemplar.

As I confessed earlier, I have a tendency to pack in too many dire situations in a short space because I think that's what Mr. Faulkner did. My solution to my own weakness is that I just don't read him while I'm writing.

You may well find you'll have to do the same thing with the author you enjoy the most. Put him or her aside while you're actively writing. Wait to read that person when you take a break from writing.

Our Weakness May Be Anything . . .

Your own weakness may be virtually anything. Let's say it's a fondness for being overly-melodramatic. If so, look at the writer you admire the most. Chances are, he's noted for his purple and flowery prose. What you may have missed is that he never quite goes over the edge in his melodrama. Which is what you're probably doing, in an either subconscious or even conscious effort to emulate him or her. When we imitate, we often end up caricaturizing, surprisingly enough.

Like I do when I'm in my "Faulkner" mode and begin a story with six murders, two lynchings, four cases of incest, and a brass band composed of musicians convicted of possession of pornography marching down Main Street. All in the first paragraph. A far cry from what Faulkner actually does! Faulkner would only have five murders in that paragraph if he'd written it. (The remainder of the paragraph would be about the same.)

Kidding! Kind of . . .

The Most Common Weaknesses I See Are . . .

Each of the following weaknesses can many times be attributed to the writer having an over-predilection for a writer that he or she either consciously or subconsciously tries to imitate. These are the most common mistakes I see in my classes, and I've been guilty of most of them myself!

Sci-fi Writers Who Think the "Story" Should be Mostly About Technology

Granted, this is one of the elements that attract sci-fi fans, but very often characterization is neglected at the expense of gadgetry. It's the people in the story that attract readers and the techy stuff should always play a subservient role to that.

I once had a young man ask me to critique his six-hundred-page science-fiction manuscript (he'd been working on it for six years!). I tried to read it at least seventeen times but couldn't get past the first twenty pages. The reason? The first five pages were detailed maps of the "universe" he'd created, complete with dozens and dozens of unpronounceable names that didn't contain any vowels. After that, the first ten pages of actual text was a lengthy setup of the entire history of his "world." When I finally reached the "story" itself, there was no inciting incident, but rather, more backstory about how his main character—a robot—had been created and what nifty things he could do. And, although the robot/protagonist was a scientific marvel with all the functions it was capable of, the machine possessed virtually no human characteristics—a humorless, programmed, technologically-sophisticated hunk of metal. But sans any semblance of a soul or heart, there was just nobody to root for or care about.

It was my painful chore to tell him that I didn't think his book would be publishable until he at least humanized his main character. He rejected the advice out of hand and somewhat angrily. I understood his being upset—it has to be disturbing when you're told something you've worked on for that long and hard doesn't work. Later, he cooled down and called me to apologize and ask what I'd advise him to do to make it publishable. I had him read Janet Burroway's advice in her craft book, "Writing Fiction: A Guide to Narrative Craft" in which she states, "Human character is in the foreground of all fiction, however the humanity might be disguised. Anthropomorphism may be a scientific sin, but it is a literary necessity. Bugs Bunny isn't a rabbit; he's a plucky youth in ears. Peter Rabbit is a mischievous boy. Brer Rabbit is a sassy rebel. The romantic heroes of *Watership Down* are out of the Arthurian tradition, not out of the hutch. And that doesn't cover fictional *rabbits*."

The same applied to robots, I told him, and to this writer's credit, he grasped what Burroway and I were telling him and immediately began a rewrite. I've seen a few pages of his rewrite, and I'm happy to report that the robot is really coming alive on the page. With his dedication to this book and his work ethic, I have no doubt he'll eventually come up with a book that's publishable.

Symbolism

Too often, writers have studied a past master in lit and English classes and the professor has concentrated on the symbolism that lies within.

They don't realize that most writers don't consciously "stick" in such symbols, but that academics "find" them after the book has been published. This doesn't mean that symbolism isn't important or that it doesn't exist, but the majority of the time, the author didn't consciously include them. They made their appearance more as a result of the author's subconscious than something done purposely. I wish I could remember who it was—I think it was Isaac Bashevis Singer—who, in speaking to an interviewer about the "symbolism" in his own work that various critics and professors had "found," said that he never set out to provide such things, but if they saw them, it was all right with him since it made him look smarter than he thought he was. He said all he was trying to do was tell stories. Don't take this to mean that you shouldn't consciously include symbolism in your work, but if you do, try to ensure that it's organic to the story and isn't too obviously contrived as such. Better, don't worry about symbols, but just write the story. You may be surprised to find that symbols will appear on their own, and when they're created in that way, they nearly always work.

Beginnings

This is the biggest single area where contemporary writers drop the ball. In fact, I teach an ongoing class on this subject online for Painted Rock. Most of the students' work I see is guilty of poor beginnings and this mostly manifests itself in opening with backstory/setup and is due to two main causes. One, the writer hasn't yet learned to trust the reader's intelligence to "get it" without these kinds of beginning explanatory setups and also from the examples they see in older novels and stories, where, in former ages when readers had more spare time than we do in these hectic days, stories could and did begin much more leisurely. Nowadays, if the story or article doesn't start off quickly, the reader moves on to something else. We just don't have patience these days for languorous or slow-paced openings, at least most of us don't.

Static Descriptions

This is a major fault that can be laid directly at the feet of imitating older work. At one time, yes, it was considered good writing to provide "window-pane" description—this term describing the kind of description one would obtain from simply peering through a window-pane and cataloging what the narrator sees—usually delivered with somewhat poetical images, full of metaphors and similes and elevated language. No more. Today, description needs to be delivered via action and incorporated seamlessly into the scene and briefly so that it doesn't slow or stop the read. This kind of writing is almost guaranteed to take you out of your own voice as you search mightily for elevated language to couch it in—the kind of language you'd ordinarily never go nearer than the International Legal Offshore Limit (twenty miles from a foreign coast).

At the end of this chapter is a list of suggested books that will help you overcome any of these weaknesses you feel you have.

Hang In Here . . . Gonna Show You an Exercise to Correct This With . . .

How to cure these weaknesses? In my classes at Vermont College which I teach online, I came up with something that has proven to be very effective. I have a mix of students there—some taking it for undergraduate credit, some for graduate credit and some for just the heck of it (no credit). A paper is required for those taking the class for credit.

I asked my students to identify what they felt were their weaknesses as writers and then research writers and writing that was especially strong in that area or writing technique. For instance, someone weak in dialogue might look at writers like Elmore Leonard, David Mamet, Woody Allen, and folks like that. If your problem happens to be not being able to write descriptive settings effectively, some good writers to study might be Ellen Gilchrist, Raymond Chandler and Russell Banks to see how they actually make setting a character in their stories. Or John McPhee for how he creates descriptive settings in his nonfiction books. For someone a bit at sea at how to effectively describe characters without stalling the read, a close look at Mario Vargas Llosa would be profitable.

The students who did these papers all progressed significantly further in their own writing skill than those who didn't. They also began to use their own voices more and more. That was exciting!

This is what I'd like to ask you to do. The same thing I asked of my students taking my class for credit. Let's call it—

A BIG Handy-Dandy Exercise

1. Figure out your own biggest writing weakness. If you're not quite sure what it might be, just ask your fellow classmates or club members to point out what they think is your chief weakness. You'll be surprised at how easy they can do this if you've shown much of your work to the others . . . and how accurate they usually are!

2. Research those who are strong in that area or technique. If you have trouble figuring out who these writers might be, you might try contacting a local college English, literature or creative writing department and asking one of the profs for recommendations. A local librarian should also be able to help. Once you find an author who can give by his or her example, evidence of strong technique in your weak area, look at blurbs and reviews of the author's works to see if there are any other writers he or she has been compared to. Those authors may be of help as well.

3. Then, write a paper on what you've learned. Make it as short or as long as you want, but I'd suggest at least ten pages. You could just take mental or actual notes, but I think you'll find that by making this a formal exercise and taking the time to write an actual paper, you'll drive home the lesson much more forcibly. Many studies have shown that when we write something down, our retention is increased significantly. We "get it" much better than by just reading it. (This is the reason we as humans are considered so much smarter than other mammals, say German shepherds. We can write stuff down and therefore retain it days and even weeks longer.) Here's the format I'd suggest for your paper.

Format For Your "Paper"

1. Begin the paper with an introductory paragraph, stating the weakness you uncovered. A good example is the one written by my Vermont College online student, Amy Jacquemard. Amy's weakness—as identified by herself, me and the other students, and a wino who washed her car windows one day while stopped at a traffic light—was that her stories lacked structure. Her writing weakness was evident to all of us. They were kind of meandering. Amy was a good writer, but her stories were just all over the map. Here's her opening paragraph:

> Throughout the years, writers have used structure to build strong stories. Structure is as important to a short story as it is to a kindergarten classroom. It's a way to control elements of a story so they do not stray from the main point, contain enough tension to keep the reader reading, and include a rhythm that enables a reader to flow through a story without annoying starts and stops.

As you see, she's identified her weakness and stated why structure is important. All things she learned from her research.

2. Your second step in this exercise is to show, by published examples, how various authors who were considered strong with their story structures, achieved this. Amy looked at writers like E.B. White, Ernest Hemingway, Harold Brodkey, Joyce Carol Oates, Tim O'Brien, and Thom Jones—all masters of structure—and provided in the paper, examples of each of their writings that illustrated concretely how they'd each stuck to the spine of their stories. You should do the same with the writers you pick to look at. Pick up on specific examples of how they achieved the technique you're studying.

3. The third (and most important!) part of this exercise paper is to then show "before" and "after" examples of your own work. "Before" examples being those passages you wrote before becoming aware of your weakness and learning new strategies and methods of strengthening them; and "after" examples being the same passages rewritten with your new knowledge. Take the time to explain in the paper what you did exactly to improve the writing. ■

This may sound to you like an awful lot of work, and it perhaps is, but consider this. Most of us don't have the opportunity to take advantage of formal education, and even if we do, most likely we won't find a class that's specific enough to address our individual needs. If you're lucky enough to be able to attend a college or university and can afford so, chances are the best you'll be able to get is a general class or two on writing. If the teacher is generous, perhaps he or she may be able (and willing) to take on your special needs in addressing a particular weakness, but even if the teacher can and will, he or she probably won't be able to give you the time or attention on it you really need.

If, however, you identify the area you need to improve in and then research and complete the paper suggested here, you'll have learned much more than you would have learned in any ten classes. Knowledge that's both practical and sticks to your writer's ribs.

Make sense?

By the way, Amy got an A+ for an outstanding paper, and now she's got structure! She's becoming a terrific storyteller.

This exercise is a dynamic tool to help improve any aspect of your writing and to get to your own particular voice much quicker. Use it for each area you feel you're weak in, and you'll be amazed at how quickly your writing improves. Also, once you've completed the paper, don't just file it away. Take it out from time to time and reread it.

Also, in your regular reading, when you come across something someone has written that you feel especially effective, jot it down. If that writer is clearly good at something you're weak in, be sure to study how he or she accomplished that. I have a file I've created for just that purpose in my Word program and I just add what I've just discovered to it. Once a month or so, I open up the file and read from it. I'm always amazed at what I'd learned or relearned a mere two months ago but had since forgotten!

(Another ability we humans have that German shepherds don't.)

Use That Education You Paid For!

You know, it's funny. We do all these papers and such for classes when we're in high school and college, and then that's the end of it. We don't grasp that we can do the same kind of thing on our own, purely for our own personal edification. I'm as guilty as anyone. We don't realize that these are proven tools for educating ourselves. Writing such a research paper is maybe the best single way to gain a writing education.

When you finish yours, give yourself an A. Nah . . . give yourself an A+! You'll know you made the honor roll when your subsequent work begins to get noticed and even published!

How good is that?

Better than a sharp stick in the eye, I'll warrant.

Don't Worship the Past

We've talked about this before—how overrespecting published writers can drive us away from using our own voices in our writing. Now let's expand upon the subject a bit further.

Literature (and writing, by extension) may well be the only field of formal and informal study that is so hopelessly (and counterproductively!) tied to its past.

That's a bold statement, but one I can prove to you.

Without Power Point and even without primitive charts such as the O.J. Simpson defense team used!

How Other Professionals Look at Their Past Masters Through Vastly-Different Spectacles

Look at other fields of study:

- A student studying internal medicine at Stanford University's School of Medicine will most likely be exposed early in her studies to histori-

cal advances and milestones in the field of healing. To better understand the present state of medicine, it's important to understand
how doctoring got to where it is today. However, do you suppose
our earnest young student spends an awful lot of time poring over
case histories in old textbooks detailing how to properly use leeches
in bleeding patients? *Not.* Even though leeches were used as recently
as the Civil War and their application at the time considered an
important means of healing? That would be like a writer-student
spending an entire semester studying Stephen Crane's books. Kind
of a waste of time . . . I suspect our med student would spend about
five minutes (if that) on leeching techniques and a bit more on
nuclear medicine.

- Picture a contemporary psychiatrist reading every word Sigmund
Freud ever wrote about how we hate our fathers and adore our
mothers and how most of our adult tensions can be traced to the
time Dad wouldn't let us buy that go-kart when we were six. Not
very likely, as many, if not most, of his theories have been discounted
by many contemporary psychiatrists.

- What of other studies? When I was a kid, we learned a skill called
typing which was done on something called a Smith-Corona. If
you're a bit older, you may have learned on a prehistoric artifact
called an Underwood. Going back even further, people learned to
set moveable type. Gutenberg was an important cat in that field at
one time. As were the Egyptians with their remarkable invention of
papyrus, which was a huge step up and an important advance over
a sharp stick and a cave wall for recording important stuff with. Do
you suppose the modern teacher in charge of what we call "Key-
boarding Class 101" takes up a lot of her students' time in showing
them how to make papyrus and gives them homework to teach them
to read upside-down so they can set type? My guess is *not.* In wood
shop, does the teacher demonstrate how to cut down trees with a
double-axe and rough-plane them into boards? Most likely *not.*

I could provide examples in just about any field of study—sociology, pharmacology, biology, rocket science, dry-cleaning lint-removal oncology—but you get the point. Writing is just about the only field in which we are urged by all who have an opinion (and hardly ever have to be asked for it for it to be delivered and whose numbers are legion!), to not only spend years and years studying the past practitioners of our craft, but even worse, to imitate and emulate them.

Just as Galileo, from what we've heard, dropped balls from the Leaning Tower of Pisa, and from that came up with his laws on kinetics and freefall motion (that would be $s = kt^2$ for you math fiends), and that led to Newton's Theory of Mechanics and his Law of Universal Gravitation, so did William Faulkner pioneer the technique of stream-of-consciousness in writing. Both Galileo and Faulkner are to be commended and honored for their significant contributions. But, as I've already noted, Newton's stuff (based in good part on what he stole from Galileo), has been discounted by new findings by laboratory mice employed by MIT.

As has Faulkner's work for a particularly apt example in our field. He was one of the pioneers in a widely-used technique, and even though today some consider his efforts not perfect in spots or even a bit clunky, he opened new frontiers in writing and should be respected a great deal for doing so.

Just as contemporary physicists bow in respect to Galileo, but don't keep looking to his "science" for the basis of conducting their own research any more, so should we, as writers, accord our writing ancestors their due respect . . . but quit looking to them so much as models for our own work.

And, keeping us from our own voices. Realize that when we study these folks, at least on a subconscious level, we are also in danger of adopting their sentence patterns and their word choices as well as other elements of their voices, at the expense of our own. Slipping into *their* voice, in other words.

Listen to what one of our contemporaries, the late, great Raymond Carver had to say about some of the icons of literature in his famous essay "On Writing."

Some writers have a bunch of talent; I don't know any writers who are without it. But a unique and exact way of looking at things, and finding the right context for expressing that way of looking, that's something else. *The World According to Garp* is, of course, the marvelous world according to John Irving. There is another world according to Flannery O'Connor, and others according to William Faulkner and Ernest Hemingway. There are worlds according to Cheever, Updike, Singer, Stanley Elkin, Ann Beattie, Cynthia Ozick, Donald Barthelme, Mary Robison, William Kittredge, Barry Hannah, Ursula K. Le Guin. Every great or even every very good writer makes the world over according to his own specifications.

It's akin to style, what I'm talking about, but it isn't style alone. It is in the writer's particular and unmistakable signature on everything he writes. It is his world and no other. This is one of the things that distinguishes one writer from another. Not talent. There's plenty of that around. (Ask any mother of your acquaintance—I'll bet she will claim to have at least one offspring who has buckets of talent in something or other, maybe even in writing. "Talent" is an element that is all around us and arrives daily through the hole in the ozone layer just above Canada.) But a writer who has some special way of looking at things and who gives artistic expression to that way of looking: that writer may be around for a time.

The End Reward

What Carver is talking about is what every editor worth his or her salt is hoping to find each time he or she opens a submission from a new writer. Someone who shows by his or her voice on the page, a "special way of looking at things."

Revealing, by your own voice, the individual you are and that readers are dying to meet on the page.

How To Spot "Copyitis"

There are many ways to find out if you're using the wrong folks for models in your own writing and thereby suppressing your own voice. Maybe even not so much the wrong writers per se, but relying too heavily on older models without putting them in context of their times and the times you find yourself in now.

Here are a couple of ways to do this.

1. Being honest with yourself, go over a piece of recent writing and mark the passages you feel are weaker than the rest. Pick up a copy of your favorite author's work, compare those passages to it, and note any similarities. For instance, pretend that the passages you marked are mostly descriptive passages. Say that your favorite author is Louise Erdrich, and that what draws you to Erdrich is something that may be considered somewhat of a "fault" with other writers: the tendency to pair adjectives for emphasis, to repeat the same idea in the same sentence with a variety of similar images, and a bit of an overly-melodramatic style. In Erdrich's capable hands, that works well. It's her voice. In another writer's, the same tendencies may be disastrous. Perhaps one of your own passages you've identified as being a bit weak went something like this:

> Joyce railed against the harsh, cruel injustice of Doc's savage, cutting words. She began to speak, to inveil against, to protest. Her voice began timidly when she first began, but then, smoothed by the sweetened coffee, Sucrets, and sips of icy water, she soon slipped into mellifluous, rich tones. Doc looked astounded, and then, even suspicious, as she began to speak faster, with more confidence, with increased assurance behind the words as she refuted his accusations. She talked in a voice that bespoke the gathering power of a spring stream, overflowing with the melt from mountain snow, the force of gravity propelling them along and out of her throat.

You look at this passage with new eyes. When you first wrote it, you may have been impressed with what you considered the "poetry" in the words. Now, at the distance of time, the passage screams out to you to have been overwritten.

You pick up Erdrich's *Tracks* and begin skimming pages. On page seven, you stop at the passage that reads:

> My voice rasped at first when I tried to speak, but then, oiled by strong tea, lard and bread, I was off and talking. Even a sledge won't stop me once I start. Father Damien looked astonished and then wary, as I began to creak and roll. I gathered speed. I talked both languages in streams that ran alongside each other, over every rock, around every obstacle.

Wow. This is *kind* of the way you wrote, wasn't it? *Kind of,* but not exactly. You recall suddenly this was one of your favorite passages when you'd first read her book, and you suspect, also suddenly, that perhaps you'd retained the words at least subconsciously.

And, Erdrich's voice entered yours.

Hers worked because it was hers.

Yours didn't, because it was also . . . *hers.*

That may tell you why those passages weren't the best in your piece—an at-least subconscious attempt to be like Erdrich.

✦ ✦ ✦

2. Ask a friend if your writing reminds you of anyone else's, i.e., a prominent, published author. Or, recall if more than one person has compared your writing to another's. If so, this should be a red warning flag to you. Sometimes, just asking this or remembering this is all that's necessary to tell you you're guilty of "copyitis."

The Cure

Once you've identified those passages in your own work that sound like someone else, mark them and try to rewrite them once again— but in *your* words this time.

Look for words, phrases, *anything* that jars you about the language you've used in the piece that lets you know this isn't really you. Check it out carefully, read whatever it is aloud and see what it "feels" like. Does it feel foreign, strained? If so, you know what to do. Experiment with other words, other phrases, until it feels natural.

In *your* voice.

Obviously, the previous example ("yours" and Erdrich's) was contrived, but I hope it gives you a good idea of what to look for in your own writing. A great many times, the weaknesses in your writing can be traced back to the author you're most in awe of. Check what you've written, identify either by yourself or with someone else's help the lesser parts, and compare those parts to writers you feel hold an influence over you.

Then . . . cut dem ties that bind!

Appendix

The following is a list of books I recommend you might look at that will help you recognize and then overcome the various writing weaknesses detailed in this chapter and help you get closer to writing in your own voice:

- Sci-fi stories that are focused too much on technology and not enough on characterization. Suggested texts: *Writing Fiction: A Guide to Narrative Craft*, Janet Burroway; *Characters and Viewpoint*, Orson Scott Card; any stories by Ray Bradbury or Isaac Asimov.
- Overt, intentional "symbolism." Suggested texts: *Narrative Design* (in particular, the sections on theme), Madison Smartt Bell; *Starting From Scratch* (in particular, the chapter titled "Myth and Symbol, as Opposed to Hit or Myth"), Rita Mae Brown; *Fiction First Aid*, Raymond Obstfeld.
- Weak beginnings. Suggested reading: *On Writing Well* (in particular, chapter nine, "The Lead and the Ending"), William Zinsser; *The Art and Craft of the Short Story*, Rick DeMarinis; *The Complete Guide to Editing Your Fiction* (especially chapter seven "Back Story and Detail"), *Michael Seidman*; the beginnings of the following stories,

novels, and nonfiction books: T. Coraghessan Boyle's *World's End*; my own "The Bad Part of Town" from *Monday's Meal*; Jamaica Kincaid's *The Autobiography of My Mother*; Marie Chapian's *Alula-Belle Blows Into Town* (as a note of possible interest, Ms. Chapian has made yours truly a character in this delightful children's book— I am "Les Fussbucket"); Douglas Glover's *The South Will Rise at Noon*.

- Static descriptions. Recommended reading: *The Cabin*, David Mamet; *Write From Life: Turning Your Personal Experiences Into Compelling Stories*, Meg Files; *What If? Writing Exercises for Fiction Writers*, Anne Bernays and Pamela Painter; *The 38 Most Common Fiction Writing Mistakes (And How to Avoid Them)*, Jack M. Bickham; the descriptions in the following stories, novels, and nonfiction books: Mario Vargas Llosa's *Aunt Julia and the Scriptwriter*; Ellen Gilchrist's *Rhoda*; E. Annie Proulx's *The Shipping News*; Russell Bank's *Affliction*; Sue William Silverman's *Because I Remember Terror, Father, I Remember You*; Frances Sherwood's *Vindication*.

CHAPTER TEN

How to Seize Control of Your Novel, Short Story, Nonfiction Article or Book and Make It Your Own

 Talent alone cannot make a writer. There must be a man behind the book.—RALPH WALDO EMERSON

This, then, is what it's all about, finally.

Putting your personality into your prose. Truly, the "secret" to getting published.

William Zinsser stresses this in his best-selling writer's craft book, *On Writing Well,* when he writes: "I wrote one book about baseball and one about jazz. But it never occurred to me to write one of them in sports English and the other in jazz English. I tried to write them both in the best English I could, in my usual style. Though the books were widely different in subject, I wanted readers to know that they were hearing from the same person. It was *my* book about baseball and *my* book about jazz. Other writers would write *their* book. My commodity as a writer, whatever I'm writing about, is me. And your commodity is you."

If your finished novel, short story, article, poem, personal memoir, bio of the latest corrupt politician or outstanding statesperson—whatever—reads as if written by another person . . . then it was.

You need to seize it and make it the work only *you* could possibly have written.

First off, however, you need to determine if your voice has, indeed, been camouflaged.

There are at least three ways to tell if this is so.

Are the Word Choices, Sentence Usages, and Phrases Employed Yours?

The first "litmus test" is to check the *language* in the piece itself.

Author Jules Renard said, "If the word *arse* is read in a sentence, no matter how beautiful the sentence, the reader will react only to that word." He's not singling out the "olde English" noun except as an example of the sort of word a writer shouldn't use unless it's organic to him and is natural to the context in which it's used. The kind of word that draws attention to itself, at the expense of the fictive dream we struggle so mightily to create for the reader. Look for those kinds of examples in your copy, and instead of reaching automatically for your thesaurus, try a different approach to coming up with a better word. One way to do this is by clustering. Write the word that needs replaced in the center of a blank sheet of paper. Draw a short, straight line out from the word, and quickly jot down the next word that pops into your mind. Do the same with that word. Do this for at least seven to eight words, then sit back and look at what you have. Oftentimes, the word you need emerges. If that doesn't work, at least change any such word that drastically calls attention to itself to something less intruding and attention-gathering.

As Anthony Burgess says, "People don't like using dictionaries when they're reading mere novels."

Jane Burroway, in her seminal writing text, *Writing Fiction: A Guide to Narrative Craft*, says much the same thing, but expands the advice even more: "When you are carried away with the purple of your prose, the music of your alliteration, the hilarity of your wit, the profundity of your insights, then the chances are that you are having a better time writing than the reader will have reading. No reader will forgive you, and no reader should. Just tell the story. The style will follow of itself if you just tell the story."

Check your text for overt evidence of a writer at work. Whenever the reader becomes aware someone is writing the piece—whether it be fiction or nonfiction—then the "fictive dream" (which applies to nonfiction as well) is interrupted and you've lost your reader at least briefly, if not permanently. You've created a speed bump, at the minimum.

Five Percent

If you can identify more than 5 percent of the language you used as being essentially foreign to your normal usage, then you're not employing your own personality on the page. That's just too many words alien to your vocabulary and it will show up as forced and unnatural. In fact, 5 percent is just about the upper limit. Go back and substitute more of your own language.

Sentence Structure

The structure you give your sentences can show you whether or not you're solidly within your voice.

If you're using complete sentences, you're probably not writing in your natural voice.

In a recent Neighborhood Connections class (local, adult-ed class) I taught, a woman who wrote otherwise wonderful prose had a sticking point with sentence fragments. She simply could not bring herself to write anything less than a complete sentence. She confessed that every time she did, the image of her seventh-grade English teacher loomed large on the screen of her mental Sony. The result was prose, that, while writ with grace, beauty and interest, nevertheless, was being strangled with formality. She was such a good writer that she was able to imbue her "Tom Wolfeian beige voice" with energy, but it wasn't until she was able to force herself to write sentence fragments within the text that her stories really began to sparkle. She "thought" in sentence fragments at the appropriate places in her writing, but she had developed the habit of editing them as she wrote to render them complete units, with subject, predicate, and all that stuff. It took almost the entire six weeks of the class for her to work through her problem, but once she overcame that inhibition, the traces were thrown off, and she confessed, after her last class, that she felt "wildly free" for the first time in her writing life. She'd been so "conditioned" that at first she couldn't even bring herself to use contractions in her character's dialogue!

Clarity

The trick to writing well? Write simply; write clearly. Eschew flowery language.

Aim for the same kind of clarity-bullseye in your own writing, whether it be a lean or lush style. The kind of writing that when the nonwriter or casual reader reads it, thinks, "Man! This writing stuff looks easy. *I* could do *this*!"

Look at other writers you admire and see if the simpleness of their language—whether lush or spare or somewhere in-between—isn't one of their strengths, too.

When rereading your work and you come to a part that has been gussied up by the over-baroqueness of your language, try rewriting it with only one thing in mind—to make it as clear to the reader as a day in Santa Monica after a Santa Ana wind has blown through. If your style requires ten words to do that and another's style uses four, that's all right. Just don't use twenty words if ten do the job, or eight, if your own style is comfortable with six. Compare the initial version and the rewritten one, and see which one you like the best. Better, have someone else read them and tell you which one they prefer.

Don't stick a Rolls-Royce hood ornament on your Chevy Lumina and try to fool people!

Second Litmus Test—Get Feedback From Others

Perhaps one of the best ways to cull out those parts of your writing where you've strayed from your own trés-cool voice is to solicit the opinions of others. If you belong to a writing group, ask your fellow writers if you can read your material to them, requesting they inform you which, if any, parts "don't sound like you." Mark through those sentences and sections with a marker (I'd suggest yellow instead of black), and then later, go through them to see if you agree. If the language has departed from the rest of the piece, you know it needs to be rewritten until it blends with the rest.

Read your material aloud, and ask yourself if you'd like to be locked up in a room with the person who wrote this and listen to the sound of that voice for several hours at a time. If not, then you're probably not putting your own personality into your prose as much as you should be. After all, we like our voices when we're ourselves, don't we? We hardly ever tell ourselves to "shut up!" when we're being natural.

Tweety in the Coal Mine

Way back when, coal miners would carry a canary in a cage down into the bowels of the mine with them. The purpose of the canary was to let the miners know if deadly gasses were present so they could get the hell out before they keeled over. They kept a close watch on Tweety, and if he fell over dead (with those little Xs for eyes), they hiked as fast as they could to the surface.

That's what you need. A canary to let you know if the "gas" of your prose has become deadly. Hopefully, your friend or writing group won't fall over onto the floor with those little Xs where their orbs used to be, but they should be able to sniff where your writing has become stifling and beige.

Beige has an odor somewhat like skunk cabbage does when you step into a patch of it. Deodorize your prose until it smells sweet—like you!

Be Alert to Critic Nag in the Room . . .

The third part of the litmus test to see if you're camouflaging your natural voice is to check the room periodically to see if Critic Nag has crept in under the doorsill or through an open window. He's usually invisible, so the only way to spot them is to read what you've written to see if he was typing while your mind spaced, as it does from time to time with us writer-types.

A good place to look for evidence that he's lurking somewhere in the room is in your character's dialogue. If you find your characters never use contractions in their speech, for instance, that's a solid clue that Critic Nag is sitting over in the corner, smirking evilly at you. If your characters always use complete sentences, wouldn't dream of using a contraction, without fail use the correct words or word combinations like "give me" instead of "gimme," then Critic Nag has probably snuck into the room with you.

Look for Critic Nag's whisper in your ear when you're writing emotional scenes. He'll try to encourage you to use lurid language and not trust your own writing ability to convey the emotion. He's a crafty little imp! When you're writing those scenes, keep in mind the advice of Philip Gerard in his excellent book "Writing a Book That Makes a Difference," where he says: "Flatten the language. The hotter the action, the cooler you want the language, to a point."

You need to choose the word that fits the situation on the page you're trying to create—whether that be description or the business or action of a scene, but you also need to choose the word that fits you comfortably. It has to carry the intent, but it also has to reflect you and your emotions. That's the only way it will ring true and be unmistakably yours.

Another clue that will tell you ol' Critic Nag has been around is if your passages of description have been overwritten and in a too-flowery style. If you read passages full of window-pane, static description, instead of active, page-turning description. This is what one of those many fiends who compose Critic Nag urged you to do way back when. He's in the room!

He's also been around if you begin to reread your stuff and unfamiliar words jump out at you. You know, those words you've never once used in conversation and look newly-purchased from that sale you visited on Dictionary/Thesaurus.com. (Or, found on ebay, most likely.)

To Reiterate . . .

In summary, there are three basic ways to seize control of your material and make it your own:

1. Check the language you've used in the piece.

Mark the words that leap up at you from the page that clearly aren't yours and come up with choices from your vocabulary.

2. Have others read your material and tell you which parts aren't "you."

Pick folks who know you well. Don't use them to tell you if the writing is "good" or make that kind of quality judgment; instead, simply ask them to let you know which passages "don't sound like you." That's all you need—someone to point out where you departed from yourself.

3. Seek out and banish Critic Nag from the room.

Begone!

Lagniappe . . .

I've lived in New Orleans more often and longer than any other single place in a lifetime of countless geographical moves and relocations, so I consider it "home." Even though I find myself currently in Fort Wayne, Indiana (mostly because that's where most of my stuff is and someone has to watch it and also, my wife and son live here and I like to be near them in case I need something important, like supper or a missing blue sock), my "spiritual" home will always be the Big Easy. In New Orleans, we "locals" have a philosophy we call lagniappe. It's a French word that means, "something extra," and it's a long-established philosophy of the local business establishments. Many places offer "something extra" to their customers in keeping with this tradition. If you've ever been to New Orleans and strolled into a gift shop down in the Quarters, you've probably been offered a free piece of praline candy, for instance. A lot of nightclubs and bars designate one night as "lagniappe" night, and provide a free spread of food for their custom-ers. In fact, if you know your clubs, you can eat free just about all week! Except, of course, during Mardis Gras, when you'll want to save all your stomach space for various libations.

I'd like to offer you a bit of lagniappe here (nonalcoholic). Some-thing you might find valuable during those times when your writing has seemed to have hopelessly moved into that beige voice and Critic Nag is perched firmly on your shoulder, digging his wicked, little sharp claws into your skin.

I'll bet many, if not most, of us began writing way back when as a way of dealing with the bullies in our lives. It's why I myself began writing as a grade-school kid—creating humorous sketches of those mouth-breathers was the only way I could deal with some of the more terrifying individuals I faced daily and felt physically powerless against. Mesomorphs ranging from the hulking schoolyard rowdy to the teacher who thought her job was to intimidate her charges into submission. I'd show these "pieces" to friends, they'd be passed around, and in more than one instance, public opinion ended those offenders' bullying careers. Even if they didn't, as in the case of a large, misshapen principal or two, just "publishing" them made me feel lots better and gave me the feedback that told me I'd gained allies from my peers. The real success came from ending the careers of schoolyard bullies. Nobody likes to push someone around if he knows he's going to get laughed at by everyone else. It just plain takes the power out of it, not to mention the fun.

My guess is that many of us here became writers from a similar motivation—because of a bully somewhere in our past. Maybe it was another kid, or a group of kids, or maybe even an adult or two in charge of us. We found we could effectively duel these kinds of folks with the written word. If we were physically weaker, we found we possessed a strength that was virtually indefensible against. The power of ideas, expressed upon the page. One of the most compelling reasons to slap down sentences on paper that ever existed, and the reason much of the world's literature exists and lives on. Some of the world's greatest books were created to battle tyranny of one form or another. An ancient tradition, from Jonathan Swift to David Sedaris.

And, in a great many cases the weapon of words was strengthened even more by the use of humor.

Which leads me to the lagniappe I promised.

When you find Critic Nag has entered the room and is influencing your words so they've lapsed into that beige voice and you're not sure how to get back to your "real" voice, try taking a few minutes away from what you're working on to crank out a short, humorous, and scathing essay blasting ol' Critic Nag dude. He's a bully, and this is the best way to rid yourself of his nasty influence.

Here's What You Do:

1. Give Critic Nag a face and body shape in your mind's eye. Preferably the ugliest face you can imagine and a wretched body with no discernable shape, other than a blob or a humongous purple insect. Make him or her huge and threatening. The kind of image that if he were to mug you, he wouldn't need a weapon other than his facial expression. Your average bully, in other words.

2. Stare at him or her in your mind's eye and begin grinning at him. It's surprising how a smiling victim can unnerve a bully! Makes 'em wonder . . . does this person have some secret weapon I don't know about?

3. Begin writing about him/her, using one or more of the approaches below. Realize that although he is one nasty-looking dude, he only exists in your mind and can't touch you, no matter what you write. Imagine you're writing this for a friend of yours, who has also been victimized by Critic Nag:

    A. Be sarcastic.

    B. Be cynical.

    C. Use caricature.

    D. Poke fun at him/her any way you feel like!

4. When you're done, read aloud what you've written about him to Critic Nag. Visualize C.R. shrinking away, sentence by sentence, growing smaller and smaller . . . until they're the size of a cockroach (great image!). Visualize your friend who has also been victimized by C.R., listening to you along with him and hear her laughter growing louder with each sentence. Then, step on him grind him into the floor. Cockroach hamburger glop.

He ain't so tough now, is he! Kinda puny, in fact. From now on, Critic Nag isn't that humongous monster, but an insignificant little pile of roach entrails.

Try it. You may even get some lagniappe from doing so by coming up with a publishable piece. Just don't write it with that (publication) in mind. Write it solely in the spirit in which you used to write those pieces back in P.S. 101—to put Critic Nag-Bully-Guy in his place.

When you return to the piece you're working on, you may be pleasantly surprised to discover your own voice has returned, all tuned up and rarin' to be unleashed.

Just always remember: *Don't let others rent space in your head*! Especially Critic Nag . . .

CHAPTER ELEVEN

What Top Writers, Editors and Agents Say About Voice

 Of course no writers ever forget their first acceptance. One fine day when I was seventeen I had my first, second and third, all in the same morning's mail. Oh, I'm here to tell you, dizzy with excitement is no mere phrase!
—TRUMAN CAPOTE

I've always been a sucker for quotes and advice from those in the writing field. For years, I've bought the current copy of *The Paris Review*, not so much for the stories, which are superb, but even more for the interviews with famous writers.

In fact, my first novel, "The Death of Tarpons," was hatched from one of those interviews. The interviewee was a French writer and I wish I could remember who it was, but hard as I try to jog that particular memory cell, his name refuses to emerge.

How did I get a novel from an interview in *The Paris Review*, you (naturally) ask?

Well, from my earliest memories, I've been in love with words. I remember as a kid in grade school, spending hours and hours ranging far and wide and deep through the dictionary, delighting at the strange and wonderful words I encountered there, sounding out their phonetic pronunciations so conveniently provided, feeling their almost-physical deliciousness taste as they tripped past my tongue for the very first time. As it so happens, in one of those serendipitous events, just a week ago my mother came to visit and brought with her that very same dictionary which she'd just come across while cleaning up the attic. She thought I might want to have it as she "remembered all those hours you used to spend reading it over in a corner of the laundry room" while she sorted underwear and my father's work shirts.

She was right.

I took the book out of her hands and clutched it like an old, long-lost friend, which it was.

I wish I could report to you the name of this dictionary from my childhood—if it was a Webster's or a Random House or even an Oxford English Dictionary (unlikely, as we wouldn't have had the money for an O.E.D.! and besides, it's not nearly big enough), but I can't. The book she returned to me was minus its covers, both front and back, and nowhere in its pages was anything that indicated the publisher. The pages are yellowed and brittle and some of them are torn. It shows heavy use. What was left of the book began on page 39 and with the word *aloin* (al′o-in), *n*, a bitter substance found in aloes, used as a purgative. It ended with page 1022 and with the word viverrine (vī-věr′ĭn), *adj.* pertaining to the civet family: *n*, a civet. A lot of the words are missing (thirty-eight pages worth!), and if I wanted to look up a word with it now that began with the letters *w, x, y,* or *z* . . . well, I'd just be out of luck.

And what does all this have to do with quotes and *The Paris Review* and my first novel? Or even the material that follows this introduction?

Hold on, we're getting there . . .

In one of his remarks to *The Paris Review* interviewer, this French writer used the word "spatterdashers." The word leapt out at me. He was kind enough to provide the meaning, which I looked up just now in my returned dictionary, and found that form of the word not there, but this form: "spatterdashes." It gives nearly the same meaning as the French writer provided, which is "leather leggings for riding; gaiters; spats."

This is a little bit off from what I remember the definition I'd originally seen, which was, "a word that denoted an article of clothing men used to wear to prevent spatter from dashing them." The French writer went on to further explain that, over time and usage, the word had been shortened to the more familiar "spats," which is a term more people are conversant with.

I loved the word!

And saw it immediately as being a word I could use for a metaphor for a book I was then thinking of writing and was stuck on how to begin. A fictionalized account of a childhood (mine) that I saw in that instant could use something like a spatterdasher to keep the "mud" of abuse from "dashing" my protagonist.

It worked really well.

And now, finally, what has all this to do with the following collection of remarks from various and noted writers, editors, agents and others in the profession of letters giving their views of the importance of the writer writing in his or her own particular voice?

Lots.

If you're like me, you want to know what it takes to be a writer and specifically, a published writer. These folks will help you see what is required in terms of voice, at least from their points-of-view as the arbiters and purchasers of work.

There's some excellent advice in what these folks have to say that you can put to use immediately.

You may even get an idea for an article, a story, poem, or a novel from something one of them says . . . just as I did with my own novel.

"You've got to be a good date for your reader," Kurt Vonnegut is reported to have said to his class at the Iowa Writers' Workshop.

Pretty good metaphor!

And, what's almost always the first suggestion your friends or even Mom or Dad usually give you when they learn you've just landed such an engagement with someone you're anxious to impress?

How about, "Just be yourself."

Which is the message you'll hear in the following pages from the kinds of folks who count in the writing game—the editors, agents, book-buyers and successful writers.

Listen carefully to what they're saying and you'll see how vital an element these people feel the writer's voice to be for the success of the writer's careers.

RICK FARRANT is an award-winning, twenty-nine-year veteran of newspapers and magazines, including *The Denver Post*, *Time*, and *The Journal Gazette* (Fort Wayne, Indiana), where he coaches writers. He is the co-author of *Crossing Over: One Woman's Exodus From Amish Life*.

Good writing is impossible in the absence of a passion and honesty that is true to the author's innate skills, lifetime observations, and inner voice.

Far too many prospective writers believe they should hold themselves to standards of fine writing established by the likes of Twain, Hemingway, Fitzgerald, and Updike. In some cases, they may even try to copy them.

But doing so is a mistake that can only lead to monumental frustration and often failure. Hemingway wrote like Hemingway because he was Hemingway; there can be no other like him.

New writers, even seasoned writers, can benefit by reading the masters, but they should avoid trying to copy wholesale the styles of others or elevating their writing to contrived levels they cannot maintain. Writing is a very personal journey that is best taken by being true to oneself and listening to the pace, rhythm, and flow of language that beats differently in all of us.

That is our voice, and it is the best tool we have for communicating effectively.

MICHELLE HOWRY is an editor for Perigree, a paperback imprint of Penguin Putnam, and is the editor of *Agents, Editors, and You*.

I'm a nonfiction book editor, so the characteristics of clarity and precision in an author's writing are particularly important to me. If a writer can offer me clean, crisp writing that delivers the ideas and does so in a compelling, interesting voice . . . that's the best of all possible worlds. A lot of my work is done by helping the writers I work with convey their ideas clearly and effectively.

Just today I reviewed a manuscript from a man who is very well respected in his field. He's been working in his area for decades, he's incredibly successful, and he's got this wealth of information . . . but he wrote in such a highbrow, academic, convoluted manner that I couldn't understand a paragraph of his book. Just deciphering each sentence was a chore! I finished the first few chapters and couldn't even have told you what the book was about.

I wonder if some writers think that using chunky words, padded phrases, and drawn-out sentences implies that their ideas are somehow weightier, too. It's just not usually the case. Writing is about communication. I get so much more out of a writer who uses words economically and effectively than I do from someone who strains to sound intellectual with needlessly complicated language.

JAMES C. VINES is a literary agent and the president of The Vines Agency, Inc.

When it comes to voice, the most important thing for any author to find is her "natural" one. That's the only voice any of us are going to want to read. Some authors are blessed with the ability to write in a few different natural voices, but for most authors, finding one true and real voice is more than enough of a gift to last a lifetime! I think it's crucial to point out that an author's natural voice might not necessarily be the one that just comes rushing out easily when she sits at her keyboard. In fact, Cynthia Ozick—an author with one of the most beautiful, natural voices imaginable—told me she once spent an entire week on a single sentence, rearranging it and tinkering with it until it was just right. That's what it can take to get to your natural voice.

For Salman Rushdie, the literary-sounding voice works; for Janet Evanovich, a sassier, funnier voice works. Both of these authors are geniuses, and both of them have figured out exactly what to write. Can you imagine either of these authors trying to fake a work with the other's voice? My best advice to an aspiring author would be to think about the books that inspire her the most in her reading life, and especially focus on the story elements and characters in those works that have had the most profound effect, because those are the kinds of things she should likely be writing about. The very things that inspire us when we read are probably going to inspire us when we write, so if your passion is James Patterson, stop writing that literary narrative non-fiction tome about the Middle Ages, and give us a hot new police detective—in *your* voice.

DENNIS **F**OLEY **started his writing career in Hollywood where he worked as a writer and producer for fifteen years. He is a member of the Writers Guild of America and The Author's Guild. His novels include** *Long Range Patrol, Special Men: A LRP's Recollections, Night Work,* **and** *Take Back the Night.* **Dennis is also a creative writing instructor for the UCLA Writers' Program and for Writers on the Net.**

New fiction writers somehow think that they need to write at a different level of sophistication or with a jacked up demonstration of the limits of their vocabulary. Couldn't be further from the truth. They aren't being graded, no teacher is leaning over their shoulder, and they aren't writing to impress. Their goal should be to communicate with the reader the same way they would when telling a story to a good friend. It is a hard habit to break, a hangover from school days, but a writer's personality and style—his voice—will only come through in his writing when he relaxes and focuses on the needs of the reader and what best communicates his intent.

My recommendation: Write for a friend, not for a grade.

JODIE RHODES is a literary agent and published novelist living in La Jolla, California. Her clients benefit from her years of experience as a former editor, creative writing teacher, and advertising executive. She also writes columns for writers' magazines, gives seminars at The Learning Annex, and conducts writers' workshops.

Voice is literally everything when considering a manuscript. Its importance cannot be overemphasized. It's what sells a book. It's what editors look for. Think of great books and it's always the voice that made them great. Dickens and Shakespeare's works are immortal because of the voice of their characters.

It's the vital element in every work of fiction and narrative nonfiction. *Gone with the Wind* is the voice of Scarlett O'Hara. John MacDonald made a fortune with his mystery series because of the voice of Travis McGee. Every successful mystery series is successful because of the protagonist's voice.

Let me tell you about two of my writers whose voice made all the difference in the world. George Pickett is a retired NYC Firefighter who sent me his memoir in August 2001. The manuscript was in such terrible shape I described it to him as an endless wasteland of garbage glittering with a few diamonds. The diamonds were his voice—distinctive, powerful, compelling. A voice that belonged to him and no one else, a voice that gave us the heart and soul of the man.

He'd been trying to sell his memoir for ten years, getting nothing but rejections. He'd paid one editor $5000 to edit it, who destroyed it in my opinion. Voice is so important that I made the considerable sacrifice of personally editing his ms (without charge, of course) and teaching him how to structure, focus, use transitions, and above all be true to his voice (writers all too often lose the voice during the writing). In fact, I ended up editing it over three times until we got it right.

But it seemed all in vain. 9/11 happened, and he went straight to NY and Ground Zero to help out. I didn't get his final edited ms until the following year. No publisher would consider it. They all had their own firefighter books by this time. More important, the timing was terrible. They wouldn't be able to get it in print and distributed until 2003—way too late.

I told him if he'd get to work building a platform for himself, getting endorsements, etc. I would go the whole nine yards with him and find a publisher.

On August 23rd his book *The Brave: A Story of NYC Firefighters* was published by a small New York house, Bricktower Press. The foreword was written by Hugh Downs. An incredible endorsement by NY Times' bestselling author and most famous firefighter Dennis Smith is featured on the inside flap.

In one short month there has been such demand for the book that it is now in its third printing. This author doesn't have a literary bone in his body. It doesn't matter. He has a voice.

The most recent story I want to tell you is that of Kavita Daswani, an Indian writer from Bombay who wrote an autobiographical novel titled *For Matrimonial Purposes*. In two short weeks it has become an international sensation, rapidly gaining fans in New York, London, Holland, Italy, France, Germany, Spain, and Japan, to name a few. Why? Because of the voice—just the voice.

It's the story of her parents' desperate search for a proper husband for her, a search that eluded them year after year, depressing everyone to the point that Kavita fled to NY and became a fashion publicist—but was so tied to her culture she still felt a failure being single. It is witty, hysterically funny at times, heartbreaking at other times, always fresh, original, authentic. We fall in love with this person.

As I write this, simultaneous auctions are being held in London and New York. The last bid in NY was $185,000—in the UK $160,000. I sold the Dutch rights to Prometheus for $10,000, the Italian rights to Mondadori for $15,000—both overnight pre-empts. Now I am not accepting any more pre-empts. We're looking for auctions in every country.

Both of these authors are brand-new, first-time writers. Both needed editing. Both won me instantly with their voice.

Most manuscripts I receive have no voice. They have boring generic characters who mouth dialogue, who act and react, but there's no voice here. There are just invented stick-figures stuck in improbable plots.

Writers have been ruined by movies and TV. They see these high-concept productions where plot is all important and think that's what sells. What they don't realize is Hollywood doesn't need a book or script with a voice. They have charismatic actors whose presence on the screen serves as the voice.

I do weekly workshops for local area writers and the most difficult writers to work with are those fluent with language and highly intelligent who have been praised for years by teachers, friends, family. They write in this high-flown, artificial literary style that's pretentious and totally empty of meaning. It's show-off writing. With few exceptions they are angry and insulted when I explain why this is all wrong. As long as they have that attitude, they will always be rejected.

Writers consistently sabotage themselves by giving us unsympathetic protagonists at the beginning of a book, thinking as they put them through problems they will evolve into finer human beings and we'll be inspired. They don't understand we'll stop reading on page one. If we don't connect with the protagonist immediately, we stop reading the book. Books are all about people. Nobody is going to read about someone they dislike.

Writers will never find a powerful evocative voice until they learn to be bone-deep honest with themselves, open and vulnerable. Every person is an individual, no one else is exactly like them. Their characters must be equally individualistic. They will not be as long as the writer distances herself or himself in the writing. The writer has to become the characters—live their lives during the journey of the book, not just describe or relate it. When writers are willing to take that leap, that big chance, only then will their characters come alive on the page. When that happens, you have magic. Because the characters start doing the writing.

Authors write bad books. Characters write great books.

SHIRLEY KAWA-JUMP is the author of several books, including *How to Publish Your Articles: A Complete Guide to Making the Right Publication Say Yes* (Square One Publishers, 2001). Over the course of her career, she has sold more than 2,500 articles to national and local publications. She is a chapter president for Romance Writers of America and writes for Silhouette Romance. In addition, she is the writing instructor for iVillage.com.

In my opinion, finding your voice is much like falling in love. There are false starts along the way, zigs and zags in the road as you experiment and grow and reach. Many times, you'll think you found the real thing only to find out later that it wasn't quite you. When you do finally and truly find your voice, you *know* it, in one of those intangible ways that is nearly impossible to explain. Suddenly the writing is as comfortable as an old pair of slippers, the words slipping easily from your mind to the page. The entire work becomes a reflection of all the different parts of you, bringing a touch of your self to every page.

There are two methods of finding your voice—through experimentation and reading. Too many writers pigeonhole themselves into one type of writing because they think that's what they should write or what they believe will sell better. They end up stifling their voices by working in a genre that isn't right for them. The writing becomes a chore and the writer's voice is lost among the drudgery of creating something that isn't coming from the heart. The key is to experiment with different kinds of writing until you find the one that is an exact fit for you.

By reading widely, you can identify other writers' voices and see how distinctive they are. Read, for example, a half dozen Stephen King thrillers and then a half dozen Dean Koontz books. Their writing voices are vastly different. It's the same with other authors. Jennifer Crusie and Susan Elizabeth Phillips both write romances with a comedic overtone. But anyone who has read both of those authors extensively would know one from the other after a few paragraphs. By identifying other voices, you recognize the importance and impact of having your own voice. From there, you can begin to work harder to find and embrace your own.

Many writers try too hard and then spoil the words. They strive for big words or picturesque phrases, convinced that lyrical writing is the key to a strong voice. It isn't. When writers try too hard, it shows. Their work is stilted and doesn't flow naturally from thought to thought.

It's important for all writers to do some "just because" writing. Sit down and write, with no thoughts about where the piece might sell or what someone might think about it. The purpose is to find your true voice and you can only do that by being an honest writer with yourself. It doesn't matter what you create (and it may even be better to create something out of your normal range of writing), all it matters is that you are writing freely. Silence the voices that judge each word and just let the piece flow. Rediscover the joy of pure creation. When you do, you'll find your true writer self.

MARIE JORDAN's latest book of poems is *Slow Dance on Stilts*. Her latest novel is *I Love You Like a Tomato*. She teaches creative writing at Mira Costa College in California, the Vermont College On-Line Life-Long Learning Program, and speaks at writing conferences across the country.

When I try to analyze with my students what makes fiction really sing, we pause for a long time on the subject of voice. My job is to help them sort through what I regularly sort through to find that "secret" ingredient for great prose. To begin to find our writing voices means to take a hard look at our own issues, concerns, and what I ceremoniously call our "truth."

I believe everything in our fiction is lodged in the writer's truth, and one way to get there is through *character*. Aristotle gives us Plot as the number one fundamental on the art of drama's hierarchy in his *Poetics,* and I am suggesting we look at *character* first

When a novel or story is lauded with reviews like, "mesmerizing," "enthralling," "captivating," we know the author has found a voice that will draw us ineluctably into her world for a lot of pages. We're drawn into that world of print first by its characters.

Consider a writer like Carson McCullers who wrote main characters she really knew nothing about. They were outside her experience. In *The Heart Is a Lonely Hunter*, her protagonists are a Jewish gay mute and a black Communist doctor. Though she didn't know any such people, she created these characters as fully alive, complex human beings, ones we can never forget.

When I say everything in our fiction is lodged in our truth, of course I also mean everything is lodged in lies. But never does good writing fudge, skirt, muff, pretend, gloss over, evade, not care, nor skip the homework. Carson McCullers didn't know her characters personally, but she *understood* them.

I have a note over my computer in my studio that reads, UNDER-STAND THESE PEOPLE. I know that if I strike out with a piece of writing, it may not be because my scenes aren't well paced, or my plot points are lagging, it may just very well be my characters are flat, unbelievable, and the reader is unable to suspend disbelief. No matter how outrageous the characters are, the writer must understand them.

Let's look at voice then as starting with the *characters* and how they move in the world, how they handle the conflicts of their world, how they create their destinies. In other words, the author's voice and personality creates real characters in real situations, whether they're dull or mad, wild or ordinary, alien, evil, or angelic.

I recently read a newspaper article about a woman who's suing her former billionaire husband to whom she was married for all of one week for child support of her three-year-old daughter to the tune of $320,000 a month (to make ends meet). The article says the woman's demands have "caused a stir among hard-working Americans."

You might think this woman is an interesting character—I do, too. But so far she's really just an empty tube with one dimension only—greed. That's enough information for public interest media, but all the stuff that make us real living, breathing human beings is missing. What she thinks like, moves like, wants, needs, loves, hates, laughs at, cries at, eats, what her past has been, what her goals, dreams, wishes, fears, are; what her weaknesses are, what her health is, what she wears, eats, sleeps in, listens to, cares about, how she affects those in her world, and more—are all missing. How does she move her head, chop her vegetables, kick off her shoes? Is she capable of a measure of kindness? Of generosity?

Newspaper reportage is what I call "skeleton" writing. Fiction needs mounds of flesh, heaps of bones. It needs spit and sweat, and it needs its characters' secrets and lies.

Aristotle talked about what he called *eudaemonia* (good spirit), a state characterized by engagement, flow, and immersion in life's activities. A student lamented to me just this week that he saw no value in taking math and geography and history and social studies when all he wanted to do was write! He wanted to know why he had to do all that general-ed junk when he planned on being the world's next Hemingway.

He didn't realize if you don't know the world, you have nothing to write about. A "good spirit" may not be something we writers walk around with all the time, but we are at least immersed in life's activities because *that's what our characters are doing.*

Hemingway hung out with Cuban fishermen, guys at the bar. His pal and boatman, Gregorio Fuentes, who just died this year, is credited with giving *The Old Man and The Sea* its title. "Look," he said, "it's about an old man. And it's about the sea," and Papa reportedly said, "Yes that's it!" Fuentes is also credited with being the model for the old fisherman: "The old man was thin and gaunt with deep wrinkles in the back of his neck. The blotches ran well down the sides of his face and his hands had the deep-creased scars from handling heavy fish on the cords. But none of these scars were fresh. They were as old as erosions in a fishless desert."

Hemingway let reality and imagination create a living, breathing, real character and his lone expedition after a great marlin in the Cuban Gulf, and readers have been mesmerized with it since its publication in 1952. True character is revealed in the choices we make under pressure. The greater the pressure, the deeper the revelation. For a work of fiction's personality to mesmerize us, does it need to have the patina of revelation?

It helps.

For over half a century, the award-winning photographer Inge Morath photographed the world and its people. "For me," she said, "taking pictures is a personal matter, a search for inner truth."

There's where the voice lies. Only humans have voices. Only humans search for inner truth. No computer or highly advanced program can do that. Inge Morath was said to make poetry out of the people and their places she photographed. One review of her work said her feeling for places as reflected in images of Boris Pasternak's home, Chekhov's house and Mao Zedong's bedroom was so sensitive that some viewers insisted they could see invisible people in the photos.

A *New York Times* book reviewer wrote, "Inge Morath possesses the priceless quality of making the world look as though it had been discovered only this morning, and she was present with her lens to record its bright freshness."

That's what we want said about our writing.

The *characters* are the personality, the life forces, the driving elements, the beauty, the focus and revelation of our writing. They mesmerize us not only with what they make happen and what happens to them, but moreover, with who they are and why.

No matter what genre you write in, always, always *understand your characters.*

And we'll hear your voice.

DAVID RUTSCHMAN is the director of the University Without Walls at Gemini Ink, an independent nonprofit literary center in San Antonio, Texas.

The main point is that for fiction to work, the reader needs to feel the presence of a live and sweating human being behind each sentence, a governing sensibility, a certain way of inhabiting the world. I buy it, too. But I think it's worth remembering that the sensibility of a story or novel—the intelligence behind it all, the moral sense—doesn't have to be precisely the author's. There's room there for some wobble, for the imagination. That's why we call it fiction.

The examples are many. I think of Tolstoy, because I can't help thinking of Tolstoy. There's something of Count Leo in every word he wrote (at least the ones he didn't cross out in his multiple revisions), but it's a different something in each case. Is he in Pierre of *War and Peace*? Yes. Levin of *Anna Karenina*? Yes. Anna herself? Of course. But each of them, each character, brings forth a different part of the author, is another angle on him, another lens into him, and into us.

You have to put your personality in your prose, absolutely. But not only one part of your personality, not only the personality you show the world. Fiction is a chance to be larger than you really are, to explore all the selves you aren't, or aren't right now. If it weren't—if fiction were *only* about each writer—then it would be called nonfiction, and it would matter less.

PHYLLIS BARBER **writes in many categories. Among her work is her memoir,** How I Got Cultured: A Nevada Memoir, **for which she won the Associated Writing Programs Award; the children's book,** Legs: The Story of a Giraffe; **story collections titled** The School of Love: Short Stories **and** Parting the Veil: Stories From a Mormon Imagination, **as well as her historical novel,** And the Desert Shall Blossom. **She is also on the faculty of the MFA in Writing Program at Vermont College.**

When I was working on my memoir about growing up Mormon in Las Vegas, it began as a collection of short stories while I was enrolled in writing workshops at the University of Utah. I'd always been fascinated about the concept of culture and whether or not it meant highbrow culture or more to the point, the culture of a particular place.

Several of my teachers were enamored with post-modernism and deconstruction, and it seemed for a time that there was a bit of prancing with the lingo of the French intellectuals. Granted, I may not have understood the underpinnings of this philosophy, but something in me rebelled. Suddenly, I wanted to throw off the whole mantle of academia and speak out in my "little old Phyllis Nelson from Boulder City, Nevada" voice. I didn't care if I fit into the academic framework anymore (if there was such a thing), and I began to pay homage to my own roots, my own way of speaking, and the most authentic voice I could find. Writing from that place proved to be tremendously refreshing for me, and I felt the burden of writing perfectly wonderfully lifted from my back.

Now, as I try to finish a memoir of my more complex "grown up" life, I find myself casting about for the voice that isn't layered over with sophisticated psychology, the myriad of probabilities, or the resorting to clever prose (a weakness of mine). How to find that more adult, and more evasive, voice . . . Maybe it has to do with the clearest speaking one can do, the speaking when one is feeling centered and brave and unconcerned with how one's voice is being received. That's a challenge for me as I'm given to trying to please.

CHARLOTTE WRIGHT is a writer who has also worked in the publishing industry for two decades. She is currently managing editor of the University of Iowa Press.

As managing editor of the University of Iowa Press, I oversee the editing of around forty books a year: fiction, nonfiction, and poetry. While the copy editors who work for me correct the usual errors in grammar, spelling, and punctuation, and even do more substantive editing at times, they maintain a constant dialogue with the authors. I instruct the editors to remain flexible when authors argue that editing some part of their work will adversely affect their style and voice. Under such circumstances, I generally override the editorial suggestions. There are often times when I feel doing so will interfere with the readers' understanding of the work, and I will discuss that with the author. But mere technical correctness and conformity to house style are less important to me than are our authors' desires to say what they want in precisely the way they want to say it.

Of course, I have the privilege here at Iowa to work with seasoned, professional writers who have long since refined their particular voice. Men and women at the beginning of their writing careers are less likely to have the confidence to reveal their own voice. They listen to people in their writers' groups or to editors and agents at publishing seminars; they read good advice in magazines and books geared toward helping writers make their way through the publishing maze; they listen to authors lecture on their own writing methods. While all these sources contain valid information about the craft of writing, the truth is that good writing is a combination of craft and voice. Beginning writers need to learn all they can about writing methods, but they should not do so at the expense of developing their own unique voice.

DR. ROBERT O. GREER is the author of the CJ Floyd mystery series, *The Devil's Hatband*, *The Devil's Red Nickel*, and *The Devil's Backbone*, as well as two medical thrillers, *Limited Time* and the soon-to-be-released *Heat Shock*. The film rights to *The Devil's Red Nickel* have recently been optioned for an HBO movie. His short story collection, *Isolation and Other Stories*, was published in the spring of 2001. His short stories have appeared in numerous national literary magazines and two recent short story anthologies showcasing western fiction. He also edits the *High Plains Literary Review*, reviews books for National Public Radio, and raises Black Baldy cattle on his ranch near Steamboat Springs, Colorado.

For the discerning reader, recognizing an author's narrative voice can become as easy as recognizing a television commentator's signature sign-off or identifying a loved one's voice on the phone. However, for the author, establishing that unique "voice" can be a difficult task. Encoding one's own narrative voice is not simply a product of time and experience, nor a function of, as some might argue, pure writing genius. Finding one's voice can be of necessity, and above all, a matter of tone recognition. In fact, for me "voice" has always had less to do with word use, wordsmithing, literary exposition, or the correct use of grammar, than with what I like to think of as word rhythm.

More often than not, once the meaning of what I am attempting to convey is established, I find the key to a successful sentence, paragraph, or even a complete written page to be not the words themselves but the rhythmic sounds the words produce. Very likely, this obsession with rhythm has a lot to do with the characters I choose to write about—black, mean streets heroes plying their trade in a world of mystery and medical suspense. The lives of these characters seem to emerge most vividly when they use the rhythmic, ethnic, working-class Midwestern vernacular, or western regional intonations I've known all my life.

For me, simple words that are rich in rhythm are all important. Most other words routinely take a back seat. And, when it becomes necessary for one voice to be heard above all others, I find it surprising, enlightening in fact, that the trappings of my own formal literary and medical education are almost always subverted by the melodic rhythms of the language of every-day working men and women. Call it retrograde writing if you will; a voice reentrenchment of sorts. However it's characterized, and whatever the name attached to it, I always seem to return to my own natural voice when telling a story, unsanitized by years of "formal" education and literary instruction. Not surprisingly, this voice appears to gather the most narrative speed when it chases the street rhythms and ethnic voices from my youth.

THOMAS WATSON lives near Grand Rapids, Michigan, where he teaches writing to at-risk students. He received his MFA in Writing from Vermont College and he also teaches a graduate online creative-writing course for educators through Indiana University. He is an associate editor for _The Crescent Review_. His short story collection, See Rock City and Other Stories, placed as a semifinalist in the 2001 Julia Peterkin Prize competition. His most recent essay, "The Bug Beacon," appeared in _Peninsula: Essays and Memoirs From Michigan_, published by Michigan State University Press in

2000. His short stories have appeared in numerous magazines and journals, including *The Southern Indiana Review and Ellipsis: Literature and Art.*

Voice is everything. Defining what voice is, though, may be best left to the politicians who can't define pornography but know it when they see it. I trust the pols have slavered over enough smut to have a firm idea of what community standards are being violated, have some criteria of how many body parts must be depicted in defined perverse ways so they can declare a particular piece pornographic. I've read enough fiction to know what voice is, but I can't point to a paragraph or sentence and say, "here is the voice," in the way I can identify metaphor or imagery. But I can hear the voice when I read a piece and if the voice of the writer works for me, I'm sold on the story.

Voice is that all-inclusive coherent which not only tells the story through character, but makes the telling of the story credible by supplying the authority needed so the reader can get comfortable with the leap of imagination he or she is asked to take in a piece of fiction. Voice is, simply, the imagination, craft, and personality of the writer on the page.

Voice begets character and character begets plot. Most of my fiction-writing students labor at first on devising an ingenious plot, in which they will next insert fantastic characters. They come to voice last as a way to make the characters and narration sound credible enough to support the plot. It upsets them when I tell them they are going about the writing of a story backward. I tell them to get the voice of the character going first, get their own voice inside the characters and narration at the onset. If they are successful at it, the plot will write itself because a real character will only tell a true story and true story means an authentic voice. No character with an authentic voice will fake an orgasm in a story.

Fake orgasm in a story is a fantastic plot, a real hummer of a tale, told with a voice that whispers to the reader, "Yeah, baby, this is the best piece you've ever got a hold of." All the while the reader knows the story is not credible because the voice of the writer is either that of a liar or is simply holding back. The reader can tell the words are just what he or she wants to hear, knows the scintillating throaty passion is worded just right, and just as well knows the author is faking it like a crafty courtesan. Nothing rings true.

Voice is the art of being true to character and the conditions of a story, writing within your own awareness and staying in context of character. Voice is letting characters or the narrator speak naturally, pertinent to the scene or setting in which they find themselves. Not "writing" so much as "talking" in print.

I was walking through the French Quarter in New Orleans recently with an old friend. He was beaming as we took in the sights on a balmy spring evening. He sniffed the air and said to me, "Can you smell it? Smell the life here?"

We both breathed in the air: shrimp jambalaya, boiled crawfish, fried oyster po-boys, azalea blossoms, voodoo incense, the steam of dancers, rum Hurricanes, a thousand different tantalizing odors of the night life and the fun people were having around us.

Then the breeze shifted and he said, "Now you can smell piss, vomit, and the sewer. Isn't the smell of life just great?" I sniffed at the fetid odors from the gutter and thought about what he said, thought about the life occurring all around us, and began to see what he was talking about. Life is always a mixture, it is never one-sided or linear. The New Orleans street we strode fostered abundant life and decay at the same time. Gumbo and garbage. Etouffee and excrement. All mixed and intertwined together all the time. I could almost see Ignatius Reilly, glutton and ideologue, hobbling behind his Lucky Dog cart, taking it all in and pontificating to whomever would listen.

When I wrote about this experience later, I didn't "write" the street and my friend's reflections. I let his words flow through me, let the memories of the sights and smells I had experienced jump onto the page *without my interfering with their proper appearance.* In other words, I tried not to be a writer so much in the technical sense of the word. I tried to get onto the page as accurately as possible the emotion behind the sensations I had experienced. And I told the story through my friend's eyes, used the very words he did, and did not filter them with the editor who lives in the back of my head all the time. Ultimately, I told the story with my own voice, but I used my friend as the vehicle to transmit his voice onto the page. And all good vehicles, characters like Ignatius, scenes like the streets of New Orleans, are mixtures of the conflicting passions of life. A solid voice in a story will encompass these sometimes paradoxical elements and produce that well-rounded, omniscient sense that the author knows what he or she is writing about. Beignets and miasma.

As an associate editor for a national fiction journal, I see too many manuscripts come across my desk that are exquisitely written and boring. The prose is so tight and polished the stories can't be called anything but technically perfect. A colleague of mine sees similar masses of flawless poetry submitted to the journal he edits. But what we read is lifeless, devoid of the smell of life and ultimately fake.

My editor friend and I agree the stuff we read has been MFA-ed to death, honed to such a fine edge after numerous workshops or revisions, the writing is professional, seamless, and all but dead. What we read is the ultimate in fake orgasm. All the sounds and motions occur in just the right places at just the right time with just the right amount of description. But, as in a bordello, the stuff we read is about mannequins making love. We leave the manuscripts unsatisfied as if we had paid our money to the madam for the best in the house, had our fun, but left feeling empty, robbed of a true experience. In short, there is no voice in the stories or poems we read. The writers have allowed their work to be MFA-ed so much that what is on the page resembles what Tom Wolfe has called a "beige voice." The stories I read show too much concern for the perfection of the craft, too much attention to the mechanics of the text; whereas, if the emphasis were directed to the voice of the narrator/character, the mechanics would largely take care of themselves. Proper language, tone and style will prevail, if the writer is skillful enough, because the voice of a story will dictate what words must be used. All the writer must do, then, is let his or her personality take the lead from the voice of the characters and let the story write itself. Sounds easy, but getting the voice right is a delicate task indeed.

So how do we get voice into our writing successfully? Aside from writing for about fifty or sixty years and finally finding the right voice, in short we must be ourselves. Too often writers forget their first task is to write for themselves and, in so doing, please themselves first. Often, writers imagine satisfying some specific but distant audience with their work, an audience who may not exist. Better to be our own devotees first because if we are honest, we will not fake the pleasure, our own pleasure, we get from our writing. We will succeed at voice only if we project our personalities onto the page through our characters and like what we are doing. Since each character we create reflects some aspect of our personality, we sell ourselves short of the writers we can be and bore our readers if we do not write with genuine emotion. If we fake orgasm on the page, no one has any fun.

FRANCES SHERWOOD's best-selling novel *Vindication* was a finalist for the National Book Critics Circle Award, and she is also the author of *Green.* Her story collection *Everything You've Heard Is True* won her two O. Henry Awards, and she is a former Stegner Fellow at Stanford University. Her latest novel is *The Book of Splendor.* She teaches creative writing at Indiana University at South Bend.

I often think of my writerly self as a medium, as if I were talking in tongues, acting as a vehicle for other voices, or giving voice to the mute. However, I suppose that the echoes I hear resonating within are, in fact, bits and pieces of myself and that the process of discovery in writing is a confrontation with the self.

CHUCK CULVER was born in and lived most of his life in Indianapolis, except for thirteen years in California (mostly in San Francisco). Two anthologies of his poetry have been published and read throughout the English-speaking world. Some thirty of his short

stories have appeared in literary periodicals all over the country and are collected in an anthology, *The Carousel Shoppe and Other Stories*. His first published novel, *We Happy Few*, was released in 1999. He is the series writer for a nationally-syndicated television show, *Game Warden Wildlife Journal*, which presently reaches one million homes on 151 stations, coast to coast. He is the cohost of *Bookends*, a literary radio show on WICR-FM, Indianapolis, and he is currently working on a new novel.

Isn't it strange how writers and teachers of writing always express the word voice in the singular? Implied is the notion that once an emerging writer finds his or her voice, the struggle is over. A mechanism is in place for all time. I quite disagree. In fact, each time a writer approaches a short story, a novel, or an essay, the search for voice begins anew in a sense, because every exercise requires its own unique voice. This is most abundantly clear when one is writing fiction in the first person. The voice of the blue-collar weekend golfer in my short story "Alexander the Great" bears no resemblance to the foppish author in my story "Hiding From the Midnight Sun" or the monied vagabond in "Following Socrates." My ideas for stories lead me all over the spectrum, and I have no compunction about making my voice young or old, female or male, principled or corrupted. And each new role I play requires taking on the appropriate and consistent voice of my narrator.

It should be obvious that first-person narrative requires its own unique voice. But so too does writing in the third person. At least it does for me. I'm well-aware that some writers, Hemingway for one, come to rely on a single voice, a signature of their work. But not everyone is Hemingway, and many of us writers see the world through complex refracted lenses. When we approach a story, it also approaches us and presses upon us its need for a particular voice. It would appear absurd to write a novel of manners set in the drawing rooms of the privileged with the voice of a Jim Harrison or a Bernard Malamud, equally absurd to write of the Battle of Guadalcanal in the voice of Henry James or Virginia Woolf.

When I wrote my first published novel, *We Happy Few*, I was compelled to find a voice that could express the lives of two disparate couples, one in their seventies, the other in their twenties. A reader could say that I simply told my story as the omnipresent narrator, a somewhat neutral voice. But I don't think that's so. I think the voice I chose allowed me to speak both for people whose decade was the 1940s as well as people from the 1990s.

A better example might be found in the evolution of my current novel, *Mary Champion*. This story originally was inspired by a poem by John Hopper about the occupation of Alsace-Lorrain by the Nazis during World War II. According to Hopper, the Germans had the notion that this province had been unfairly snatched from them by the Treaty of Versailles and was technically their property. Therefore, its citizens were German citizens and, they reasoned, the young men of the province should be eligible for conscription in the German Army. But the young men still thought of themselves as Frenchmen and, in their attempts to avoid the draft, were willing to risk the consequences of hiding or even of suicide. My thought was that there might be one boy who cooked up the idea of willingly submitting to the draft, with the idea of waiting until the appropriate moment in combat and then taking out as many as his "fellow" German soldiers as possible. A true hero.

But there were some problems with this scenario for me. First, though I had been to France several times, I'd never specifically been to Alsace-Lorrain. That could be easily remedied with a quick trip to the region and some research. But, more than that, my voice in all of my previous work, even as an omnipresent narrator, had been along the lines of a street-smart contemporary American. I supposed I could bridge that gap and develop more of a European or international voice. But why? Wouldn't it be far easier to convert the dilemma of the Nazi occupation of Alsace-Lorraine into something that could happen in the modern American business world, which I knew, and set in San

Francisco, a city where I once lived? And so my story became one of a high-ranking executive fired by his fellow officers and forced into a new life. Not quite as traumatic a prospect as being overrun by the Nazi Blitzkrieg, but traumatic enough for an individual going through it. And, as long as I was taking liberties, why not make my protagonist a woman? Just to be different.

Wasn't I concerned about taking on the voice of a woman? No, not nearly as much as would becoming an eighteen-year-old youth in eastern France in 1940. American professional women are probably the demographic I know best besides my own. I've been around them all my life. I still think the potential for the story is there, but much more manageable for me to develop.

So, if we accept my notion that it is the story that drives the voice, one is left with two options: (1) to seek potential stories that are adaptable to one's natural voice or (2) to develop versatility in creating voices. Either way, what is most obvious to the writer is that this writing game, as we well know, is damned difficult indeed.

A Consensus

Seems to be unanimous, doesn't it? The importance of the writer using his or her own individual voice. Publishers, editors, agents, book sellers—the whole lot of them are in agreement.

Their message?

Get *your* personality on the page! *Your* voice.

CHAPTER TWELVE

A Disclaimer . . .

We are all apprentices in a craft where no one ever becomes a master.—ERNEST HEMINGWAY

One of the problems I've personally had with many of the how-to writing books I've collected over the years (an estimated 714 pounds worth!), was the absoluteness of the author in ladling out his or her wisdom.

A tone, often, that proclaims authoritatively, "I am the Way, the Truth, and the Light." Oops. That's another book . . .

Except . . . that's sometimes the "message" the reader receives.

It's intimidating.

Makes the writer/reader feel that if she doesn't follow the author's advice, she's doomed to describing her novels, articles, short stories, poems, etc., as being available "only in my room."

Won't get published unless we follow the author's advice . . .

It occurred to me that some readers might get the same notion about *this* book, *this* writer . . .

Uh-oh . . .

What to do! About the "I am the final authority" tone. A tone I've been guilty of myself in teaching my classes and in lectures and talks to other writers. Most of us who teach and write books of advice like this are probably guilty, at least at times, of such a stance.

Further, what I put forth in these pages is largely experiential, derived in no small part from a lifetime of writing and teaching and yes, research, informal and formal. You can find just about every book written on the art and craft of writing in the past fifty years or so somewhere on my messy bookshelves. If not there, then there's a good chance at least a few are buried in the piles of books that regularly seem to accumulate in my writing space!

But, the fact remains that lots and lots of what I say here comes from my own personal and individual experience.

Another's experience may be somewhat or even quite different than mine.

Who's right if I'm at odds with another of us writer-type "authorities"?

Well . . . I venture to say that neither of us is, at least in total. The person who's right is . . . *you!* What I mean by that kookie-sounding statement is that this is exactly why writers and those whose aim it is to become an author should read everything on the subject they can get their hands on . . . let everything kind of percolate like dark-roast coffee grounds . . . and then make their own java!

It may well be that when this book comes out, an editor or a publisher or an agent or another writer or even just a learned student of writing will take me to task for stating something he or she disbelieves and even refute something said with vigor.

Go for it.

Better, write another book and I'll buy it and I'll read it and I imagine I'll get something of value from it, even if I disagree with you.

It's how we progress in this writing game. We learn from each other.

Or, take what works for you from me and what works for you that you've gained from another and brew your own cup of writer's wisdom.

It just seemed to me that I should address this—to let know you that not only is your own voice oh-so-important, but so are your own writing instincts.

The thing is, nothing is absolute. Especially in writing! Not even death and taxes are absolute. Just ask every third person you come upon in the Cayman's about taxes, and Shirley MacLaine will probably be happy to give you another opinion about that death thing.

And this is what I came up with.

A disclaimer.

Far more than we should be, as writers, we're unsure of ourselves. That's been the gist of this book. Trying to get you not to "overrespect" writers on the shelves and to use your own voice. It seems to me that I might be guilty of the same thing by saying, "Hey! Listen to me! I know what's best for you. (Over)respect me."

Well, maybe I do know what's best for you . . . and maybe I don't . . .

Don't get me wrong. I firmly believe what I've been telling you to be valuable and valid and I'm not saying to disregard all that. I'm just admitting out loud that I'm not God. That's what any of us as writers should do, I think—take any advice we get with at least a small grain of salt. Trust our own instincts more, when push comes to shove.

In my own writing career, if I'd taken the advice given me at every turn by just about everybody, to "turn off your left brain" and "just get the stuff down," then I'd still be fighting my own writing style and instincts and probably be a lot less successful. Luckily, I chanced upon a writing guru who advised the opposite, and I was given an instant key to freedom.

With that perfect, infamous 20-20 hindsight, I realized I should have trusted my own instincts more. The older I get and the better at this writing thing, the more I realize I should have done so in any number of things.

All I'm saying is that none of us is infallible. That includes me.

I hope that whatever I've said in these pages makes sense to you and helps you achieve your own voice. That you agree with me at the end of our time here that your own voice has worth and is perhaps the biggest asset and strength you have as a writer. That *your* voice is the one thing editors, publishers, and readers want from you.

Truth.

To pay attention to my words of wisdom, yes, and use what you find useful, but not to buy anything whole hog. Unless, of course, you agree with everything. That would be cool . . .

Nah. It wouldn't.

Listen to what one of the most-respected names in the writer-teaching business, the esteemed John Gardner, had to say on this very subject to perhaps his most famous student, Raymond Carver. Carver relates this anecdote in his essay "Fires."

From "Fires"

> Recently, we [Carver and Gardner] had dinner together in Ithaca, New York, and I reminded him of some of the sessions we'd had up in the office. He answered that probably everything he'd told me was wrong. He said, "I've changed my mind about so many things." All I know is that the advice he was handing out in those days was just what I needed at the time.

How about that! John Gardner admitting that "everything he'd told (Carver) about writing was wrong"! That's obviously not true—probably most of what he'd passed on to his student was valid and valuable, but the thing is, even Gardner recognized that writing and the writer both change and evolve into a different thing as each grow. He could "take back" what he'd said in person to his student Carver, but a book is forever entombed in amber. Or at least reordered into infinity by Barnes and Noble and Borders if it keeps on selling, and you can be sure until it falls into particles of dust the library will still be checking it out.

Mr. Gardner was a moral man. I think that if he'd had the chance, he might have recanted at least some of the advice he gave in his books in the same spirit as he did at his meeting with the older Carver. Most likely, if he'd lived longer, he'd have revised his earlier writing books or written a new one, based on his new understandings of the craft.

Here's another quarter heard from . . .

> If I had to give young writers advice, I'd say don't listen
> to writers talking about writing or themselves. —Lillian
> Hellman

Ms. Hellman perhaps overstates the case; in reality, we gain much of our knowledge of our craft by listening to other writers. In fact, she makes an absolute statement . . . against absolute state-*ers*! And she herself gave out plenty of writing advice in her day. Fairly authoritatively, the rumor goes . . . What she is saying, however, carries the essence of truth. She might have said it more accurately if she'd said, instead, "Don't listen to writers talking about writing or themselves, *unless you buy what they're saying and it works for you.*"

Which is what I'm suggesting here. If it works for you, put it in your writer's toolkit and take it home. If it doesn't, leave it on the shelf.

Just please don't write me letters telling me I'm all wet if that's your opinion. I get enough of that here at home . . . Some of it deserved.

◆ ◆ ◆

When I began writing, I was a high school student and a high school basketball player on the side, and we still had a center jump after every basket then (back during the mid-Neolithic Period, for those of you uncertain with your historical landmarks), to create a sports metaphor that may be illustrative. Today, that style of play seems hopelessly moribund, when nowadays the Pacers and Knicks just take it out-of-bounds and push it up court (for a three-pointer by Reggie Miller . . .). I don't begin a story with backstory or setting any more than the Indiana University center heads to mid-court after a score for a center jump. The fans at that kind of game would go nuts, and the fans of a story begun with much backstory at the beginning (literary version of that old centerjump) would have the same reaction.

I'm glad I know about the center jump, though. It makes me appreciate the fast-paced, frenetic game I enjoy today even more. I'm also glad I've read stories with languorous openings written in the past, as well. It makes me appreciate the skill of the contemporary writer who plunges me into the fray instantly and covers all that backstory with a few quick strokes later on in the read when I'm ready for a bit of a time-out.

Get it?

Read books on writing and craft. Read lots of 'em. Even the worst of the genre usually has at least one thing of value you can use that's worth the cost of the book and the time you spent digging it out. The more you read such books—both good and bad ones—the keener you'll develop your sense of which dog hunts and which dog you'll want to leave back home on the porch.

And not only books on craft. Books . . . in general. Novels and short stories and poems and biographies and articles and memoirs and grocery lists and . . .

You get the point. Read everything you can get your mitts on!

In other words—pilot your own writer's starship, Cap'n Spock.

Always remember you don't have to be Tom Clancy to get published. In fact, if you try to be Clancy in your prose, you probably won't be. Clancy did because he only tried to be himself. Successful writing and besting the competition is kind of like playing golf safely in bear country. If a bear charges your foursome, you don't have to outrun the bear. You just have to outrun the slowest member of your group.

Run at your best speed and *write with your own marvelous, individual voice*. It's how you beat the bear.

Suggested Craft Book Reading

My wife, Mary, and my son, Mike, and I have a regular outing just about every week of the year. When Mary gets home on Saturday afternoons from her hairstyling job, we pile in the van and head for one of three bookstores we like here in Fort Wayne. Either Barnes and Noble, Borders, or Little Professor. Once in a while, we depart from our usual haunts and visit Village Books, a wonderful used bookstore just down the street from our house for a change of pace.

We spend a couple of hours browsing and usually end up with each of us buying at least one book apiece. Oh—Mary always gets a cappucino and I get a double latte with half a shot of Irish cream. Mike sometimes gets a decaf latte. Mike just turned thirteen and he's been doing this with us for every one of his thirteen years, and I'd venture a guess he's read more books than just about anybody in his class! He reads an average of three books a week. He's for sure become an avid reader, and that may be the best legacy I could have helped instill in him. In fact, for about the past six years he's been on a "program" I began when he was seven, wherein if he reads a "classic" from a list I make up and then writes a one-page book report or synopsis on it, he earns five bucks. And, none of those insipid "simplified" versions of those books count. He knows he has to read the original.

Which he prefers.

Once, when he was eight, he read one of those versions and put it down before he'd read ten pages, declaring, "They wrote this for babies!"

I concur . . .

At five bucks a pop, he's collected a lot of money over the past six years!

After we leave the bookstore, we go out to eat at a restaurant we choose "democratically." The way "democracy" works in our family, is that Mike and I voice our opinions of where we'd like to go . . . and then Mary decides. Usually we end up at Casa d' Angelo's or the local Don Pablo's. Sometimes I'll have a beer with dinner, but more often, not. I've found I can't write as well when I've imbibed, even a single beer, and so I've pretty much cut out all liquor consumption. I'll probably write some when we return home, so it's a fairly rare occasion when I knock back a Bud.

My first stop wherever we hit the bookstore is always the "writer's" section. It gets tougher and tougher to find something new as it seems I've already accumulated just about all the books on the writing craft that I find on the shelves each week. (You writer people need to be putting out more books and faster! Drink more coffee—stay up later!)

One thing I usually notice when I visit the writer's craft section is at least one person standing there looking over the selection. Lots of times, it's evident the person really doesn't have a clue what he wants. I imagine for something that will help unlock the "secrets" of this marvelous art. I know that's what I'm looking for! I watch the person pick up one book, then another, and finally, with what seems to be a bit of unsureness, he makes his selection and heads to the front counter.

And those books (with writing secrets) are there. It's just sometimes a bit difficult to know which is the best book to spend our hard-earned money on.

Also, most of us as writers are somewhat isolated. By that, I mean we don't get to see and talk to a lot of other writers in our normal day-to-day existences. We just don't see many other writers who could perhaps help us out with suggestions of books on craft they've read that they found helpful.

With that in mind, I thought it might be helpful for at least some of the readers here to give you my own list of the books on craft I've read and found useful. I won't "rate" them, mostly because while, yes, the quality varies from the excellent to the fairly good, I've uncovered something enriching and valuable in each and every one of the books I'll list and I think you will, too. The following is a list of some of the books I've found personally enriching and helpful in my own development as a writer, and so I thought I'd pass them on to you. You will note that included are a few texts on screenwriting, which I also write. I've included them simply because many of the techniques they provide, such as how to write dialogue that isn't "on the nose," or how transitions are written effectively, along with several other writing tips, are valuable to writers working in other forms as well. Some of the texts are obviously intended for a particular genre, but I've included them as they all contain advice and information every writer should find beneficial.

While I won't rate the majority of the larger list that follows, I will list the "best baker's dozen" of books I felt helped me the most.

My "best baker's dozen" are:

1. *Writing Fiction: A Guide to Narrative Craft*, by Janet Burroway. (The rest of these and the rest of my "recommendations" that follow could be arranged in any order, but Burroway's book, in my opinion, is the single best text on writing craft in print at this time.)

2. *The Art of Dramatic Writing*, Lajos Egri.

3. *What If? Writing Exercises for Fiction Writers*, by Anne Bernays and Pamela Painter.

4. *Fiction First Aid*, by Raymond Obstfeld.

5. *Your Life as Story: Discovering the "New Autobiography" and Writing Memoir as Literature*, by Tristine Rainer.

6. *On Writing Well*, by William Zinsser.

7. *Follow the Story: How to Write Successful Nonfiction*, James B. Stewart.

8. *On Becoming a Novelist*, John Gardner.

9. *Revision*, David Michael Kaplan.

10. *Writing a Book That Makes a Difference*, Philip Gerard.

11. *The Power of Myth*, Joseph Campbell.

12. *Story*, Robert McKee.

13. *Aspects of the Novel*, E.M. Forster.

13A. (Okay, so I cheated. So sue me . . . I just had to get this one in here. Think of it this way—you're getting a big, fat baker's dozen . . .) *The Art of the Novel*, Milan Kundera.

13B. (Okay, okay! So I'm a big fat liar and my pants are on fire! How's that for a couple of clichés I for one never hear enough . . . How can I leave this one out of my top tomes?) *Writing in General and the Short Story in Particular*, Rust Hills. (If you haven't read this, after you do I dare you to tell me I shoulda left it out . . .)

◆ ◆ ◆

Remember, these are only my selections and are based on my own needs as a writer. Your list may and probably will be, quite different. These are just the books I return to, time and again, and except for

Fiction First Aid, which came out relatively recently, I've read and reread the others for years. I expect to do the same with Obstfeld's book as well.

The following are all books I own and found useful.

1. *The 38 Most Common Fiction Writing Mistakes (And How to Avoid Them),* Jack M. Bickham.
2. *Magazine Writing That Sells,* Don McKinney.
3. *Starting From Scratch,* Rita Mae Brown.
4. *Writers and Company,* Eleanor Wachtel.
5. *Write From Life: Turning Your Personal Experiences Into Compelling Stories,* Meg Files.
6. *Finding Your Writer's Voice: A Guide to Creative Fiction,* Thaisa Frank and Dorothy Wall.
7. *Characters and Viewpoint,* Orson Scott Card.
8. *Drinking, Smoking and Screwing: Great Writers on Good Times,* edited by Sara Nickles.
9. *The Right to Write: An Invitation and Initiation Into the Writing Life* and *The Artist's Way,* Julia Cameron.
10. *Thinking Like Your Editor: How to Write Great Serious Nonfiction—And Get it Published,* Susan Rabiner and Alfred Fortunato.
11. *Building Fiction: How to Develop Plot and Structure,* Jesse Lee Kercheval.
12. *The Associated Press Stylebook and Libel Manual,* edited by Christopher W. French.
13. *How to Write a Book Proposal,* Michael Larsen.
14. *The Oxford Companion to American Literature,* edited by James D. Hart.
15. *Spider, Spin Me a Web,* Lawrence Block.
16. *You Can Write a Memoir,* Susan Carol Hauser.
17. *Strictly Murder: A Writer's Guide to Criminal Homicide,* Martin Roth.
18. *How to Write and Sell Your First Nonfiction Book,* Oscar Collier with Frances Spatz Leighton.
19. *The Marshall Plan for Novel Writing,* Evan Marshall.

20. *Stein on Writing,* Sol Stein.
21. *Novelist's Essential Guide to Crafting Scenes,* Raymond Obstfeld.
22. *Inventing the Truth: The Art and Craft of Memoir,* William Zinsser.
23. *Writing the Thriller,* T. Macdonald Skillman.
24. *Words and Things: An Introduction to Language,* Roger Brown.
25. *Plot,* Ansen Dibbel.
26. *Writing Down the Bones: Freeing the Writer Within,* Natalie Goldberg.
27. *Writing the Novel: From Plot to Print,* Lawrence Block.
28. *Novelist's Essential Guide to Creating Plot,* J. Madison Davis.
29. *Poets in Their Youth: A Memoir,* Eileen Simpson.
30. *The Forest for the Trees: An Editor's Advice to Writers,* Betsy Lerner.
31. *The Complete Guide to Editing Your Fiction,* Michael Seidman.
32. *Narrative Design,* Madison Smartt Bell.
33. *Plotting and Writing Suspense Fiction,* Patricia Highsmith.
34. *The Art and Craft of the Short Story,* Rick DeMarinis.
35. *Turning Life Into Fiction,* Robin Hemley.
36. *How to Tell a Story: The Secrets of Writing Captivating Tales,* Peter Rubie and Gary Provost.
37. *The Writing Life,* collection of essays and interviews of National Book Award authors.
38. *Freelance Writing for Magazines and Newspapers: Breaking In Without Selling Out,* Marcia Yudkin.
39. *The Writer's Digest Handbook of Novel Writing,* edited by Tom Clark, William Brohaugh, Bruce Woods, Bill Strickland, and Peter Blocksom.
40. *Writing for Young Adults,* Sherry Garland.
41. *Writing to Sell,* Scott Meredith.
42. *The Magazine Writer's Handbook,* Franklynn Peterson and Judi Kesselman-Turkel.
43. *The Writer's Guide to Conquering the Magazine Market,* Connie Emerson.

44. *Creating Unforgettable Characters*, Linda Seger.
45. *On Writer's Block: A New Approach to Creativity*, Victoria Nelson.
46. *How to Write a Damn Good Novel, II*, James N. Frey.
47. *Editors on Editing*, edited by Gerald Gross.
48. *12 Keys to Writing Books That Sell*, Kathleen Krull.
49. *Writing From the Body: For Writers, Artists, and Dreamers Who Long to Free Your Voice*, John Lee with Ceci Miller-Kritsberg.
50. *Writing the Blockbuster Novel*, Albert Zuckerman.
51. *Dare to be a Great Writer: 329 Keys to Powerful Fiction*, Leonard Bishop.
52. *Get Published: One Hundred Top Magazine Editors Tell You How*, Diane Gage and Marcia Coppess.
53. *Scene of the Crime: A Writer's Guide to Crime-Scene Investigations*, Anne Wingate.
54. *The New Well-Tempered Sentence: A Punctuation Handbook for the Innocent, the Eager, and the Doomed*, Karen Elizabeth Gordon.
55. *How to Write and Sell True Crime*, Gary Provost.
56. *From Pen to Print: The Secrets of Getting Published Successfully*, Ellen M. Kozak.
57. *Structuring Your Novel: From Basic Idea to Finished Manuscript*, Robert C. Meredith and John D. Fitzgerald.
58. *How to Sell More Than 75% of Your Freelance Writing*, Gordon Burgett.
59. *Telling Lies for Fun and Profit*, Lawrence Block.
60. *Scene and Structure*, Jack M. Bickham.
61. *The Crime Writer's Handbook*, Douglas Wynn.
62. *Techniques of the Selling Writer*, Dwight V. Swain. (This one almost made my "best baker's dozen" list.)
63. *Writing a Thriller*, Andre Jute.
64. *Fiction: The Art and Craft of Writing and Getting Published*, Michael Seidman.
65. *Conflict, Action, and Suspense*, William Noble.

66. *How to Write a Mystery,* Larry Beinhart.
67. *Write the Perfect Book Proposal,* Jeff Herman and Deborah M. Adams. (And Mr. Herman turned down the proposal for this book when I sent it to him for possible representation!)
68. *The Elements of Style,* William Strunk Jr. and E.B. White.
69. *If You Can Talk, You Can Write,* Joel Saltzman
70. *The Career Novelist: A Literary Agent Offers Strategies for Success,* Donald Maass.
71. *The Elements of Storytelling: How to Write Compelling Fiction,* Peter Rubie.
72. *Three Rules for Writing a Novel,* William Noble.
73. *Bird by Bird* and *Traveling Mercies,* Anne Lamott.
74. *Writing Successful Self-Help and How-To Books,* Jean Marie Stine.
75. *Self-Editing for Fiction Writers,* Renni Browne and Dave King.
76. *The First Five Pages: A Writer's Guide to Staying Out of the Rejection Pile,* Noah Lukeman.
77. *How to Write Crime,* edited by Marele Day.
78. *The Joy of Writing Sex: A Guide for Fiction Writers,* Elizabeth Benedict.
79. *Writing for Story: Craft Secrets of Dramatic Nonfiction by a Two-Time Pulitzer Prize Winner,* Jon Franklin.
80. *Willa Cather on Writing,* Willa Cather.
81. *Random House Guide to Good Writing,* Mitchell Ivers.
82. *Conversations on Writing Fiction: Interviews with Thirteen Distinguished Teachers of Fiction Writing in America,* edited by Alexander Neubauer.
83. *For Love and Money: A Writing Life,* Jonathan Raban.
84. *Screenwriter's Bible,* David Trottier.
85. *Zen and the Art of Screenwriting,* William Froug.

◆ ◆ ◆

There you have it. A starting point for writing books to read. I think you'll like the majority of them. Even in the ones you don't particularly like, I feel confident you'll find at least one thing you'll be able to take back to your writing desk and use profitably.

I know I've left out some worthy texts, and for that I apologize to any author whom I've slighted. It was unintentional, I assure you. About the time this goes to press, I'll think of a book that not only should have been on the list, but probably should have made my top choices. Ah, well. Blame it on my worsening case of CRS (Can't Remember . . . er, Stuff).

Also, if you feel compelled to pick up quill and parchment to write me a scathing letter along the lines of, "You illiterate, undereducated cretin! How could you possibly have overlooked_____!!!??" let me hasten to qualify my list as merely being the books I currently have on my shelves and look to on a regular basis. I've also left off some forty-odd other books on writing also on those same shelves for various reasons. Some I didn't feel were worth the time and money, and others, while good books, were too far outside the purview of this humble list. Etc., etc.

Happy reading!

Index

Get the Instruction and Inspiration You Need!

The Pocket Muse—Here's the key to finding inspiration when and where you want it. With hundreds of thought-provoking prompts, exercises and illustrations, it immediately helps you to get started writing, overcome writer's block, develop a writing habit, think more creatively, master style, revision and other elements of the craft.
ISBN 1-58297-142-0 ✳ hardcover ✳ 256 pages ✳ #10806-K

Snoopy's Guide to the Writing Life—Inside you'll find more than 180 heartwarming and hilarious Snoopy "at the typewriter" comic strips by Charles M. Schulz, paired with 32 delightful essays from a who's who of famous writers, including Sue Grafton, Fannie Flagg, Elmore Leonard and more. These pieces examine the joys and realities of the writing life, from finding ideas to creating characters.
ISBN 1-58297-194-3 ✳ hardcover ✳ 192 pages ✳ #10856-K

Writer's Guide to Places—Imbue your settings with authentic detail - the kind of information that only an insider would know! Inside you'll find information on all 50 states, 10 Canadian provinces, and dozens of intriguing cities. From small town squares to city streets, you'll find great places to set a scene, the foods your characters eat, where they shop, and more.
ISBN 1-58297-169-2 ✳ paperback ✳ 416 pages ✳ #10833-K

The Creative Writer's Style Guide—Textbook rules about punctuation and grammar can be difficult to apply to your novel, short story, personal essay, or memoir. There are special considerations that normal style manuals just don't address. The Creative Writer's Style Guide is a revolutionary resource. It provides the answers, advice and rules you need to edit your manuscript with confidence.
ISBN 1-884910-55-6 ✳ hardcover ✳ 240 pages ✳ #48054-K

These books and other fine Writer's Digest titles are available from your local bookstore or online supplier, or by calling 1-800-448-0915.

More of the Best From Writer's Digest Books!

45 Master Characters—Make your characters and their stories more compelling, complex and original than ever before. This book explores the most common male and female archetypes—the mythic, cross-cultural models from which all characters originate—and shows you how to use them as foundations for your own unique characters. Examples culled from literature, television and film illustrate just how memorable and effective these archetypes can be—from "Gladiators" like Rocky Balboa to "Maidens" like Guinevere. ISBN 1-58297-069-6 ✻ hardcover ✻ 256 pages ✻ #10752-K

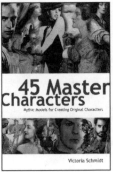

Careers for Your Characters—To create realistic, well-developed characters, you have to write with authority, describing their professional lives with the accuracy and detail of an insider. Here Raymond Obstfeld shares the hard-to-find specifics for 50 intriguing occupations, including professional jargon and buzz words, education requirements, salaries, benefits, perks, expenses and more! ISBN 1-58297-083-1 ✻ paperback ✻ 326 pages ✻ #10765-K

Howdunit—Howdunit illuminates the dark side of human nature and the methods used to confront it. An all-in-one writer's crime reference, it compiles twenty classic chapters from the original series with nine all-new pieces. You'll find information on investigative techniques, surveillance techniques, street gangs, causes of death, interrogation, profiling, terrorism, murder, and more. ISBN 1-58297-015-7 ✻ paperback ✻ 416 pages ✻ #10696-K

The Writer's Idea Book—This is the guide writers reach for time after time to jump-start their creativity and develop ideas. Four distinctive sections, each geared toward a different stage of writing, offer dozens of unique approaches to "freeing the muse." In all, you'll find more than 400 idea-generating prompts that are guaranteed to get your writing started on the right foot, or back on track! ISBN 1-58297-179-X ✻ paperback ✻ 272 pages ✻ #10841-K

These books and other fine Writer's Digest titles are available from your local bookstore or online supplier, or by calling 1-800-448-0915.